OBSESSED

M. WILLIAM PHELPS

PINNACLE BOOKS
Kensington Publishing Corp.
http://www.kensingtonbooks.com

PINNACLE BOOKS are published by

Kensington Publishing Corp.
119 West 40th Street
New York, NY 10018

All Kensington Titles, Imprints, and Distributed Lines are available at special quantity discounts for bulk purchases for sales promotions, premiums, fund-raising, and educational or institutional use. Special book excerpts or customized printings can also be created to fit specific needs. For details, write or phone the office of the Kensington special sales manager: Kensington Publishing Corp., 119 West 40th Street, New York, NY 10018, attn: Special Sales Department, Phone: 1-800-221-2647.

Pinnacle and the P logo Reg. U.S. Pat. & TM Off.

ISBN-13: 978-0-7860-3246-4
ISBN-10: 0-7860-3246-4
First Kensington Mass Marked Edition: March 2014

eISBN-13: 978-0-7860-3247-1
eISBN-10: 0-7860-3247-2
First Kensington Electronic Edition: March 2014

10 9 8 7 6 5 4 3

Printed in the United States of America

HIGHEST PRAISE FOR M. WILLIAM PHELPS

BAD GIRLS

"Fascinating, gripping . . . Phelps's sharp investigative skills and questioning mind resonate. Whether or not you agree with the author's suspicions that an innocent is behind bars, you won't regret going along for the ride with such an accomplished reporter."

—**Sue Russell**

NEVER SEE THEM AGAIN

"This riveting book examines one of the most horrific murders in recent American history."

—*New York Post*

"Phelps clearly shows how the ugliest crimes can take place in the quietest of suburbs."

—*Library Journal*

"Thoroughly reported . . . The book is primarily a police procedural, but it is also a tribute to the four murder victims."

—*Kirkus Reviews*

TOO YOUNG TO KILL

"Phelps is the Harlan Coben of real-life thrillers."

—**Allison Brennan**

LOVE HER TO DEATH

"Reading anything by Phelps is always an eye opening experience. The characters are well researched and well written. We have murder, adultery, obsession, lies and so much more."

—*Suspense Magazine*

"You don't want to miss *Love Her To Death* by M. William Phelps, a book destined to be one of 2011's top true crimes!"

—*True Crime Book Reviews*

"A chilling crime . . . award-winning author Phelps goes into lustrous and painstaking detail, bringing all the players vividly to life."

—*Crime Magazine*

KILL FOR ME

"Phelps gets into the blood and guts of the story."

—**Gregg Olsen**, *New York Times* best-selling author of *Fear Collector*

"Phelps infuses his investigative journalism with plenty of energized descriptions."

—**Publishers Weekly**

DEATH TRAP

"A chilling tale of a sociopathic wife and mother . . . a compelling journey from the inside of this woman's mind to final justice in a court of law. For three days I did little else but read this book."

—**Harry N. MacLean**, *New York Times* best-selling author of *In Broad Daylight*

I'LL BE WATCHING YOU

"Phelps has an unrelenting sense for detail that affirms his place, book by book, as one of our most engaging crime journalists."

—**Katherine Ramsland**

IF LOOKS COULD KILL

"M. William Phelps, one of America's finest true-crime writers, has written a compelling and gripping book about an intriguing murder mystery. Readers of this genre will thoroughly enjoy this book."

—**Vincent Bugliosi**

"Starts quickly and doesn't slow down . . . Phelps consistently ratchets up the dramatic tension, hooking readers. His thorough research and interviews give the book complexity, richness of character, and urgency."

—**Stephen Singular**

MURDER IN THE HEARTLAND

"Drawing on interviews with law officers and relatives, the author has done significant research. His facile writing pulls the reader along."

—*St. Louis Post-Dispatch*

"Phelps expertly reminds us that when the darkest form of evil invades the quiet and safe outposts of rural America, the tragedy is greatly magnified. Get ready for some sleepless nights."

—**Carlton Stowers**

"This is the most disturbing and moving look at murder in rural America since Capote's *In Cold Blood*."

—**Gregg Olsen**

SLEEP IN HEAVENLY PEACE

"An exceptional book by an exceptional true crime writer. Phelps exposes long-hidden secrets and reveals disquieting truths."

—**Kathryn Casey**

EVERY MOVE YOU MAKE

"An insightful and fast-paced examination of the inner workings of a good cop and his bad informant, culminating in an unforgettable truth-is-stranger-than-fiction climax."

—**Michael M. Baden, M.D.**

"M. William Phelps is the rising star of the nonfiction crime genre, and his true tales of murder are scary-as-hell thrill rides into the dark heart of the inhuman condition."

—**Douglas Clegg**

LETHAL GUARDIAN

"An intense roller-coaster of a crime story . . . complex, with twists and turns worthy of any great detective mystery . . . reads more like a novel than your standard non-fiction crime book."

—**Steve Jackson**

PERFECT POISON

"True crime at its best—compelling, gripping, an edge-of-the-seat thriller. Phelps packs wallops of delight with his skillful ability to narrate a suspenseful story."

—**Harvey Rachlin**

"A compelling account of terror . . . the author dedicates himself to unmasking the psychopath with facts, insight and the other proven methods of journalistic leg work."

—**Lowell Cauffiel**

Also By M. William Phelps

Perfect Poison

Lethal Guardian

Every Move You Make

Sleep in Heavenly Peace

Murder in the Heartland

Because You Loved Me

If Looks Could Kill

I'll Be Watching You

Deadly Secrets

Cruel Death

Death Trap

Kill For Me

Love Her to Death

Too Young to Kill

Never See Them Again

Murder, New England

Failures of the Presidents (coauthor)

Nathan Hale: The Life and Death of America's First Spy

The Devil's Rooming House: The True Story of America's Deadliest Female Serial Killer

The Devil's Right Hand: The Tragic Story of the Colt Family Curse

The Dead Soul: A Thriller (available as eBook only)

Kiss of the She-Devil

Bad Girls

ACT ONE
THE EXPOSITION

CHAPTER 1

SUSAN RAYMUNDO WAS used to her daughter calling her Florida winter home at least twice a day. Anna Lisa was good that way. She liked to stay in close touch with her parents, even just to say hello, things are fine.

"She was a very thoughtful daughter," Anna's father, Renato, later said. "She was a perfect daughter . . . an excellent human being."

Smart too: Anna Lisa held a bachelor's degree from Harvard and a master's from Columbia University.

On November 8, 2002, retired pediatrician Susan Raymundo was at a local hospital near her Florida home with her mother, who was undergoing a routine procedure. When she returned to the house, Susan noticed the light on the answering machine blinking. During that ride home, Susan later recalled, she'd had an uneasy feeling. She couldn't put her finger on it, but something was nagging at her.

Something was wrong.

Tossing her keys on the counter, putting her handbag down, Susan hit the PLAY button and listened, knowing who it was.

Anna . . .

"Hi, Mom and Dad. I just want you to know what's going

on. I know you're busy with Grandma, but I'll talk to you sometime."

It was 10:34 A.M., Susan noticed, when the message came in.

After getting herself situated, Susan called Anna Lisa back. The line rang several times, but there was no answer.

Odd.

Anna worked from home on Fridays. She was always there, especially during the day. Susan and her husband had purchased the Connecticut condo for Anna Lisa, closing the deal back on March 15, 2000.

I'll try again later, Susan told herself, perhaps subtly sensing, if only with a motherly intuition, that something was amiss. During the car ride home from the hospital, was that feeling she had related to Anna?

CHAPTER 2

THE WOMAN SOUNDED FRANTIC. She was in a terrible hurry. Inhaling and exhaling heavily, as if out of breath. Yet, strangely enough, she cleared her throat before speaking for the first time.

"Yes, hello . . . ," the woman said after the Stamford Police Department (SPD) 911 dispatcher beckoned her to speak up. "Yes . . . the guy . . . the . . . he attacked my neighbor."

"You mean someone attacked your neighbor?" dispatch asked as the caller blew two gasping, dramatic breaths into the receiver.

Whoosh . . . whoosh.

"Yes, yes . . . ," the caller said, but she sounded sheepish, as if uncomfortable for some reason.

"When did this happen?" dispatch queried.

It sounded as if the caller said: "I saw a guy go into the apartment at 1-2-3 Harbor View . . ."

Dispatch noted the address. Then, not quite understanding, the police operator asked: "One twenty-six Harbor View—"

But the caller interrupted, correcting the dispatcher in

an angry tone, yelling over the dispatcher's voice: "One twenty-*three* Harbor View!"

"Okay," dispatch said. "Don't yell, because I cannot understand you."

Almost in tears now, the seemingly frantic 911 caller spoke once again over dispatch: "One twenty-three Harbor View."

"Listen to me . . . 123 Harbor View . . . what is your friend's name?"

"I don't know her name, but she's my neighbor and she lives in apartment 1-0-5."

"She lives in apartment 1-0-5?"

"Right! And the guy was in there, and he . . ."

"He what?"

"He *attacked* her."

"Okay. Can you tell me what the guy looks like?"

"I just don't know. I heard yelling. I heard yelling."

There was a clicking sound next.

"Hello?" dispatch said. "Hello? Hello?"

The line was dead.

This strange call, in its entirety, lasted one minute, thirty seconds.

CHAPTER 3

HE HAD JUST finished eating lunch. It was near 12:30 P.M., November 8, 2002—that same Friday. The weather was rather mild for this time of the year near the Connecticut shoreline, the temperature ranging from 46 to 57 degrees Fahrenheit. The air was dry and sharp, a slight breeze, with winds of approximately six miles per hour rolling in off the Atlantic Ocean. The sun was bright and blinding. There was a waxing crescent moon (7/8 full), nearly visible in the illuminating blue skies. By all accounts, a resident could call it a picture-perfect late fall day in one of Connecticut's more prominent, upscale, seaside communities.

The cop drove a marked police cruiser. He was dressed in full uniform. The area that twenty-two-year veteran police officer David Sileo patrolled was indeed exclusive. Officers called it "District Three." Stamford had seen a sharp economic resurgence in recent years; its downtown was revitalized and injected with a bit of vitality—shops and businesses thriving. The bubble all around them might have burst, but Stamford seemed to be still floating. This particular region just outside downtown, where Officer Sileo headed, was known to locals as "Cove/Shippan," located south of Interstate 95, in between Cummings Park and Cove Island Park.

Yachts and fishing rigs and houseboats.

Money and status.

The dwelling at 123 Harbor Drive sat in an inlet, a cove, southwest of West Beach, just across the waterway from Dyke Park. It was not Harbor View, as the caller had suggested. People walked their dogs here. Docked their massive sailboats and Bayliners and Sea Rays, cruise liners and immense pleasure boats. Men and women jogged in expensive sweat suits, earbuds pushed in deeply for privacy, minding their own business. Families had picnics and tossed Frisbees, lay out in the sun when weather permitted. Stamford, Connecticut, by and large, is a wealthy region within a small state of 3 million-plus residents. Stamford is the sister to the more select, more elite, and perhaps even snootier Greenwich. By big-city standards, Stamford boasts a small population of about 120,000. Median income holds steady at $75,000. Taxes are high. The streets are mostly clean. Crime rates in certain areas are low. Housing prices fluctuate, depending on where a person wants to live within the city limits.

Officer Sileo was dispatched to 123 Harbor Drive, unit 105, specifically, after that strangely cryptic 911 call moments before, wherein an anonymous woman had maintained that a neighbor—someone she apparently knew—was being attacked by a man.

Those three facts were clear: *neighbor, attack, man.*

When Sileo arrived, another officer pulled up behind him. They agreed to knock on the door. See what the hell was going on—if anything—inside the condo.

The unit at 105 Harbor Drive (not Harbor View) sat atop a three-car garage. Visitors walked up a few steps to the front door.

Officer Lawrence Densky, who had arrived as Sileo did, knocked on the screen door. Sileo looked into the condo through the side-window panels on the left side of the door.

Neither officer heard or saw anything.

So Sileo rang the doorbell.

They waited.

Nothing.

With no answer, Sileo attempted to open the door. He turned the knob.

It was unlocked.

Sileo watched as his colleague, Officer Densky, pushed the door open "a few inches," took a quick peek inside, and then yelled, "Stamford Police . . . is anyone home?"

No response.

It was eerily quiet—especially for a domestic incident, the type of which had been called into 911. If two people were arguing, where were they?

Pushing the door fully open, Densky spied a ghastly sight, which prompted him to immediately draw his weapon.

Officer Sileo stood directly behind his colleague, hand on his sidearm.

Both cops made eye contact with each other and agreed silently with head nods to enter the condo slowly, barrels of their weapons leading the way.

CHAPTER 4

NELSON SESSLER WAS hired in September 2000 by Stamford-based Purdue Pharma, a major player in the pharmaceutical world of developing medications. Purdue stakes claim to being the industry leader in pain management. For Nelson, who held a doctorate in pharmacy from the Massachusetts College of Pharmacy and Health Sciences (MCPHS), Purdue was the ideal company to work for. He could pursue his passion for research and development, and ultimately carve out a career he could excel in. At the same rate, he could take some pride in the work he was doing.

At thirty-five years old, Nelson Sessler had hit his prime. He was a good-looking man. Tall, thin, handsome. He took care of himself, working out and working hard. Purdue was one of those companies so big, with an employee list of so many diverse individuals, that cliques kicked up within the group an employee worked for. Nelson had no trouble making friends. And in December 2000, merely months after he started with the company, he met and quickly began dating a fellow employee, thirty-two-year-old Anna Lisa Raymundo. Anna Lisa was a bright prospect from a family of well-educated high achievers working within the medical field. Philippine by descent, Anna Lisa had beautiful dark, shiny skin, eyes to match, a cheerful demeanor, and a smile so large it was hard not to like the woman and feel her magnetic charm the moment she was introduced.

"You look at a photo of Anna," a good friend later said, "and although it displays her beauty and perfect skin, no photo I ever saw of her captured how beautiful she truly was."

With a master's in public health, Anna had been working at Purdue for several years. She liked Nelson Sessler the moment she met him. They hit it off.

Nelson shared an apartment in town with several men, about three miles away from Anna Lisa's Harbor Drive condo. By November 2002, however, as their relationship hit its stride, going from its highest and lowest points, he had been spending most of his time over at Anna Lisa's condo.

"Five to seven [days]," Nelson said later. "The majority of the week."

In February 2002, Anna Lisa left Purdue Pharma and went to work for a New Jersey company, Pharmacia. There was a time when Anna was actually commuting back and forth to New Jersey from her Stamford condo, spending four hours per day on the road. By November, however, Anna Lisa had worked it out with Pharmacia that she could work from home and head into the office for meetings on an as-needed basis.

Nelson Sessler was the first to admit later that his relationship with Anna Lisa had maybe run its course by November 2002. They had hit a stride, sure, but it was more or less lined with complacency as he, anyway, was going through the motions. As long as Nelson had known Anna, he had not given up his room at the apartment across town he shared with three other men. And that alone said something about how Nelson Sessler felt.

For Nelson, there was that feeling of going through the motions with Anna, but there was also a secret Nelson had been keeping from Anna: He had been sneaking around, sleeping with one of his coworkers at Pharma. She was a rather elegant, highly intelligent, dark-skinned woman, who had told most of her friends that she was Italian and French, perhaps not wanting to share that she had spent fourteen years in the Middle East as a young child, which was where her parents were actually from. She had long, flowing, curly tar-black hair. Nelson had met her socially at the local bar Pharma employees hung out at in town after work for happy hour. Nelson had been having a fling with the thirty-two-year-old woman since the summer of 2001, almost a year by then—although, by November 2002, according to Nelson, it had been over for some time. He had made it clear to the woman he wasn't interested. While their relationship had been hot and heavy that spring and early summer, Nelson couldn't really see his concubine too often because, he later explained, she "had a handicapped brother—a mentally challenged or retarded brother that she took care of—and elderly parents, and volleyball. And that those three items took up most of her weekends. . . ."

So by late summer, Nelson had decided to devote himself once more to Anna.

CHAPTER 5

JUST BEYOND THE DOOR, inside that Harbor Drive condo the SPD had been summoned to during the early afternoon of November 8, 2002, Officers David Sileo and Lawrence Densky immediately entered through the unlocked front door with their weapons drawn. They had been lured into the condo by what was a horrifying sight before them, right there near the foyer of the front door.

"The apartment was in disarray," Sileo explained later. "There were signs of a violent struggle."

Violent struggle didn't even begin to describe what they would see next.

Before them was a hallway filled with "blood and broken glass," Sileo said in one of his reports: *And the victim appeared to be bleeding from the head and face areas.*

Indeed. The body of a young female was stretched out on the floor, her legs spread open: One leg was propped up on a box, the other on the floor. There was blood all over; smears and smudges and spatters on the white tile underneath her body, as if beet juice had been spilled and tossed around by a child playing in it. The walls and carpeting had blood smears and spatter, too, all the way down the hallway heading toward the bathroom. There was blood on the victim's jeans, on her bare feet. She was fully clothed, but her white shirt (a sweater) had been pulled up to her breasts (not in a sexual manner, mind you, but amid some sort of struggle for life). On the wood floor by her foot was a barbell, a ten-pound chunk of steel, essentially. Next to that was a plant, with its dirt out of the pot. The soil was spread all over the place by what was a very deadly encounter, one would guess.

The woman lay adjacent to the stairs heading up to a second level inside the home and the front door. A laundry basket was tipped over, as were other pieces of furniture. There were boxes and everyday items found in any home scattered around, as though there had been a terribly violent, extended scuffle.

A fight to the death.

These smudges of blood on the floor, however gruesome they were, told a story these officers were immediately familiar with: There had been a terrific battle *after* blood was present.

Several additional officers were on their way to the scene within those moments after Sileo and Densky entered. The troops had been called in. It was put out over the radio by dispatch that the SPD's Bureau of Criminal Investigation (BCI) was needed fast at the Harbor Drive scene.

"We got a ten-one," a superior officer announced over the radio.

As one officer drove toward the scene at a high rate of speed, he knew what that meant: *A 10-1 equals homicide.*

As he headed toward Harbor Drive, however, this particular officer was soon called off.

"We need you to head out to the Duchess Restaurant to secure a pay phone there," dispatch ordered.

"Ten-four."

Seemed like a strange request, but the officer shifted his destination and took off on his way. The Duchess, he knew, was only about a half mile from the crime scene.

Back at the Harbor Drive condo, it became obvious that the dead woman on the floor had been ambushed, or attacked by surprise. The scene just had that feel to it. But what also made sense by quickly analyzing the scene around the woman was that it had taken a while for her to be murdered. It wasn't quick. The scuffle had started in one place and finished in another. She fought, which was obvious in the way things were tossed around and blood was spattered and smudged all over. It wasn't as if she was murdered in the spot where an apparent argument took place. The fight—and that was what this was, for certain—started in a place and went throughout the home and ended where she had been found lying on the floor.

Officer David Sileo, gun in hand, eyes darting in all directions inside the condo, with Lawrence Densky covering him, reached down and checked the victim for vital signs.

There were none.

The wounds appear fresh, Sileo thought. The blood had not had time to begin coagulating. Puddles of blood were shiny and wet. Tacky. The victim herself appeared to be still bleeding out.

Whatever had taken place inside this home had perhaps happened within the hour—a few at most.

The officers knew what to do next. They had been trained. The first thing an officer did when he entered a residence with a possible dead body (DB) was to clear the remainder of the home. Make sure there were no additional victims or a perpetrator hiding out, waiting to attack anyone coming into the home.

After a cursory search of the condo, Sileo was confident they were alone with one victim.

Next, Sileo and his colleague sealed off the front door, not allowing anyone in. They'd greet the team of investigators on their way to begin the process of finding out what in the name of God happened to this woman and, more important, who did it.

CHAPTER 6

THE WOMAN WITH WHOM Nelson Sessler had been cheating on Anna Lisa became somewhat of a nuisance in his life as the summer of 2002 progressed. He grew tired of her. According to Nelson, by that June, he and his mistress, Sheila Davalloo, the coworker whom he had been sleeping with when Anna wasn't around, had stopped having sex altogether.

"I saw her a number of times to walk her dog," Nelson later explained. Sheila had purchased a dog that spring. "And she asked me to come to her place . . . to walk the dog on a couple of occasions, where she had something going on and couldn't get home."

"Stamford (Connecticut) to Pleasantville (New York) is quite a ride," one law enforcement officer said later. "I cannot believe Mr. Sessler was going all that way just to walk her dogs—and *not* getting laid."

Sheila Davalloo had turned thirty-three on May 11, 2002. Her lover, Nelson Sessler, was a research pharmacist, his work revolved around the research-and-development side of Purdue: the development of drugs, the marketing of drugs, and the use of programs to educate physicians about drugs. Sheila, on the other hand, was a manager of medical coding and thesaurus administration, a select group within Biostatistics and Clinical Data Management (BCDM). She did not conduct formal scientific (bench) research, in a traditional sense. According to one source, Sheila's role at Purdue "dealt with pharmaceutical adverse event reporting and how to code adverse events in a uniform way so that they could be more easily analyzed." She lived in Pleasantville, New York. From Stamford, where Nelson lived, Sheila's apartment was about a forty-minute drive south on I-95, before heading north on I-287, up through White Plains, New York, and Hawthorne, along the Hudson River. That was on a good day. With traffic, an hour at least. Still, it was a nice backcountry drive: the pine trees, oaks, and maples; the plush landscapes and bubbling waterways; the trendy new homes; People around here worked mostly in New York City and the financial districts of Stamford and Greenwich. Pleasantville, in particular, is one of those perfect places to raise kids and live a happy-ever-after life, devoid of any big-city problems or politics. The people are kind, considerate, loving. They look out for one another and enjoy the peace and quiet they've worked so hard to live around.

For Sheila Davalloo, however, she'd had her share of problems and issues over the years—boy, had she ever. It was Nelson Sessler, Sheila had said on more than one occasion, making her life a bit easier, a bit more managable. Sheila made great money at Pharma, in the six-figure range. She had the looks. Age was on Sheila's side at this point; time had been okay to her. Yet, there was something within Sheila that just didn't seem (or, to her, feel) right. Sheila would show signs of not being able to deal with loss or rejection. She was the first to admit that she had major issues where men were involved.

Nelson Sessler would go over to Sheila's condo—after

they had apparently stopped having sex and were more friends than anything else, according to Nelson—to grab Sheila's dogs and take them for a walk around the neighborhood. Nelson felt bad for Sheila. She was alone, she'd explained to him, and didn't like it. Life since their breakup was something she didn't want to think about. How could she go on without the love of her life? Nelson Sessler had hit every note for Sheila. He was all she could think about—that one guy who was going to give her life a happily-ever-after ending.

Except that for Nelson, it just wasn't meant to be. Sheila was lucky he was still hanging around. He felt bad for her. And, beyond that, he was with Anna, who was actually pressuring him to buy her a ring that coming Christmas holiday.

Sheila knew about Anna Lisa and Nelson. He said later that while Anna worked at Pharma, they rarely shared their relationship with anyone, including Sheila, because they felt it might negatively impact what people thought of their work and passion for their chosen professions. But since Anna had taken that job in New Jersey, Nelson was more "open," as he had once put it, to admit and talk about his relationship with her. As the summer of 2002 continued—and his relationship with Sheila became more like one of friends (with possible benefits) rather than the love story Sheila had sought—Nelson was leaning more toward marrying Anna. At least that's what Nelson later said. He and Anna had settled into a routine, and he was beginning to enjoy it.

In the spirit of Nelson and Anna Lisa becoming tighter, and Nelson and Sheila growing apart, Nelson decided he wanted to introduce one of his good friends to Sheila. The guy was coming down from Boston to attend a Yankees game in the Bronx with Nelson.

Maybe he and Sheila will hit it off? Nelson considered.

And perhaps with that introduction, Nelson could get rid of Sheila and refocus his life on Anna.

"I invited Sheila to join us so that [my friend] could meet her," he explained later. "My friend is a big sports fan."

Sheila had expressed a great interest in volleyball to Nelson and had told him she was on a women's team in town.

"I figured if Sheila was this big sports fan, spending most of her time [as she had always said] doing this volleyball, that maybe they would be a good match."

So they all went to the game. Sheila, perhaps more than Nelson's friend, seemed interested—on the outside, anyway.

The friend went home after the weekend and Nelson forgot about it.

A month later, near the end of the summer, his friend contacted him.

"Your friend keeps e-mailing me," Nelson's friend said. "I'm *not* interested in her."

Sheila had refocused her desires and attention on Nelson's friend. In a series of e-mails that the friend shared with Nelson, all of which had been penned by Sheila, she had detailed a trip she wanted to take with the friend to West Virginia to go white-water rafting. After that, there could be a trip to a bar to watch a soccer game. There were other trips, too, that Sheila said she wanted to plan. It seemed Sheila had turned her attention on this new guy, even though he wasn't interested.

In each one of these e-mails, however, and in the trips that Sheila wanted to plan, she asked the friend to "make sure" Nelson joined them. It would be the three of them.

Sheila wasn't giving up on Nelson that easily.

Right around Halloween, near the first week of November 2002, Nelson Sessler knew he had a problem with Sheila and her not being able to let go. Nelson had gone down to North Carolina with a colleague on a business trip. Lo and behold, when he got there, he realized Sheila had "arranged business with the same vendor, at the same time." She had essentially followed him to the state.

How did she even know where he was going to be working? He had not shared the trip with her.

"What are you doing here?" he asked when he "ran into" Sheila.

"We're in the same work group, right?" she said.

Turned out that Sheila had not only volunteered to be in Nelson's work group at Pharma, but she had also volunteered to be part of the team on the project he had been working on.

Nelson had known nothing about it.

During that overnight trip, Nelson later claimed, he did not sleep with Sheila. Nor did he have much interaction with her. He couldn't understand what was going on. According to him, he had never told Sheila he loved her. Not once. Moreover, he said, he had never even bought her a gift. Or taken her to meet his parents. Never discussed living together. Never talked about them being some sort of item someday.

According to Nelson's evaluation of the relationship, he and Sheila had met at work, hooked up at a bar one night when he was at a down point in his romance with Anna, and had sex several times. It was a fling—a one-night stand that lasted a little longer. It was just some fun in the sack to forget their troubles. They were adults. They had sex. Sure, Nelson might have been considered a dog to treat Sheila like she was disposable. He might not have been the best guy in the world while using her for sex. He could claim that while he and Sheila were sleeping together, he and Anna were just dating and not exclusive. He might have to sit down someday and take a look at his morals and maybe change.

However, if anyone asks Nelson Sessler, he'll say that he never made any suggestion to Sheila Davalloo that he was in love with her, or that there was a future for them. It was a damn workplace affair. Why wasn't this woman getting over it and moving on?

Sheila had viewed the relationship quite differently. And there were so many secrets she had kept from Nelson, so many aspects of her life he had not a clue about. When the closet opened up and all those skeletons fell out, Nelson Sessler was going to wish he had not only never slept with this woman, but had never met her.

CHAPTER 7

BY 12:30 P.M., emergency medical services (EMS) specialist Tom Manning had arrived at the Harbor Drive scene with several paramedics.

"She's gone," Manning told Officer David Sileo.

The inside of the condo had to be maintained; it was a massive crime scene. Potential evidence was everywhere.

As Sileo stood, he watched Detectives Greg Holt and Yan Vanderven, colleagues from the BCI, pull up. Within the next ten minutes, a dozen or so seasoned investigators, decades upon decades of detective work experience among them, would arrive and begin to figure out the best way to approach a crime scene of such massive magnitude.

With nearly thirty years with the SPD, Richard Colwell was a highly skilled investigator and decorated officer. Colwell had seen a lot of murder in his day. As Colwell heard the call go out for Harbor Drive, he grabbed SPD captain Richard Conklin and headed out the door.

The officers and investigators already at the scene when Conklin and Colwell arrived explained that the victim was still inside where they had found her. By this time, crime scene tape had gone up, a swarm of patrol officers had blocked off the area, and neighbors and bystanders had begun to emerge on the other side of the flapping yellow tape. There was an ambulance parked near the garage. As Conklin and Colwell walked up to the door, however, they were told the ambulance was unnecessary.

"She's dead."

First thing they did after that was walk through the entire scene and make certain the condo had been thoroughly searched for "suspects and any additional victims." It was a more thorough exploration than the responding officers had done in haste.

Procedure.

As they did this, Conklin realized what an enormous crime scene they had before them. The struggle the victim had been involved in had begun in one portion of the condo and seemed to encompass several rooms throughout the main level.

When they were finished with that somewhat laborious inspection of the condo, Colwell gathered up a few officers and explained, "I need a unit to get over to the Duchess Restaurant."

Since they'd left the station, Conklin and Colwell had learned that the 911 call, which had sparked interest in this entire crime scene and murder investigation, had been made from a local Duchess hamburger/hot dog restaurant in Stamford, there on Shippan Avenue, just up the road from the condo complex. There was an officer up there already, but Conklin wanted additional officers to protect and preserve that scene.

They needed to find the person who made the 911 call.

"That was where dispatch told us the 911 call had come from," Colwell later explained. "So we wanted to see if the caller was still there and see if there was any evidence at that scene."

Good move.

The caller was likely waiting in the restaurant for cops to arrive.

The other officer arrived at the Duchess just as several additional officers had. There were two telephones located on the Shippan Avenue sidewalk, out in front of the restaurant. A sergeant on scene already told the officers, "I need all units to begin canvassing this entire area. I also need someone to find out about any videotape the restaurant might have."

The 911 caller was nowhere to be found.

They needed to know who had made the 911 call—and, better yet, why that person was hiding from police? There's that whole "I don't want to get involved" sense some people live by. But considering what had happened back at Harbor Drive, this caller held one of the keys to the case.

The "man" mentioned on the call.

One officer spoke to both managers of the restaurant, asking for any surveillance tapes from the day and the night before.

"No problem," they said.

A man walked over to the officers securing the telephone scene.

"I saw something," he said.

"You what?"

"I witnessed a possible assault that happened on Harbor Drive by the boat slips."

Had the scuffle Anna Lisa gotten into actually started at the boat slip and concluded inside her condo?

"Get him down to HQ," the sergeant ordered.

The witness was asked to give a complete statement downtown.

He agreed.

* * *

Meanwhile, Captain Richard Conklin became concerned about something as he began studying the crime scene: namely, its size and scope. The SPD was not equipped to dig into such an expansive crime scene, with what looked to be evidence from the kitchen to the living room to the bathroom and all points beyond. They had the manpower and experience, but they were in great need of help. The Connecticut State Police (CSP) had a mobile crime scene truck as big as some small-town brick-and-mortar units. It was the size of a recreational vehicle. The SPD could handle large crime scenes; that was not the issue. Conklin knew his crime scene investigators (CSIs) were competent, capable evidence techs who could do the job, and do it well. But the size, again, was intimidating.

Especially when they had a vicious killer at large.

"So we considered something a little bit out of the ordinary [for us]," Conklin said later. Conklin didn't tell anyone, but he began to think about calling in the Connecticut State Police Major Crime Squad Crime Lab to assist in the processing. The CSP's crime lab is an enormous operation, with the potential to bring its state-of-the-art mobile crime lab to the scene, on top of its resources. None other than Dr. Henry Lee was involved with the lab on the forensic and crime scene reconstruction side. Having them possibly process what was a complicated scene with evidence all over the place, Conklin felt might be the right move. The question he had to ponder seriously, though, was: How would it go over with his crew? He did not want to cause any division among the troops. Especially now, with what appeared to be a major whodunit in front of them.

Captain Conklin had a rather interesting climb up the law enforcement ladder and found himself, when not at work fighting crime, consulting with none other than James Patterson, the megafamous thriller author. Conklin was even a character in some of the novels. His name? Richard Conklin, and in *The Women's Murder Club* books Conklin has been called "Inspector Hottie." In the *11th Hour,* Patterson writes, *Conklin is good with people, especially women. In fact, he's known for it.*

"You can tell it's all fiction," Conklin said with a chuckle, describing his Patterson character, "because they describe me in the books as six-one, dark hair . . . slim. . . . My hair's gray at this point. I'm not anywhere near six feet." He laughed.

Put aside the razzing the guy took when those books were released, and it's clear to say that a person doesn't get the gig of captain by asking for it; it's earned. And Richard Conklin, despite the over-the-top character Patterson created in his image, is a top-notch cop. There's nothing Hollywood about Conklin. He's sharp and does things by the book. If Anna Lisa could have chosen the cop she wanted to manage the investigation of her murder, she could have never chosen a better investigator than Conklin to lead the task and begin delegating jobs to his crack team of BCI detectives.

Conklin was no rookie when it came to high-profile cases. He would ultimately run the Charla Nash investigation in 2009. Charla Nash was attacked by Travis, a chimp one of her friends owned and kept at her house. The victim's face was literally torn off. She was blinded; her hands were chewed off. She had no nose, no ears, no eyes. There was nothing left to her scalp. It was an international news story, garnering coverage around the world. Conklin and his team were left to cipher through it all and come to a conclusion. He's done projects with National Geographic Channel, History Channel, Animal Planet, and many others.

Conklin had been with the SPD since 1980, working his way into heading BCI. He was born and raised on Long Island. He started his life as a commercial fisherman. One year out of college, though, the fishing industry collapsed and

Conklin found himself looking for work. Law enforcement was a thought that soon turned into reality when Conklin realized he was being called.

Climbing the law enforcement ladder, he ran narcotics and organized crime units before the position of captain was created for him. It's really not just BCI that he leads, but "all investigative units."

This type of horrendous murder Conklin and his team were looking at inside unit 105 at 123 Harbor Drive was not something the SPD was accustomed to investigating. Sure, the crack boom of the 1980s and the gang wars of the 1990s brought with it lots of death and destruction to the city. The murder rate was higher at that time than anybody would have liked to admit. But this—a seemingly senseless act of violence perpetrated inside the home of a woman, in what was the middle of the day, in a high-end, exclusive area of the city—wasn't something the SPD saw a lot of.

That 911 call became an important part of the investigation immediately. The caller, a female, had said she was a neighbor. And yet, as Conklin thought about it, "She wasn't that familiar with the terminology one might use if you're familiar with that neighborhood."

It was very strange.

So Conklin sent out some officers to canvass the condo facility, door-to-door, to see if anyone would admit to making the call.

True, the dispatcher had to pull the information out of the caller. It did not come naturally as part of their conversation. That was a red flag, the dispatcher noted. In all the years this dispatcher had fielded calls, very rarely did someone call, claim to be a neighbor, but not get the address correct and not really know what they're talking about.

There is something to that. . . . Conklin believed this right from the get-go. He knew it was going to become a major part of the case.

As Conklin and several investigators looked more closely at what they had, it appeared that Anna had been "brutally attacked . . . stabbed repeatedly. . . . There was so much blood [and] things overturned."

But if the killer used a knife, there was no murder weapon in clear sight.

Conklin stopped and thought about it. He looked at the furniture, the door left open, unlocked, and the things banged around.

"It was obvious to us that the place had *not* been ransacked."

Plus, there were valuables lying around.

"Yeah, it was clear that this was not a burglary or robbery. There're no drawers opened and gone through, things like that. So right away, you're thinking, 'I need to learn more about the victim. Circles she traveled in.'"

Victimology: Place the victim in the middle of the matrix and begin to work the case outward, talking to family and friends, neighbors, anyone who could paint a picture of who Anna Lisa was and where she hung around, who her love interests might be. The scene had the feeling of an argument that turned deadly. Two lovers, yelling and screaming, going toe-to-toe, and then one became violent.

That 911 call: *a man.*

Conklin had seen this before, and the way in which Anna was murdered indicated overkill. Someone was angry with her, completely enraged. People might say, *"Oh, she was perfect. Everyone loved her! She did not have an enemy in the world."* Well, with a scene as brutal as the one before Conklin and his team, there was one thing crystal clear about Anna Lisa Raymundo: There was indeed someone out there who did not care for her.

Conklin surveyed the crime scene. It was near 1:00 P.M. As he walked around, his gut spoke to him: *This is going to be a forensic case.* . . .

Within that condo—somewhere—was the answer to the mystery.

CHAPTER 8

IF ASKED, SHEILA DAVALLOO would have no trouble describing her role at Purdue Pharma pre-2002 as the company's "star employee." Sheila considered herself one of Pharma's top performers—someone upon whom the company relied as a go-to worker, eagerly fighting her way up through the company's corporate infrastructure.

Nothing could be further from the truth, however, if one looks at Sheila's life leading up to those days when she and Nelson were becoming friends *without* benefits and she found herself in a terrible funk. According to Sheila, life had dealt her a weighty blow. With Nelson, she thought she'd found true love, her soul mate. And Sheila was definitely one who could talk for hours about lost loves and bad relationships of the past. In Nelson, Sheila believed the entire package was there before her. But that's the thing with relationships: They need two to tango. And Nelson didn't feel the same way. He had been in it from the beginning for a good time, the steamy sex, the thrill of a workplace affair that they were keeping secret. Nothing more. He was sowing his oats. Whatever cliché a person wants to drop into this situation would work. Nelson wasn't exclusive with Anna Lisa, he said, they were dating.

And Nelson was testing the color of the grass on the other side.

But love and marriage and a home with Sheila?

Uh-huh. No way.

Not ever.

As the summer of 2002 wound down, Sheila was beginning to—if not accept—at least realize her chances with Nelson were over. She was finally admitting to herself that Nelson was not interested. And that admission, alone, had led Sheila down a path of great melancholy.

She later said she felt alone and hopeless.

"I was taking advantage of my position in the company," Sheila explained. "Not functioning one hundred percent. Not responding to e-mails. Basically not working at all. And I was extremely, *extremely* depressed."

Sheila claimed that since the age of fifteen, she had suffered from depression. She'd always deal with it accordingly, doing the things most people with depression do; but as the fall of 2002 arrived, this time was different. She and Nelson were obviously never going to be together—even their friendship was just about over—and Sheila found herself "hitting an absolute bottom."

Part of what she did was leave the office, head home to take the dogs out for a walk, then hit the couch for a little afternoon nap. She would close her eyes, drift away, and forget about life for a while.

Sheila had worked in the pain management field at Pharma. She especially knew which drugs were best for which condition. It was her job to know those things. And throughout that year, Sheila later said, she had developed a hunger for some of those meds.

"During those months where I had severe lows, I would continue to take . . . basically Valium, Dilaudid, and I had a slew of other medications at home," Sheila explained.

Dilaudid is known on the street as "hospital heroin." It is a very potent drug, if heading on the freeway to Never-Never Land is what a user is game to do. People pop Dilaudid pills, sure. Lots more crush it up and snort it, or cook and inject it.

Vicodin was originally prescribed to Sheila after a surgery she had for some back pain during which, according to Sheila, the doctors "severed three nerves in my back [and] upper thorax." To combat that unbearable pain, Sheila said, she started using Vicodin and Dilaudid. Both drugs are in the narcotic (opioid) family and Sheila was taking them "regularly." As many as "fifteen to twenty pills of Vicodin, sometimes, a day, and others. I had other medications at home. I had Valium that I would take regularly. I had Xanax that I would take regularly. I had Percocet I had bought over the entire time—I had a box full of medications at home."

Both prescribed and not prescribed.

Sheila, it could be said, was a prescription drug addict with a lot of money in the bank, a darkness settling on her, and slowly was beginning not to care about herself or the world in which she inhabited.

Sheila, if what she says holds any truth, was far below her bottom.

Nelson Sessler met Anna Lisa Raymundo in December 2000 during happy hour one night at a spot where people working at Pharma tended to hang out. It was downtown Stamford. A group got together. Anna and Nelson talked. Liked what the other had to say. Had some things in common. Started dating.

Things became serious between them as November 2002 approached. Although Nelson "had some clothes, a tooth-brush . . . some weights, barbell weights" over at Anna Lisa's, and she paid all the bills at the condo, he still considered

himself living there most of the time. And his former affair—
which he believed Anna had not uncovered—with his
coworker Sheila Davalloo was completely over. Nelson and
Anna were back, heading toward a life together.

If there was one thing about Anna, Nelson later explained,
she kept the condo clean—especially the bathrooms and the
downstairs living area.

"Spotless," Nelson said.

When Nelson and Sheila talked about their lives, Anna
never came up. Nelson never mentioned her. As far as Sheila
knew, he lived with his buddies on the other end of town.
Sheila did not even know Anna existed. At least that is what
Nelson believed. Yet, when an objective person steps back and
looks at the situation, it was pretty clear that Sheila knew
Nelson was dating Anna. For Sheila, there needed to be a
reason why she had been rejected. It couldn't just be that
Nelson hadn't fallen for her or didn't share the same feelings.
There had to be that other element—another woman.

But then there was that business trip Nelson took to North
Carolina during the week of November 1, 2002, where he ran
into Sheila and she explained how she was now in the same
work group and they just *happened* to run into each other.
Sheila thought about that one day. It was too much for the
guy. She had pushed too far. Nelson knew he could not see
her anymore, not even as friends. She couldn't handle it.

That relationship, whatever was left of it, was completely
over. Still, Nelson Sessler had to wonder if Sheila Davalloo
was ever going to leave him alone, and just what was he prepared to do if she didn't.

CHAPTER 9

THERE ARE WAYS to handle a crime scene as large as the one the SPD faced on November 8, 2002, at 123 Harbor Drive. Captain Richard Conklin made the right call when he decided to ask the Connecticut State Police to come in with their sizable crew of CSIs and forensic investigators and begin processing the scene. There were far too many blood droplets, smudges, smears, spatters, and items that needed processing, bagging, and tagging. There was fingerprint dusting that needed to be done just about everywhere. Drawings had to be made. Photographs snapped. Reports written.

There were answers here in Anna Lisa Raymundo's condo. With the right mind-set and patience, the SPD would find that clue leading them to a person of interest (POI). Maybe several clues, actually.

"It was the one and only time I have even done it," Conklin commented, thinking back to that moment when he made the decision to call in the CSP. "And I'm very happy I did."

After conversing with his lieutenant and sergeant within the BCI, Conklin called the CSP crime scene unit to get over to Stamford as soon as they could gas up the supersize CSI rig and get it parked in front of Anna Lisa's unit. Still, Conklin knew there was a political aspect to calling in the CSP, and there could be fallout if the situation was not handled with respect and dignity to his men. Was he dissing his forensic unit by asking the "big boys" to come in and help out? That was certainly never Conklin's intention.

But would it come across that way? Would the department's CSIs feel slighted?

"What do you think?" Conklin asked his lieutenant after explaining his decision.

"It's probably a good idea," the lieutenant agreed.

"Our guys will work *with* them, you know."

"Yeah."

So the two teams of CSIs—the CSP and the SPD forensic and crime scene unit—would work as one team to sift through what was a mountain of forensic and potential trace evidence. But even more than that, whenever the Connecticut State Police responded to a crime scene to assist a local department, along with the CSP forensic team and the mobile crime lab came five detectives and a sergeant.

"And that alone, we knew," said one investigator on the scene, "was going to play a major role for us here in getting some answers. If we had to do it alone, we would have been at the scene for days."

Conklin took it to his sergeant next, who was completely on board. Then he met with his forensic team and explained what he was thinking.

"No animosity, no drama . . . nothing like that," Conklin said of that chat he had with the SPD crime scene unit.

Total professionals. Everyone was focused on the goal of solving the case and delighted to have the extra help.

That's how great investigatory teams work.

In doing what he did, Conklin had no idea, however loud and clear his gut was speaking to him, just how important that one decision they made to call in the CSP would be in the years to come. In many ways, it was a turning point, a game-changer, within the scope of what was going to be an investigation the likes of which the SPD had never conducted.

Back at the Shippan Avenue Duchess Restaurant, something was happening. Sergeant Ken Jarrett grabbed one of his investigators, Yan Vanderven, and pulled him aside. Vanderven, who had been at the condo scene with his partner, Detective Greg Holt, had driven down to the Duchess to help out.

"We have a witness here that says he saw a fight on Harbor Drive and he also claims to have witnessed an 'elderly lady' finishing a phone call on that nearby pay phone approximately sixty seconds before we arrived on scene. Get over there and interview him."

Vanderven walked across the parking lot toward the witness, Max Hendrix (pseudonym). He was a forty-one-year-old local who said he worked at nearby IBM on Harbor Drive.

"I was driving back from work when I passed the parking lot here with all the boat slips, just west of Magee Avenue," he explained as Vanderven took notes.

"What'd you see?"

"An older guy, white, late forties, maybe early fifties. He was with a younger guy. Big guy. Six foot. Black hair. Mustache. He wore blue jeans. . . ."

"What were they doing?"

"They were fighting."

Vanderven had a report that another officer had pulled concerning a man who had been stabbed just recently on Shippan Avenue. He didn't say anything to Max Hendrix about the report, keeping the SPD's cards close. Instead, he let him talk.

"Did you notice any vehicles?"

"Oh yeah. There was a dark-colored pickup and gold station wagon in the parking lot at the time."

"Did you stop?"

"No, sir. I continued down the road until I got to the Duchess. And that was when I saw this elderly lady, probably in her late sixties, white shoulder-length, perm hair, on the pay phone on the east side of the restaurant, near the sidewalk on Shippan." Max pointed to the pay phone the SPD had cordoned off. "She hung up and got into a white car, like an older-model LeSabre. It had a handicap placard hanging from the mirror. She left. You guys showed up about a minute later."

Vanderven noticed that a black male was sitting in Max's car, a 1990 Lincoln. The passenger had a large dog with him. The man and his dog seemed to be waiting for Max to finish up.

"Who's that?" Vanderven asked.

"Him? Oh, a friend from Florida."

"Was he in the car with you when you witnessed all of this?"

"Yeah, but I don't think he saw what happened."

Vanderven spoke to the guy. Took down his vitals: date of birth, name, Social Security number, and address. Then asked the guy for an ID.

"I don't have it on me," he said.

"You see anything?" Vanderven asked.

"Nope," he said without much feeling, as if he didn't want to help. "I was sleeping."

Both guys seemed a bit sketchy, but their backgrounds checked out and any information to go on at this point was better than no information. Vanderven thanked the men and told them the SPD might be in contact for a follow-up.

Word had come back to those investigators at the Duchess that there was an eighteen-minute time span between the moment the 911 call had come in and when police had arrived at the Duchess scene—so there was no way Max Hendrix had witnessed the woman making an exit after making the

911 call. The 911 caller had made the call before the elderly female. Long before, actually.

Vanderven and a colleague wrapped up a few more interviews at the Duchess scene and headed back to 123 Harbor Drive. That was where a major investigative team was assembling, taking on those imminent and seemingly mundane responsibilities that go along with a murder case of this scope, heading out to canvass the local neighborhoods in search of information—while the CSP and SPD crime labs teamed up to begin the daunting task of going through the crime scene, inch by inch.

When Vanderven and his sergeant made it back to Harbor Drive, a "black female," as she was described in Vanderven's report, approached them.

"I live upstairs," she said, pointing. Anna's condo was above her unit, which was just below. Some of the living areas were over and under each other. They were neighbors.

The SPD was interested in the neighbor's story. A talk with a neighbor could yield big results. Maybe she heard something? Saw something? Knew something? Was there a history of loud arguments . . . anything?

Was she the 911 caller?

"I closed on the condo back in October," the neighbor explained. "I've been getting it ready to move into."

"So you're not completely in there yet?"

"No. I have been working on it every weekend, though."

Good. That meant she was around.

"Do you know anyone in the neighborhood here, like the woman in unit 105?"

"No. They're noisy, though," the neighbor said. She gestured toward Anna's condo. It wasn't that they were periodically loud, she seemed to suggest, but whoever lived there made a racket. "I just went up there last Monday to speak with them. They stomped around a lot. They made a *lot* of noise."

"Anything else?"

"When I went up there on Monday to talk to her, I could hear a loud guitar in the background that sounded like it was inside her apartment."

"Did you speak to Miss Raymundo?"

"No, no, a guy answered the door."

"What did he look like?"

"Oh, five-ten, maybe. He was skinny. Late twenties, perhaps. Lighter, sandy-colored hair—and he had a possible English or Australian accent."

"Had you seen him before?" Vanderven asked.

"Never. I'm new here, though. He was nice. I didn't get his name. He told me it was his computer making the [guitar] sounds."

"Have you ever spoken to Miss Raymundo?"

"I've never even seen her."

"Why are you here today?" The woman had said she only came by on the weekends to work on the condo.

"The building manager was supposed to send some painters out here for me to meet."

"We might need you. You think you could identify the male if you saw him again?"

"Probably I could, yeah."

Several officers were sent out, door-to-door, knocking and asking those residents at home if they had seen or heard anything out of the ordinary. The officers kept their focus on those units facing Anna's, along with those in the direct vicinity. This can be tedious work—lots of questions, writing, and reports. But sometimes a gem can come from asking those simple questions of people who thought they hadn't seen or heard anything.

Many residents weren't home. And for those that were,

most did not have much to report. It seemed like just any other day along the exclusive Stamford coast of Harbor Drive. That was, of course, until the fire trucks, ambulances, emergency medical technicians (EMTs), and police showed up.

Vanderven and another officer went to see the superintendent of the building. It was as good a place as any to start poking around to find out who Anna might have been dating and/or living with, and who that male was that had answered her door. Not only would the guy have to be notified that Anna had been found dead, but he was the most likely suspect the SPD had at the present moment. Looking at the crime scene, sizing up the possibilities, the fact alone that the door was unlocked and there was no forced entry into the condo made some think that Anna Lisa and her lover had gotten into an argument and the boyfriend snapped. The anger and hatred and violence associated with the scene were all too obvious to overlook. Smart investigators—and the SPD major crimes unit was full of experienced, intelligent cops with thousands of hours of investigatory skills among them—knew that this sort of situation played out more than not: a jilted, jaded, and enraged lover who allowed his emotions and anger to take over loses control and goes crazy. A shouting match turns into a pushing event that turns into a beating that turns into what?

Violent murder.

The condo superintendent, Pete Heap (pseudonym), reported that he had seen Anna's "boyfriend" around, noting, "He drives a green Nissan Pathfinder. I just saw him this morning leaving for work about, I don't know, eight-thirty or so."

"What's his name?"

"Oh, I only know both of them by face. That's how I know most people around here." Too many names. Too many tenants. The guy couldn't remember everyone. Impossible.

"How long have you been working here?" Vanderven asked.

"Two years."

"Can you describe him for me?"

"Sure. Yeah. Five-ten, skinny, white, sandy hair, twenty-seven or twenty-eight years old. He likes to leave for work early and return really late."

"You notice if he is foreign at all?"

"No. He has an American accent. He's white."

"Anything else you have for us? Like, you ever see him drive the woman's car?"

"Yup. Not too often, though. She has a Mustang, I think." He was right. "Maybe two times I seen him driving it. Something like that."

"There's a security gate here on premises, right?"

"Yeah."

"Do you have a record of who enters and who leaves?"

"Nothing like that. It's a keypad type of thing and some tenants have, like, a garage door opener device that allows them access. Sorry."

Investigations are full of monotony. The SPD was a few hours into it and didn't have anything to go on. This was not unusual. Time was going to play a role here, investigators were certain. As the day progressed and that "first forty-eight" ticking clock, which cops are all too familiar with, clicked away, it was a definite possibility that Anna's boyfriend would at some point show up at the condo.

Either that or the guy was never coming back at all, because he had a damn good reason to run.

CHAPTER 10

ALL COPS HAVE those cases haunting their dreams: nightmares startling them awake; the cases that, no matter how hard they try, they can never shake. Most involve the exploitation and/or murder of children. It is something every investigator, at some point, must face: the terribly violent, gruesome, sad, heart-wrenching murder of a young person not yet even out of grammar school. Those crimes have a way of enveloping a cop's soul. The images they see of the dead child morph into Polaroids, popping up at unexpected times, sharply putting into focus the preciousness of life and how evil murder is to that balance.

Forty-nine-year-old Greg Holt was part of the SPD's BCI major crimes unit and, arguably, one of the department's most effectual investigators. Greg had that fatherly warmth—and stepfatherly crassness—about him, depending on who was describing him. With a carefully manicured, pronounced dark black beard and mustache, framed around a smile that invited sincerity, a radio voice oozing charm and comfort, Detective Holt worked those characteristics to his advantage when investigating any major crime. He had a way of tearing into a case and relentlessly pursuing leads until he found that nugget—the one accidental clue that led to the next and opened up an entire new way of looking at a case. And yet, for some, it was that same passion and stubbornness of Holt's that rubbed them the wrong way. If ten people were asked, there might be one or two in the bunch saying Greg Holt came across bold and forceful, and that alone turned them off. But an 80 percent likability factor was more than anyone could ask for.

Either way, there was no mistaking the tenacity and drive or compassion that motivated this cop to solve crimes perpetrated against the people of the town he worked in. Holt was a doer. He believed in working cases the old-fashioned way: Hit the bricks. Track down sources. Bang on doors. Ask questions repeatedly. Allow his gut to guide him. And when he thought he'd exhausted every possible lead, every palpable clue a case had given up, he would dig even deeper, go over it all again, and find that missing link—that one needle sending him running toward an entirely new haystack. For Holt, a cop didn't stop because the answers were hidden. He persevered and made them emerge.

When asked to recall, without thinking too hard about it, the case that kept him up at night, Holt said it involved a child on her birthday. Detective Holt was new to the major crimes unit then. He was working the day shift. "I fielded a call from a detective outside Richmond," Holt remembered. Richmond, Virginia—a long way from Stamford, Connecticut.

"Hey, Greg, nice to meet you. I'm working the drug task force down here on I-95. We collared a guy who says he has information on a homicide in your town."

Sometimes, that's how it happens: a scumbag is arrested hundreds of miles away and decides he wants to trade information. There's no loyalty in the world of crime, no matter what any criminal says. To save his own ass, a career criminal will do what it takes.

"Well," Holt said, "of course, we'd love to hear it. Details . . . the year, the neighborhood, what did he say?"

As the cop explained, the case came back to Holt as if it had happened the day before. It had been years. Holt was working patrol. A neighborhood girl was celebrating her seventh birthday. The memory played back almost as if in slow motion. Holt could see the girl walking outside her home, laughing and being a kid. There were people around, family and friends. Everyone was celebrating. Congratulating the youngster on another year. She got herself a slice of her birthday cake. She started walking back to the kids' table to sit down and enjoy the cake. Yet, as she sauntered innocently across the lawn, a stray bullet from a gang war—a group from New York City and one from Stamford fighting for turf— whizzed by and went up through the plate she was carrying and into her head. The rival gang battle was taking place along the street adjacent to the courtyard where the little girl had been enjoying her birthday party.

The girl was killed instantly.

While celebrating her seventh birthday.

A horror show.

A heartbreaking case for any cop. Makes one wonder: a split second earlier, a pause to say hi to a relative, a stop along the way to sneak a quick bite of her cake, and she would have been allowed to celebrate her eighth birthday. The bullet could have entered the side of the house, and then everyone could have gone about their day, a little wiser, a little more aware of the danger of living in the city amidst a gang war.

The case the cop from Virginia was calling about involved another blowhard Greg Holt was chasing on the same day the little girl was murdered—a crime in which nearly every cop in town was sent to the scene. A guy, a drug warrior, had been capped at the local train station. Middle of the day. Bullet in the back of the head while walking into the depot. Years went by and both cases went unsolved. And then, with this one phone call, the doors opened and both cases served arrest warrants.

Ask Holt if he's seen it all, and the inquirer will get a nervous laugh out of him.

"I've seen my share," he has explained, "which is plenty."

The major crimes unit within the SPD worked rotating schedules, alternating: one week 8:00 A.M. to 4:00 P.M., one week 4:00 P.M. to midnight. A normal day—quite an interesting choice of words here—for a major crimes detective consisted of a meeting in the morning, paperwork, fielding calls on cases from potential sources and witnesses, field interviews, and also responding to breaking crime scenes. They all took turns "catching" cases. Simply put, "catching" means what it sounds like: It was as if a cop went up to bat and the next case that came into the strike zone was his to take a swing at.

The major crimes unit has four detectives, a sergeant, and a lieutenant on any tour/shift. They are always ready. If the unit needed additional investigators, they'd call in other cops from the Internet crimes and sex against women and children divisions. Everyone chipped in when the crime called for it.

On the day Anna Lisa Raymundo's murder had been called in, Detective Greg Holt and his partner, Yan Vanderven, were working the streets of Stamford doing routine outreach to the community, letting residents know of their presence, while sending word to the dopers that they were out and about. When they weren't working cases, the SPD did a lot of outsourcing into the neighborhoods where crime was prevalent.

The call they heard first as Holt and Vanderven drove around downtown was for a domestic disturbance/possible violent crime on Harbor Drive. A fairly common call to hear coming in over the radio. Couples fought. Sometimes—no matter how much money they had in the bank, how many degrees tacked to the walls—violence entered the home.

It happened.

But then, as Holt and Vanderven continued cruising the neighborhoods, a few moments went by and Holt heard a senior officer put out a "homicide" call on the radio.

"And, of course, everything changed," Holt said.

What had struck Holt first as they drove out to Harbor Drive, parked, got out, and headed up the stairs and into Anna's condo was that the homicide hadn't occurred in one of those gang-saddled neighborhoods, where cops expected these types of calls. It was Harbor Drive. A visitor looked around the parking lot and saw cars and SUVs that cost as much as some condos in other towns. And that alone, Holt understood, made the case all that much more unique and potentially difficult as it evolved.

The wealthy, Holt knew, held their secrets a lot closer to the vest.

"Harbor Drive is *very* upscale," Holt commented. "It's in a section of the city we call Shippan. . . . And, for all intents and purposes, Shippan Avenue is a long straight street that goes all the way down to the point and overlooks Long Island Sound. And then there are various streets that go off to the left or right. But it's very nice, very upscale, and exclusive. Shippan Yacht Club is down there. Where this scene was, was right at the top, right at the mouth of Shippan Avenue—which is nothing but high-rise condos, town houses, and they're all connected to yacht bases—in other words, every condo has its own slip."

Ka-*ching*.

There were scores of cops inside the unit as Holt and

Vanderven arrived. As he walked up the steps leading to Anna's front door, Holt noticed something.

"Very, very minute particles of evidence—some crushed glass and other evidence that wasn't that big."

Not easy to see, either.

Greg Holt and Yan Vanderven were part of that original team searching the condo for other potential victims and/or a second perpetrator. Others got there before them, and still others arrived after. But they were now entirely invested in this massive crime scene.

After Vanderven had gone up to the Duchess to help out, Greg Holt stayed behind and took a moment to catch his breath and begin processing in his mind what the SPD was looking at. First impressions are sometimes all a detective has. The place would never look the same a day or two later. Checking out Anna's unit, Holt thought: *The victim is not that big, but—man, oh, man—she fought for her life.*

It was clear that Anna had fought.

I cannot imagine how long this went on for, Holt wondered as he walked around, studying the scene as CSIs got busy collecting evidence.

"It wasn't like she opened the door and was shot or something," Holt added.

Stunned, Anna got up from what she was doing, answered the door, and whatever happened began right there. Or, she got up from what she was doing, an argument ensued, and blood was spilled.

Next, Holt noticed the foyer into Anna's condo, how big it was, and how "every square inch of it had been destroyed. There was a good rumble that went on in that location."

Upstairs, Holt checked the sliding door, which turned out to be another way into the condo. That, too, was intact. Which told him the perpetrator was definitely let into the home downstairs through the front door.

Likely by Anna.

"Somebody knocked on her door and she let them in," Holt assumed. "It didn't appear to be a blitz attack right there at the door, but she let them in."

Or perhaps Anna's killer had a key?

CHAPTER 11

NELSON SESSLER HAD secrets. One, in particular, was something he had kept from Anna Lisa, and now it was too late to fess up and admit he was "that guy"—*a playa*. Not many men can admit to being *that guy*. Most that are—they just don't see it. They kid themselves and make excuses. But in the end, when faced with the prospect of losing what they have at home, they suddenly feel as though the grass wasn't greener on the other side, after all. What they had all along was a blessing, the best thing that ever happened to them. In Nelson Sessler's case, however, his blessing in disguise was dead. There would be no redemption.

It was over.

A dapper-looking man, with business-cropped brownish black hair groomed around the ears, parted on one side, and dark, round eyes, set on a fair complexion cast over a boyish face, Nelson Sessler was a smart guy. Nobody would argue with that. But bad decisions are generally made with the highest intellect at the ready, in the spur of the moment. For Nelson, who carried himself well—although some claimed he came across as cocky and one of those *"I'm smarter than you"* types—every decision from here was going to reflect the type of person he was at heart.

Nelson had gotten rid of that thorn, Sheila Davalloo—or so he thought.

For Sheila, she saw things a little differently.

"I had no idea she was obsessed," Nelson said later. "We never had that kind of relationship, where we shared the word 'love.' It was completely left field for me."

And yet, if one is to take a peek at some of the letters Sheila later wrote to Nelson, the word "love" was all over many of them. In fact, her signature sign off was "Love Always."

As of November, though, Nelson had found himself back settled in with Anna. He was now focused on Anna and rebuilding the intimate relationship he had almost allowed to slip away. On the very same morning of Anna's murder, November 8, 2002, before the superintendent saw Nelson leave for work, Nelson and Anna "had sex," Nelson would soon explain to police. They had not made love, no. That's not what he said. To be exact, Nelson put it rather superficially, kind of tritely, and as positively terse as he could, explaining: "I woke up early in the morning and we had sex, Anna Lisa and I. Then I went to work. . . ."

For a day that was about to end on an entirely different note, that was how Nelson's morning began. When Nelson walked out the door, he claimed, Anna was knitting. This was the last time he saw Anna. She sat, fussing with some needles and yarn. Truthfully, Anna loved to knit. She would sit and think about her life, her work, and the things she had to do that day. This was Anna's time to contemplate and reflect. It brought her incredible peace and comfort to make something from nothing. Known to her family as the "bright star," Anna was said to have brought "life, enthusiasm, and energy" into any event or gathering she attended. Friends and family called Anna "smart," which goes without saying, really. She was more in the highly intelligent column. "Sincere and independent" was how her mother, Susan, once described Anna. If there was one thing that made Anna who she was, it had to be her knack for setting a goal and achieving it. Anna never talked about what she was *going* to do, ruminating on tomorrow and what *might* be. She never fell into that *"Oh, well, someday I'm going to write 'the Great American Novel' or travel the world."* Anna did what it was she yearned to do and did not allow any obstacle or resistance to get in her way. She cared not what people thought about her or what they said—only that she was fulfilling the values she had set for herself. One friend later said there were always two Annas: There was the one who liked to go out with friends to clubs in Manhattan and have a ball dancing and talking and laughing. Anna was often the leader of the group, watching out for everyone. Then there was the more docile and homebound Anna, who liked to be a recluse, neatly tucked inside her home with her man, knitting, reading, cooking, dreaming of marriage and kids one day. And it appeared, if what Nelson Sessler had to say was true, that the latter Anna was the person Nelson left that morning.

On the day Anna Lisa Raymundo was murdered, as her mother, Susan, drove Anna's grandmother home from the hospital in Florida, Susan was suddenly overcome with a sense of dread, fear, and terrible grief. It came on like a blast of cold air from the car's dashboard vent, quite startling. The feeling was so all-encompassing that while driving, Susan abruptly started crying.

"What's wrong?" Anna's grandmother asked her daughter.

Susan had "no words to explain it." She couldn't understand. It was a heavy feeling weighing her down, as if someone was pushing her, squeezing her heart. She actually felt the drag and slouch of her shoulders curling over. There was something speaking to her on an emotional, telepathically charged manner, beckoning Susan to think that something big was going to happen. And she had better be prepared.

When Susan got home, it was Bernadette, Anna's sister, who called and relayed the terrible news that Anna had been murdered. And then Susan knew. The ride home from the hospital now made sense. As she thought about it later during those dreaded, dark hours, as Anna's murder settled on her, Susan considered it was "an angel" coming down to warn her in the car that day, to somehow communicate to her soul that a tragedy was awaiting her at home. That was the weight. Or, perhaps, Susan wondered, was it "Anna Lisa herself"? And if it was Anna, Susan thought, was it during that exact moment when poor Anna was struggling for her life that Susan was overcome with those heavy feelings? Was Anna simply saying good-bye, letting her mother know it was all over? Was Anna conveying that she was at peace now, no more pain, leaving this terribly violent world for a much better place?

Either way, Susan Raymundo knew her Anna Lisa had always maintained an "undying love for her family." Anna was a daughter who always thought about her mother and father. She was a sister who always considered her siblings—not herself, not Anna. She was as unselfish as one could be. Caring, delightful, full of life and love, Anna always focused on those around her.

Anna was born on September 11, 1970, inside Brooklyn Cumberland Hospital in New York. It was just three short miles across the Brooklyn Bridge and into Manhattan, near Park Row and the World Trade Center Tower area. Thirty-one years after the day she was born, Anna would celebrate her birthday as those two towers burned and imploded into the ground while the world watched in horror. Anna, with her "vibrant presence," was Renato and Susan Raymundo's first child. She was baptized a Catholic at St. Saviour's Church in Brooklyn, on Eighth Avenue, in Park Slope. Anna was five when the family, chasing medical vocations, moved to Troy, Michigan. Eventually, in 1982, they settled happily in Bloomfield Hills, Michigan.

As Anna knitted quietly on that morning, after having sex with the man she loved (but was also, unbeknownst to Nelson, questioning friends whether he was cheating on her or not), she was no doubt meditating on her day ahead and the work she had to do. Meanwhile, Nelson walked out the door of the condo and got into his car. He stopped first at the Donut Delight up the street to get a coffee and morning pastry.

From there, Nelson claimed, he parked his vehicle in Purdue Pharma's parking garage and entered the building using his key code card with a magnetic strip. Employees have to swipe the card through a holder, like when using a credit card to pay for something at the market. Every entry and exit is recorded and logged. One cannot leave the multistory Purdue building without Big Brother Pharma recording it.

"Then I went into my office," Nelson explained.

Another typical day in corporate America began. Many thought that with all the security the building had in place, Purdue was a facility that somehow housed the drugs the company developed. However, it was not. The Purdue building in Stamford was the brain behind the operation—the main hub where the numbers were crunched and analysis performed. It was not a drug factory.

Nelson Sessler worked on the seventh floor. His morning was purposeful and routine. It was about noon when Nelson got up from his desk, took the elevator down several floors, and attended a lecture in the company auditorium. Several coworkers saw him. Nelson had nothing to hide. He was at work. He logged into the system. His every move was being tracked, traced, and recorded by the company he worked for.

"Most people go and get their lunch and bring it, and then we listen to somebody do a talk," Nelson explained. "So I went to the cafeteria and went to the auditorium and sat with other colleagues and listened to the talk for the day."

According to Nelson's keypad card, he did not leave the building all day.

At some point that day, Nelson couldn't later recall what time exactly, his desk phone rang. He looked down and saw that it was Anna's number at the condo. That didn't mean it was Anna calling—only that it was someone from that home who was calling Nelson at his desk.

Nelson stared at the number.

One ring . . .

Two . . .

Then it stopped before he picked it up.

No message. No callback.

So Nelson, not thinking anything of it, went back to work. If it was important, he surmised, Anna would call back.

At five o'clock, as the day ended basically the same as any other, Nelson collected his things and left.

The ride home was unremarkable. Nelson drove the same route he had many other nights when he was planning to stay at Anna's. He hit traffic at all the same locations. Listened to the same boring drive-time talk radio and music. He stared out the window at the same local scenes of buildings and homes and strip malls passing him by in a blur. Driving home from work every day is a metaphor for life: a cycle and a circle, all at once. Not much of anything happens in most lives from day to day. And most people take for granted how pleasant that silence and routine can be in the scope of what *could* happen—as Nelson was about to learn. It's not until a person's world blows up in front of his very face that he yearns for the return of that subtle boredom and monotonous sameness that everyday life offers.

As Nelson pulled into the parking lot of Anna's Harbor Drive complex, the image of his life exploding appeared before him—he just didn't know it yet.

"There were probably twelve police cars, maybe even more . . . parked around the building."

Nelson became instantly nervous. His heart pounded. His stomach rose into his chest. That same feeling like when someone startles an individual unexpectedly. He was shaken up. And Nelson didn't yet have a clue as to why.

He parked in a space away from the entrance to Anna's. Sitting in his vehicle, looking at all the blue and red lights flashing, the yellow crime scene tape—the same as he saw on television crime shows—cops walking around, the immense mobile State Police Crime Lab RV, Nelson Sessler decided he had better phone Anna's number and see if she could tell him what in the heck was happening. It was almost as if Nelson knew. Or, more likely, he had an indication that something bad had occurred.

The line rang three times before the answering machine picked up. "Listen . . . I'm worried," Nelson said into Anna's voice mail, his voice frantic and fragile. "I'm not quite sure what's going on up there."

As he exited his vehicle and walked toward the building, Nelson tried the number again, thinking: *Geez, maybe I dialed wrong the first time?*

He didn't know exactly what he was doing. It all seemed surreal and dreamlike. This scene in front of him unfolding: It was so, well, Hollywood. Like a movie set.

Halfway up the pavement toward the steps leading into Anna's condo, a cop stopped Nelson. It was 5:25 P.M.; the cop noted the time in his report.

"Who are you?" the officer asked.

"I'm . . . I'm her boyfriend," Nelson said, pointing to Anna's door. "I was on my way up to see her."

"Wait here," the cop said.

Inside Anna's condo, Yan Vanderven and Greg Holt were notified of Nelson Sessler's arrival. Nelson would soon be referred to as "the boyfriend" among investigators—truly, he was their only prime suspect at this point.

"All we had before this was two vehicles that appeared to be owned by Anna Lisa, and this very busy condo complex," Greg Holt said. "You have UPS and FedEx in here all day, an on-site manager to the complex roaming around, landscapers all over the place. There had been a piece of furniture delivered immediately next door to Anna's condo unit. Cleaning people coming and going. Husbands and wives coming and going. Activity around the place *all day* long."

But at first blush, as the interviews came back and investigators started hearing what people inside the complex were saying, nobody had seen or heard anything.

And now investigators headed down the stairs to speak with Nelson Sessler, the last person to see Ann Lisa alive.

CHAPTER 12

THE ORIGIN OF the phrase "person of interest," which has somehow replaced "suspect" in the lexicon of investigations being publicly pumped out over live-television airwaves, is unknown. Merriam-Webster's Dictionary claims the phrase's first known use was in 1937, but it gives no source. If one thinks back to the terrorist attacks of 2001 and the fallout from the fear the United States suffered afterward, "person of interest" became then-U.S. Attorney General John Ashcroft's go-to expression for describing potential terrorists, either homegrown or abroad—namely, Dr. Steven J. Hatfill, who underwent a relentless trial by media as the chief suspect in the anthrax attacks cases post-9/11. There is no legal definition for "person of interest"; yet, to be honest, it is widely used today in the place of "suspect," so talking heads and pundits can point a guilty finger at someone and not worry about being sued for slander or libel. Turn on a television during a high-profile breaking news crime case and watch the coverage.

The boyfriend of a murder victim, if he doesn't have a rock-solid alibi immediately at the ready, has to be considered the main suspect for committing the murder. If the victim is the bull's-eye, then the boyfriend is the first ring around that center point. At the beginning of any investigation, a good cop follows the odds. And the odds are that a murder such as the gruesome, violent homicide the SPD studied at 123 Harbor Drive in Stamford was solved easiest when they stayed within the parameters and painted by the numbers. Nelson Sessler, rolling up to the scene of the crime, wanting to go in and see his girlfriend after calling and leaving her a voice mail, was looking fairly good right now as the only human being with a motive for murdering such a well-respected, quiet, smart, kind woman—a person who did not seem to have an enemy in the world.

Along with several other investigators, Sergeant Richard Colwell walked down the stairs leading up to Anna's condo and met with Nelson Sessler just outside. They stood on the pavement in front of Anna's condo. Cops and crime scene technicians walked in and out of the condo. It was a busy scene.

"What's happening?" Nelson asked. He didn't seem too antsy or eager. He was calm—considering all that was occurring around him.

"Come with us," Colwell said. The plan was to bring Nelson down to a boathouse/restroom attached to Anna's condo complex. It was located in the same building structure as Anna's unit, at street level. Basically, it was just around the corner from the entrance to Anna's condo, but far enough away to provide privacy, away from the actual crime scene. There was a push-button lock system allowing residents access into the boathouse, the combination known only to those who lived in the complex.

Anna Lisa was still upstairs in the exact spot where she had breathed her last. Her body had not been moved. The CSP crime lab was busy working the scene. It would be some time before Anna was taken away and brought to 11 Shuttle Road in Farmington, Connecticut, the office of the chief medical examiner (OCME), where CME Harold Wayne Carver would either do the autopsy himself or assign it to another ME.

"An officer told me there was a murder . . . ," Nelson said as they walked toward the boathouse. "What's happening?"

Nelson was wearing a rust- and beige-colored button-up plaid shirt, gray khaki-type pants, and brown shoes. He had left his coat in his car and, at some point, asked if an officer could retrieve it for him. His clothes did not appear to be dirty or, more pointedly, bloody.

Still, investigators thought, he could have changed.

Yan Vanderven and several investigators were with Colwell and Nelson in the boathouse. They sat Nelson down, asked him if he needed a glass of water. Something to eat? Cup of coffee? It was clear from the tone and amount of people that this was serious.

"No . . . no," Nelson said. "What's happening? Tell me what's going on here." The words he spoke might have suggested urgency, but the officers listening to him later said Nelson Sessler didn't come across as a concerned boyfriend in a hurry to find out about Anna. He never asked about Anna specifically, several investigators later noted. Instead, he kept repeating: "What happened?"

"Listen, Mr. Sessler, your girlfriend, Anna Lisa Raymundo, she's been murdered," Colwell explained with as much compassion and instinctive sensitivity as he could muster, without allowing Nelson Sessler to feel as though the SPD wasn't looking at him with one eye squinted. There was a fine line here for a cop, teetering on being sympathetic to the victim's significant other and also looking at the guy as a potential suspect on the top of what was a very short list.

As the news struck him, every officer present later reported that Nelson Sessler "did not seem overemotional" about what he learned. He did not cry. He did not get angry. He did not stand up and start pacing frantically, stomping around, crying out, *"Why, why, why?"* He did not do what most people do when they're told the person they love—in this case, the SPD had recently found out, the woman whom they were planning on becoming engaged to—had been slain viciously inside her condo.

Instead, Nelson asked, "Where is her body?"

The cops looked at one another. They couldn't answer the question in the specific manner he seemed to want.

"Was there a burglary?" he queried next, as if trying to figure out if they knew more than what had happened.

"Miss Raymundo's body is still in the apartment," Colwell noted, giving the guy as much information as he could.

"Was there a burglary?"

"Mr. Sessler . . ."

"Are you serious?" he said next, changing the subject, more or less talking to himself. Then: *"Was* there a burglary?"

"We're investigating now, Mr. Sessler," Colwell said.

"Was there a *burglary*?" This fact seemed important to the guy.

"We're not certain. We are, though, going to need your help in this investigation," Colwell said.

"Are you . . . is this . . . are you *serious*?" Nelson asked, running a hand through his hair. He was referring to—again—the crime itself, not his potential role in helping. The totality of the situation was beginning to sink in.

Anna was gone. She had been the victim of a brutal, bloody homicide.

When Colwell felt that Nelson Sessler had somewhat collected his senses and began to act somewhat like a lover should, the sergeant asked deliberately, "Where were you today, Mr. Sessler?"

No hesitation: "At work."

"What time did you leave for work this morning?"

"Oh, I don't know, same as I do on most mornings I stay here—between seven and nine."

Colwell studied his suspect.

"Can I go into the condo and see Anna?" Nelson asked.

"No."

The boyfriend turned away.

"Would you come down to the station and give us an interview?" Colwell asked. This was probably the most important question of the moment. What would he say? *"I want a lawyer."* Or, *"Sure, I'll do whatever you need."*

"Yes . . . yes," Nelson announced, looking at everyone. He was willing to help. "But someone," he added, "someone . . . Can someone contact Anna's parents and let them know what's happened here?"

Colwell told Nelson they would appreciate it if he waited in the boathouse until they were ready for him. They had other things to take care of right now, but one or two detectives would be back to transport him downtown as soon as possible. And, yes, Anna Lisa's parents were being notified, if they hadn't been already.

Nelson Sessler agreed to wait.

Outside the boathouse, Colwell told Vanderven to grab another officer and watch Nelson Sessler. Don't allow him out of their sights. Yeah, he said he wanted to help; but was the decision born out of protecting himself, or catching Anna's killer?

As they waited, Vanderven walked about the boathouse, looked around, while another investigator watched Nelson Sessler. The entire unit—building—had been taped off and considered prime territory for evidence. Vanderven wondered if maybe Anna's killer had used the boathouse or entered it for some reason. As he walked around, Vanderven spied "what appeared to be a drop of blood upon a white trash disposal can in the ladies' restroom." So he called up to the condo on his cell to send forensics down.

Had Nelson Sessler used the ladies' room while they had him down there for questioning? Had anyone seen him inside the ladies' room?

As they waited, Nelson said he didn't want any food when Vanderven offered again. "But I'll have a cup of coffee."

"Sure."

It was getting late in the evening, much darker out now as that dense winter night air off the ocean came in from the Atlantic and put a haze over the entire scene. Big, bright lights were propped up by the CSP, and the scene now teemed with cops of all kinds walking around, taking photos, making notes, interviewing passersby and residents.

Nelson Sessler waited in the boathouse to be escorted to the SPD station house. He asked very few questions and remained rather quiet. By all accounts, it was going to be a long night for everyone.

As Nelson took a sip of his coffee, Vanderven watched. It was then, as Vanderven studied him, that the seasoned investigator noticed "what appeared to be several markings on [him]." For one, Nelson Sessler had what Vanderven described as a "red, swollen mark on his right hand, middle-finger knuckle . . . and a red mark on the right side of his head in front of his right ear, which wrapped behind the ear."

If this cop didn't know any better, it would appear that Nelson had been in a scuffle of some sort just recently, or had injured himself some other way.

The coffee was hot, tasted like shit, but as Vanderven watched Nelson drink it, he couldn't help but consider how a guy might have gotten those marks.

* * *

Back upstairs, inside Anna's condo, Sergeant Richard Colwell and Detective Greg Holt continued to study Anna's body. There was a "sizable pool of blood around [Anna's] head," where she lay on the floor. Her body was now stiff from rigor mortis. At one point, a cop tried to open Anna's mouth to see if she had any internal oral injuries, but rigor was too set up. Her arms and legs were likewise frozen in the time of her death, unmovable. She had blood—dried and smudged—and scores of lacerations about her face and neck, a clear indication she had been stabbed repeatedly in the face.

Somebody hated this woman, Greg Holt thought, staring at Anna.

Stabbed in the face meant the crime was personal. Injuries such as those on Anna's face don't come from a home-invasion type of sexually motivated crime. A stealthy attacker would not, by most accounts, stab his victim in the face either before or after he was finished raping her. It just didn't happen that way. It was hard to murder somebody by stabbing her in the face.

Interestingly enough, there was "dirt and/or potting soil on [Anna's] pant legs," which had most likely come from the struggle and fight she endured, as Anna and her attacker knocked over the houseplants. Anna's killer, most on-scene investigators believed, was a powerfully built, strong person. Not meek or feeble in any way. Anna fought, yes; but her attacker kept coming and coming.

"Get down there and bring Mr. Sessler to the station," Colwell told Holt. "Get him in the box and let's see what he has to say."

Greg Holt nodded and left.

Nelson Sessler had fallen asleep, surprising as that might sound, "several times while waiting" for Detective Greg Holt and his partner to arrive at the boathouse.

He slept? Holt asked himself after he heard. *The guy fell asleep? Hell, it isn't that late.*

The guy's girlfriend had been murdered; her body was still in the same building; and he was down in the boathouse sleeping?

Another one of Holt's partners was Detective Tom McGinty. McGinty has that clichéd cop look: gray hair, slight potbelly, five feet eight (maybe nine) inches tall, solid build, hard-as-stone upper body, and a sad, weathered look from all the crime scene scars he carried around. There was also a sense of solitude about the guy. Like Holt, McGinty wore a suit and tie and thought about things intuitively before ever uttering a theory or reason for doing something within the boundary lines of an investigation. These guys did a hell of a lot more thinking as a case unfolded than they did reacting. When his colleagues are asked, they'll answer that McGinty has always been a cop's cop, a guy who takes things to heart and allows them to fester and ripen. But, like any good cop, if there was one thing McGinty hated, it was when he discovered a suspect or witness had lied to his face, either by withholding information or downright making something up.

Nelson Sessler was now waiting in the ladies' room, and Holt and McGinty rustled him up and asked him if he was willing to go downtown under his own free will. There was nothing wrong with asking this question too many times. Nelson was under no obligation legally to go anywhere. But McGinty and Holt made it clear that they would be driving him.

Anna's boyfriend said he was willing to help in any way he could.

"Good," Holt said. "Let's go."

Before leaving, Holt frisked Nelson as a normal course of procedure.

He was clean.

"I didn't like Mr. Sessler right away," Holt admitted later.

This was vintage Nelson Sessler—he left that kind of impression on people who didn't know him. They would meet the guy and, straightaway, they didn't *want* to like him. He had this cockiness about him, most said, that was hard to get over.

As soon as McGinty, Holt, and Nelson Sessler took off downtown, somewhere around 10:40 P.M., crime scene investigator EJ Rondano processed the boathouse scene. First he photographed the entire exterior and interior of the boathouse. Then Rondano went to work collecting swab samples from the garbage can in the ladies' room and other fixtures throughout the place. While he did this, back inside the condo, Yan Vanderven went through Anna Lisa's caller ID and took down each of the numbers that had called over the past several days, dating back to November 6. Immediately Vanderven noticed something peculiar: At 3:16 P.M., on November 7, the day before she was murdered, Anna took a call from that same pay phone down the road at the Duchess Restaurant that the 911 caller had used to call in the murder.

What did this mean? Why had someone from that pay phone called Anna's condo the previous day? Was it that same neighbor (the one they couldn't find)?

Vanderven took down the information and brought it back to headquarters, where Holt and McGinty, the two main detectives now leading the charge to find Anna's killer, were preparing to interview Nelson Sessler.

CHAPTER 13

THE STAMFORD POLICE DEPARTMENT is a fine-tuned law enforcement machine that runs smoothly and efficiently, unlike a lot of city departments that can seem to be chaotic and discombobulated. There are old-school jail cells, with metal beds and metal sinks and open toilets and old Western-style cell bars, lining a section of the downstairs basement near booking, where the "bad guys" are locked up and held until their chance to plead their case in front of a judge comes up. Go down farther into the bowels of the building and there's even a shooting range, where officers qualify and practice on moving and stationary targets.

Nelson Sessler's day—maybe his life, no one yet knew—had been turned on its head. It was close to 11:00 P.M. on November 8, 2002. It was cold and dark outside; a fine mist in the air made it humid and dreary. The woes of winter had moved stealthily into New England without much pomp or circumstance. Nelson Sessler's girlfriend—or, rather, fiancée, no one was yet clear which—had been murdered, he knew, but not much else had been explained. What was clear to Nelson from the start was that this case was the top priority for the SPD. The local news stations had already run with it, leading off the eleven o'clock nightly news. The radio stations were blaring scant details. Stamford had not seen a murder such as this in quite some time. A local girl, highly educated, comfortably wealthy, living in an exclusive section of the city, from a solid family of two physician parents in Michigan, had been murdered. The question residents were asking as they went to bed: Was there a ferocious, ruthless maniac lurking in the city, in search of his or her next victim? Should residents sleep with one eye open, knowing this was a one-off murder and not the beginning to a spree?

If Holt and McGinty were asked—and they weren't at this time—their response would have been a resounding *"no need to worry about a monster out on the streets in search of his next victim."* To them, this crime spoke of a concerted, concentrated, evil effort to dispose of Anna Lisa—and Anna Lisa only. Anna may have been liked by all, but there was at least one person in the world who hated her enough to bludgeon and stab her repeatedly. That much these two experienced cops knew as they walked down the hallway toward the small room where their main suspect sat in wait.

Most police departments call the interrogation room "the box," and the SPD was no different. Box, however, is an appropriate way to describe this room the SPD used to question potential suspects in major crimes. The actual room itself is about twelve feet long by eight feet wide, so it is not that much bigger than a small bedroom in a modest home. There are black walls covered with an egg carton–type material that recording studios use to soak up noise. There is a one-way, covered window at one end of the room for outsiders to view an interview, and a blackboard on the other side of the room. Then there is the standard box stuff: clock, oblong table with chairs, a computer for statements to be taken, and a telephone, which is "usually placed down on one of the chairs," Holt explained. There are two doors, one into the major crimes office space, and the other into booking. The entire room is "very basic and barren," Holt added, "and is intended to be so." The focus while in this room is to gather information, of course; but it's also to send a message to the interviewee that everything said in this room will have an immediate impact on his life, whether he's done anything or not.

"Can I get some water?" Nelson Sessler asked as they got under way.

"Sure," McGinty said.

Greg Holt watched Nelson closely. Holt did not have a good feeling about the guy. He was hiding something, Holt felt. It was clear in his body language and the way he spoke. Holt had interviewed countless suspects and witnesses. When a professional does that for years and years, he develops a sixth sense about people in general. He's able to read human beings fairly accurately. Obviously, it's not evidence, but it gives a cop an upper hand.

It bothered Holt that Nelson Sessler had gone to sleep while waiting in the boathouse, merely a few hours after hearing that his girlfriend had been murdered. Another thing on Holt's mind as they began asking Sessler questions was the fact that Nelson Sessler had never "charged the yellow tape line and cried out upon coming up on the scene . . . ," Holt added, "At first, there in front of the condo, as he came up on us all standing there, he never asked what happened, where she is, demanded to go into the house, why we're all there. . . ."

Those questions came later, down in the boathouse.

"And then he goes to sleep?" Holt said. "Come on."

Nelson had an extreme monotone vocal characteristic. He spoke at one level, all the time, never raising or lowering his voice to accompany a certain feeling or emotion.

"Can I use the restroom?" he asked. "I need to stretch my legs and get some air," he said at one point.

They let him.

Back inside the box, McGinty encouraged Nelson to go

through his day from start to finish. Plot out the entire thing, moment by moment. They needed to lock the guy down to a narrative. Get him set in stone on what he did, so they could track it all down and back it up or rip it apart.

"I left for work later than usual, about nine," Sessler explained. "I had a meeting scheduled for that morning early, but it had been canceled the night before."

"Okay, and what did you and Miss Raymundo do before you left for work?"

Nelson first said, "We had sex, and then I took a shower and went to work." But a bit later, when they asked him to describe once again what he and Anna did that morning, he said, "We had sex, took a shower together, and then I left." And yet still, when they pressed him further on into the night (well into the next morning, November 9, actually), he changed that story again, adding, "We had sex. We took a shower together. Then she sat on the bed and knitted, and I went to work."

"Okay, where did you go immediately after leaving the condo?"

"I went down to Donut Delight . . . at Elm and McGee. . . . I arrived at work shortly after that and remained there, until I left there at five to go back to the condo."

"You live there?"

"I stay there, but I maintain a separate residence [on the other side of town]. I live at Anna's full-time, except when her parents come to visit."

The investigators wondered if Anna's parents didn't like him.

"They're devout Catholics," he explained. "They'd be really upset if they knew I was living with her."

As the night progressed and Nelson took breaks to use the restroom and clean up and grab some fresh air outside, Holt and McGinty focused on a feeling they both had that Nelson Sessler was hiding something important. He just had that swagger about him—an uncanny way of not showing any of his cards. As McGinty later described it, "Emotion welled up inside. . . ." It was strange. Nelson would be on the brink of crying, but he would never let loose.

"I did not kill my girlfriend," he said after being asked the first time.

"Okay. . . ."

"She was alive when I left for work!"

"What happened, you think?"

"I don't think she's dead," Nelson said as they began talking about who could have killed her. "Wait, I have no idea who killed her."

He seemed confused and disconnected.

"What do you think happened, Mr. Sessler?" Holt asked.

"I don't know. How did the person get into the condo? Was anything taken?"

"We cannot answer that, Mr. Sessler."

He looked at them with a quizzical expression.

"You never left your building all day?" Holt pressed.

"Nope. Not once."

They took a break. It was 1:05 A.M., November 9. Nelson Sessler was becoming unruly and shaken up. They had hit a benchmark. The next several hours were going to tell the detectives if they were dealing with a killer or a confused individual who simply acted strangely.

Not long after the interview with Nelson Sessler got under way in the box, in another part of the SPD station house, Sergeant Richard Colwell sat at his desk, staring at the telephone. This was the part of the job that made Colwell sick to his stomach. It was his duty to notify the family. They deserved to know the moment the SPD was able to release the information—which meant, Colwell knew, a family, sound asleep in their Florida winter home, counting sheep and dreaming of another Florida day in the sunshine, was about to get that midnight call no parent ever wanted. The phone was going to ring, wake the Raymundos up, and they would, like anyone, immediately think that something terrible had happened.

And this time they'd be right.

"Mr. Raymundo," Colwell said softly, empathetically, "this is Sergeant Colwell with the Stamford Police Department in Connecticut."

Silence. Then Renato Raymundo cleared his throat, realizing perhaps who was calling, the weight of Colwell's professional title settling on him. "Yes, Sergeant, can we help you?"

Colwell delivered the news.

Renato Raymundo later explained how, at that moment, his body "went numb" and he started "trembling" as he began to accept this his daughter, his beloved Anna Lisa, had been murdered inside her condo. This was what the sergeant was telling him. Those were the words coming out of the cop's mouth on the other end of the line—"Your daughter has been murdered inside her condominium"—and yet none of this seemed to be happening in real time.

"As parents, we were hoping this news couldn't be true," Renato said later. "I felt weak. My heart was pounding hard."

Standing, with the phone in his hand, Renato believed he was having a heart attack. His heart was thumping quickly and aggressively in his chest. The anxiety and pain the news brought were unbearable.

"Thank you, sir," Renato said after some time. He had to get off the phone, Renato explained. He and Susan Raymundo had to console each other. They had to figure out what to do next.

"I understand," Colwell responded. He hung up the phone, took a deep breath, sighed, and stared at his desk.

By 2:35 A.M., the medical examiner had arrived to remove Anna Lisa from the Harbor Drive scene. It was time for her body to be transported to Farmington, an hour away, where further examination and investigation could occur. The workers from the ME's office placed brown paper bags over Anna's hands and feet, which were bare to begin with. She was rolled over on her side, which "revealed" several "lacerations to the back of her head."

Photos were snapped, flashes going off in the darkened room, as the ME's office photographed close-ups of Anna's head and where she was lying on the floor. Within twenty-five minutes, or 3:00 A.M., Anna was being wheeled outside to the ME's van. By three minutes after three o'clock, that same morning, Anna Lisa Raymundo was driven one final time away from the condo she loved so much.

CHAPTER 14

GREG HOLT HAD not necessarily lost his patience with Nelson Sessler—that is, without coming on too strong and overbearing—but the detective was beginning to feel that the interviewee had better open up or he was going to have some big problems. As of now, they were going around in circles. When they returned to the box after a break, Holt started right in on Nelson.

"He did not like me," Greg Holt said of Nelson Sessler. "The feeling was mutual."

Holt sensed some sort of secret that Anna's boyfriend was keeping; and as the night went on, that feeling for Holt grew. Holt was fairly certain it did not have anything to do with murdering Anna Lisa, but there was something major the guy was not sharing.

McGinty and Holt went through a series of questions regarding Nelson's former girlfriends, his and Anna's close and not-so-close friends, and anyone else Nelson thought could be capable of having a reason to kill Anna. They needed a motive. Sometimes that reason for murder is buried within the context of relationships, and those involved don't even realize it's there. Maybe Nelson knew something without knowing it.

"Was there any discord in the house between you and Anna?" This was as good a place as any to start.

"No."

"Any family, friends . . . any issues we need to know about?"

"None that I can think of."

"Does she have an ex-husband, an ex-lover . . . *anyone* who might be jealous?"

"No, no . . . it's just me and Anna Lisa."

As the three of them went back and forth, tit for tat, Nelson became "frustrated and angry," McGinty described in his report of the interview. And then, without warning, Nelson Sessler said: "I want a lawyer."

The interview was stopped right there. Greg Holt walked out of the room.

McGinty and Nelson were alone in the box. "Do you think I need a lawyer?" Nelson asked McGinty.

"I cannot tell you yes or no on that," McGinty explained. "It's a decision that's entirely up to you."

Nelson and McGinty continued to talk. Nelson said he had no problem carrying on a conversation without a lawyer. The problem, maybe, was Greg Holt. Nelson was growing impatient with the investigator and how Holt seemed to be badgering him—if not with words, certainly with his tone and those deep stares.

Greg Holt returned at some point later.

"Do I need a lawyer?" Nelson asked Holt straightaway.

Greg Holt reached down onto the chair in the room where the phone sat, picked it up, and handed it to the interviewee.

"Call your lawyer," Holt said sharply.

Nelson dialed. The detectives left the room.

When they returned, Nelson said, "I will continue to talk to you without a lawyer."

"Who did you call?" Holt wondered.

"My voice mail. I wanted to see if the Raymundos or anyone else called."

"So you *don't* want a lawyer, then?" Holt asked.

"Nope. I understand what you're doing and why you're questioning me, and I want to be as much help any way I can."

Such a sudden change of heart, Holt thought. *Huh.*

"Look, I'll even take a polygraph, but only with my lawyer here."

The interview went well into the following morning. At one point, Nelson asked for some water and Holt went out to get it. As he closed the door to the box behind him and looked down the hallway, Holt saw several of his colleagues—including his bosses—waiting around.

"They were thinking, definitely, 'When is that confession coming? Have you guys broken him yet?'" Holt walked past the men, got the water, then stopped there in the hallway.

"Bizarre," Holt said. They all looked at him. "This guy is bizarre."

Nelson Sessler had a "very atypical response to everything," Holt recalled. "Aloof, cool, but also very respectful to us. He didn't like me. He took to Tommy McGinty right off the bat."

Continuing, Holt said, "Sessler wouldn't give us anything. We knew there was something there, but he wouldn't tell us. In my opinion, I think he knew who killed Anna Lisa Raymundo, and I have no doubt that Nelson Sessler was an accessory *after* the fact. I cannot say, or cannot speculate whether or not he knew beforehand. He may have surmised. But I cannot say he knew beforehand. But he *knew.* . . . He knew. . . ."

Nelson Sessler agreed to give a written statement about halfway through the night. McGinty swore him into record. Then the cop read him his rights. After that, they got down to it. Nelson Sessler put down on paper basically everything he had told them thus far.

Done with that, he agreed to strip down to his underwear so the SPD could photograph his body. And this was where things got a bit interesting.

Detective Tom McGinty, studying their prime suspect's body, noted in his report that Nelson Sessler had what appeared to be "scratch marks over his right shoulder," of which the younger man had no explanation for and could not say where they had come from.

"Do you own a Graham and Lockwood green tie and a size-sixteen . . . beige-and-white striped shirt?" one of the detectives asked after Nelson got dressed and prepared to leave. This question was important. They had found clothing items at the scene.

"I don't know the brand names. I had worn clothes that color earlier this week, and they would have been in the laundry basket downstairs. . . . The tie might have been folded by the piano downstairs, but I'm not sure."

"What about workout clothes?"

"Yes."

"What type?"

"Plastic, nylon pair of pants, gray."

"Sneakers?"

"Nike, size ten and a half, and two other pairs, one blue and red, and the other white . . . sizes eleven and eleven and a half. I don't know the brand names of those."

"Will you come in and give us blood and hair samples in the future if we need you to?" McGinty asked.

Nelson thought about it. "Yes, I will."

They cut him loose.

As Nelson Sessler was brought back to the condo to pick up his vehicle, Greg Holt and Tom McGinty were left to wonder what it was that the guy was hiding. It was implicit in his demeanor and the way he explained himself. They both felt it.

What McGinty and Holt didn't know then was that, strangely enough, in his written statement nor in any of the conversations he had with police that night, Nelson Sessler had never mentioned the affair he'd had with his coworker, Sheila Davalloo. During the course of the night, he had given them the names of two other females he had dated in the past, both of whom Nelson said "had suffered from depression." However, he systematically and deliberately chose to leave Sheila out of it. Yes, the lusty affair between them had been over, but Nelson Sessler didn't think it important enough to tell police that he had dated Sheila.

This made one wonder: Wouldn't he want to tell them if his goal was to help the SPD locate Anna's killer—or was he hiding something?

CHAPTER 15

SHE WOULD SNEAK up behind him, throw her arms around his waist, and stealthily whisper in his ear, "I love you, Daddy." Dr. Renato Raymundo later remembered that heartfelt exchange with his daughter.

Anna.

No father should have to sit and recall the moments of his daughter's life after she has unexpectedly, tragically, and violently left the world by the hand of a maniac. It upsets the balance of natural order for a parent to bury his or her child.

When asked about Anna Lisa, and the most glorifying quality he had taught his daughter, Dr. Raymundo recalled, "As I look back and review in my mind all the things I had shown her, taught her, and inspired her, I think the most enduring was that to serve and love mankind is to love and serve God."

As doctors and Catholics, the Raymundos would go on missions, bringing medical and surgical services to the less fortunate of the world. Anna Lisa would sometimes go. It was a calling, to serve the poor and sick and not expect anything in return. Anna Lisa was never one not to show how much she loved the world and the people in it by giving totally of herself.

"While in college," Renato said, "she volunteered in the soup kitchen and the Center for Women. Anna Lisa was very friendly, and she never thought negatively of others. Her laugh, affectionate cheerfulness, lifted us up, especially in sad times. She was very respectful to me, my wife, and to other people and friends."

Renato called his daughter "exceptionally gifted, with a sharp mind and intellect." This was a trait in Anna Lisa, he reiterated, that both he and Anna's mother witnessed while she grew "from infancy to childhood."

Anna was twenty-five years old when she began working at an executive level, which is unheard of in the pharmaceutical field in which she had chosen as her life's work. With Pharmacia, she had become the associate director of Global Health Outcomes and Applied Outcomes Research at the time of her death.

It was ten in the morning on November 9, 2002, and Anna Lisa Raymundo was naked. Her body was stripped of its clothing after a careful inspection for trace evidence, and she was ready for associate medical examiner Dr. Thomas F. Gilchrist to begin the task of finding out what exactly killed her—and what additional evidence Anna's body would surrender.

Anna Lisa would be known from this point on as "the victim."

Case: 02-13082.

The victim was X-rayed and negative findings of foreign objects, investigator EJ Rondano, who was there to witness the autopsy and write a report for the SPD, jotted down in his notes. This meant Anna had not been shot. Nor had she been violated with an object.

The "once-white" shirt Anna had been wearing was thought

to contain bloodstains around the rim—or collar—of the neck area; but as they checked it after the ME removed it from Anna's torso, it was found to be "near completely red stained with blood. . . ."

Anna was wearing a necklace with a pearl pendant, but the pendant was missing. As the ME searched Anna's head, however, the pendant turned up in her hair—an indication that at some point Anna's killer grabbed the pendant, or the knife used to kill her had cut it off and lodged it in her thick black mane of hair.

Rondano collected two body bags, both white. One of which the ME had used to transport Anna's corpse to the medical examiner's office; the other one was used to "roll the victim" onto it at the scene "to examine" Anna's back. Rondano noted, *Both bags were heavily coated with blood on the interior surface.*

Documenting Anna's injuries was next, a part of this procedure Greg Holt and Tom McGinty would be greatly interested in, once the information became available. Injuries can tell a lot about the killer. The way in which a person is stabbed to death might explain if a male or female committed the crime, or what, perhaps, the killer had been motivated by: hatred, lust, jealousy, or pure rage. The "why" would come later; but knowing the "how" was equally important in the earliest stages of any investigation. Not to mention a driving factor for cops.

Rondano and Gilchrist counted a total of nine stab wounds in the area of the face, left cheek, neck, and shoulder areas.

The fatal wound, Rondano wrote, with the ME in agreement, *[was] to the chest, inches left of midline.* Upon further examination of Anna's interior midsection—effectively cutting her open to look inside—Gilchrist found that the fatal knife wound had a "straight entry" as the blade "struck" the left lung, left pulmonary artery, the interior ribs, and muscle in the back.

This proved Anna's killer was powerful and strong: The stab wound that killed her had entered her chest and nearly exited out her back. She didn't have a chance after this wound had been inflicted. Anna could have fought for some time with superficial stab wounds to her face and neck—however painful and deep, providing none nicked one of her carotid arteries—but a wound like the one she sustained to her chest was fatal every time. There was no coming back from it.

This injury caused a lot of internal bleeding, Rondano wrote.

Another strong indication that Anna put up a fight, based upon what Rondano wrote, were *bruises . . . visible on the left forearm and smaller lacerations/cuts . . . on the right forearm. Bruises were also visible on the left shins.*

Anna had put up her arms to defend herself.

But those shin injuries told another story. At some point, Anna ended up on the floor and her attacker still felt the need to continue pummeling her.

How did they come to this conclusion?

Gilchrist conducted a careful examination of Anna's head after shaving her hair. As soon as he did that, it became clear that Anna's killer was likely a novice, someone for whom killing was the means to an end, not necessarily something he or she had done before.

Rondano noted: *Dr. Gilchrist discovered five (5) blunt trauma injuries at the back of the head. The largest wound being approximately three (3) inches long at the center of the head. There were two (2) additional smaller injuries to the left of center and two to the right of center.*

Anna's murderer had bashed her head in at some point.

These injuries were not consistent with a fall to the floor.

* * *

Meanwhile, Greg Holt was busy tracking down Nelson Sessler's supervisor, Bernie Offman (pseudonym). Holt was interested, of course, in locking Nelson down as soon as possible to his story. Anna's boyfriend was, in every regard, the SPD's only viable suspect. Although still considered quite early in the race, after Nelson Sessler, there was nobody on the SPD's immediate radar screen.

This was the part of the job that Detective Greg Holt took to: gumshoe police work. Wearing down that shoe leather. Cases weren't solved by sitting on one's ass, scrolling through Internet sites, and reading reports. Knocking on doors and asking questions—that's what got law enforcement closer to a resolution at this early stage. This technique had worked for hundreds of years. After a cop exhausted all of his up close and personal possibilities with interviews—and with this case, Holt knew already, the amount of people to interview was going to be daunting—he would go back to square one and start over, perhaps using slightly different methods, and yet always returning to that core tool in a cop's arsenal: interviews.

"Personally, I like talking to people," Holt explained. "I study and have studied people and their responses/body language for years. If you are trained (I have been to many training schools for this) and know what to look for, you can find an interview invaluable. Deception is fascinating to me, and there is no feeling better than an interview that results in great info or a confession."

Holt checked the phonebook and found one man listed under the name that Nelson had given them for his supervisor. Accompanied by Yan Vanderven, Holt took a ride over to the guy's house. This was an important moment in the investigation. It would begin to tell the SPD who Nelson Sessler was and, probably most important at this juncture, what, if anything, he was hiding.

"Actually, we have another location we can check," Vanderven said after he and Holt got no response at the first address.

"Let's go."

Nobody was home at the second location, either. So Holt and Vanderven left business cards, hoping Nelson Sessler's boss would do the right thing and call them when he returned.

As Dr. Tom Gilchrist continued with Anna's autopsy, sifting carefully through her hair, he found what appeared to be glass fragments and other seemingly essential material he associated with the potted plants turned over inside Anna's condo. After studying it, Gilchrist and Rondano agreed it was soil, with those little white balls that look like Styrofoam used in potting soil fertilizer.

Also discovered in the hair was a single contact lens with a blue tint.

Anna's or her killer's?

Interesting.

Rondano made a note of it.

Then, as Gilchrist forced Anna's mouth open and examined the inside, he uncovered what was described as "a small piece of white metal" (possibly stainless steel) in the corner of her mouth.

Could be important, Rondano thought.

Gilchrist, too, considered this to be important.

Both fingernails from Anna's middle fingers had been broken. Another result of a struggle and fight. Gilchrist scraped the remaining fingernails and placed all of the clippings into bags. If Anna scratched her killer's face or chest or any other part of his or her body, forensics would have DNA.

Gilchrist was pretty certain about his findings as he completed the autopsy. As in every autopsy he's conducted, there were answers.

"Any idea what type of weapon was used?" Rondano asked.

Snapping a latex glove off one hand, Gilchrist took a moment and thought. Then: "The weapon would have had approximately a one-half-inch-wide blade that was four to five inches long and . . . well, very thin in width."

Rondano considered what type of weapon the doctor was describing. It would have been flexible. Very efficient if an assailant was using it to stab someone.

"Maybe a fillet or boning knife?" Rondano suggested.

Gilchrist agreed it was a possibility.

Interesting that Anna was murdered with a knife used to fillet fish. After all, her condo was so close to the Long Island Sound. There were fishing boats and fishermen hanging around the area all the time. Could it have been a lone stranger? Someone hanging around the docks, looking for work on a fishing boat. Maybe he happened upon Anna's condo for some reason? Did a local fisherman stalk Anna for weeks and then figure out how to get into her condo? Once she turned away his sexual advances, he killed her in a fit of rage?

Any scenario was possible.

"The stab wound to the left lung," Gilchrist further explained, "was the fatal wound. Although, the injuries to her head may have resulted in death if the victim had survived the stab wounds."

"How long do you think she would have survived, given that the stab wounds didn't kill her?"

"Oh, approximately four to seven minutes *after* the stab wound to the chest."

Equally interesting was the fact that Anna had no wounds on the back of her body. All her wounds were to the front. She had not been attacked from behind. Another indication that Anna's killer did not chase and surprise her. Her killer went directly at her.

Anna knew what was happening.

When all was said and done, Dr. Gilchrist gave EJ Rondano a "Notification to Police" outlining his findings regarding the cause and manner of death for Case: 02-13082.

The cause was "multiple stab wounds/blunt trauma of head"; the manner certified as "homicide." Dr. Gilchrist gave his proverbial stamp and signed the documents. Rondano left with the official statement and death certificate, along with twenty-seven individual packets, all of which had been tagged as supporting evidence and on their way to the lab for further testing.

Later that day, Greg Holt got a call from Bernie Offman, who apologized for not being around earlier to speak with them.

"You can come over now," Bernie said. "I'm home."

Holt and Vanderven left right away, arriving at Bernie Offman's house near nine-thirty at night.

"Come in . . . come in," he said, opening the door. The weather had been mild in the Stamford area the past several days. Although cooler by the shore, with temps in the high 40s and low 50s Fahrenheit, it made going out at night a bit easier, save for that unmistakably heavy as San Fran haze coming in off the Long Island Sound.

"Have you spoken with Mr. Sessler?" Holt asked, strategically sizing this guy up, making judgments, trying to figure out whose side he was on.

"I have," the supervisor said. He and Nelson had spoken

earlier that day. "He told me what happened was a 'great tragedy.' He and Anna were supposed to go to New York City to have dinner that night. They had plans."

"Did he mention anything about his day?"

"He did. Nelson said that as he arrived home from work, there were lots of police cars, and that's when he found out what happened."

"How was he . . . you know, his demeanor?"

"Oh, his mood went up and down as we spoke."

"Talk to us about Friday—yesterday at work. When did you first see him?"

"When he came in around nine, nine-thirty. We passed each other in the hallway."

"How did he seem?"

"Normal. Nothing struck me as being out of the ordinary with Nelson."

"Do you recall what he was wearing?"

Fridays were dress-down days in the office, but Bernie could not recall if Nelson wore a tie or not. As Holt listened, he knew everything Nelson's boss said could be by design. He didn't yet know if Bernie Offman could be trusted. A detective had to be prepared for anything during those early moments of an investigation. Holt put every ounce of himself into a case for the first twenty-four to forty-eight hours. "And obviously longer, like years, if that's what it took," Holt explained. "Everything goes on hold and you run to catch up as the perp is already ahead of you." Greg Holt thrived on the adrenaline rush that came from a case like this. He had been awake and working Anna's case since he got that call to head over to her condo. "I could go strong for long periods with little or no sleep. I worked thirty-two hours the first day, home for three, back for twenty-four-plus, and then sixteen-hour-plus days, and I did this for a long time after Anna Lisa's death. I knew there were answers out there. We just had to find them."

"Nelson generally dresses pretty casually," Bernie explained.

"Now, throughout the day," Holt said, "did you see him, or converse with him at all?"

"Oh yeah. I saw him periodically throughout the entire day. I was with him at a lunch conference, from, like, noon to one. It was a big group we were with. Then there was another meeting after the conference, which narrowed the group down to about fifteen to twenty people. That meeting lasted from about, I don't know . . . oh, one to two-thirty or so. But I cannot tell you if that was the *last* time I saw him, however. I cannot recall."

The opportunity was there for Nelson to commit the murder—at least going by Bernie Offman's brief, albeit tenuous, timeline of the day.

"What type of person is Mr. Sessler?" Holt asked.

"Nelson? Oh, he's definitely a driven individual. He's always at work early and leaves relatively late. He generally arrives at seven in the morning and leaves around six or even seven at night."

The guy worked twelve-hour days at a salaried job. So far, Nelson Sessler was scoring pretty well.

Holt took out a photograph of Nelson they had taken of him during the interview the previous night. It was important to establish if Nelson had changed his clothes on that Friday at some point during the course of his day.

"Was he wearing these clothes? Do you recall that now, looking at the photograph?"

"I believe, yes, those were the clothes he had on yesterday," Bernie said.

He didn't sound too confident.

"But I cannot be positive," he added after staring at the photo.

"We'll need to figure out how to get the times Mr. Sessler entered and exited the building for that entire day," Holt explained.

They asked a few questions and left.

When Greg Holt and Yan Vanderven got back to the station house, Bernie Offman called. He said he had just remembered a few things.

Vanderven listened and wrote it all down.

"Hey," Vanderven told Holt after getting off the phone with Bernie, "our guy just called."

Holt sat back, all ears.

"He said he had thought of two ex-boyfriends of Raymundo's that we might want to find and talk to. One's a theology grad at Yale, shoulder-length brown hair—that's all he recalls about him. The most recent boyfriend"—Vanderven looked down at his notes for a moment—"and she dated him before or at about the time Sessler came into the picture, is a chief pediatric medical resident at Columbia University Presbyterian Hospital. Offman says Raymundo had a 'tumultuous relationship' with this guy."

"Interesting," Holt said. They needed to look further into both leads. "Did he have any idea what times Mr. Sessler was in and out of the building—I mean, that's gonna tell us a lot."

He didn't.

Holt began to think about this new information. A theology student and a resident physician, two highly respected jobs—men who were more inclined to honor the sanctity of life—in other words, not take it.

CHAPTER 16

NO MATTER HOW FOOLISH OR WEAK a lead might seem, law enforcement has to check out anything that comes in, Detective Greg Holt explained.

Indeed, it's the one time you don't that you'll get burned.

That said, Greg Holt knew those ex-boyfriends of Anna's weren't going to amount to much. And sure enough, when all was said and done, both boyfriends had excellent alibis and in no way could have killed Anna Lisa Raymundo.

In the earliest stage of a murder investigation, one of the most time-consuming and "boring," Holt explained, "parts, especially for the patrol division . . . but absolutely essential and important, is the neighborhood canvass."

By this, Holt meant knocking on doors and asking people in the neighborhoods what they had seen, what they knew, maybe even going to sources and confidential informants (CIs) on the street and pressing them about what they've heard.

The problem is, however, "People may shut down and tell you nothing, because of being afraid of retaliation."

Amid this strenuous and oftentimes fruitless work that

takes man- and womanpower, there might also be that one nugget—the one piece of information—that will send investigators like Holt and McGinty in the right direction.

The other end of it is maybe a call comes in later on because some cop on patrol made a connection with some door knocking out on the street.

"Being out there on the street, 'working it,' is so important," Holt said. "An example is the recent 'pushing' of a civilian onto the subway tracks in New York. The perp was a male black, possibly an EDP (emotionally disturbed person), and the police had only a grainy surveillance camera photo. But they stuck to the neighborhood canvass around the clock and, sure enough, someone soon recognized the photo, which led to a collar."

That's how it works. It's that unexciting, unromantic, unadorned, routine police work that viewers *don't* see glamorized on television that ultimately solves murders.

Along with several other investigators, Holt was hanging around Anna's condo the following morning, November 10, studying the scene, walking the parking lot, trying to figure out if anyone could have seen something and perhaps didn't realize it was important.

Yes, more canvassing.

"We just dug right in," Holt added.

The condo complex that Anna lived in, the complex next door to it, both needed canvassing. Same as the street that led up to it.

Anywhere they could find someone to speak to.

Then there was Purdue Pharma. The SPD began letting everyone in that facility know there was going to be lots of questions coming about Nelson, Anna, and anything else anyone could recall. There were a few cops on their way down to New Jersey to begin speaking to people at Anna's employer.

"We interviewed *every*body."

The goal was to interview anyone and everyone Anna Lisa could have had contact with throughout her life, especially in those days and weeks leading up to her murder. Somebody had an idea who killed her. That info was out there somewhere. They just needed to find it.

Not to mention, it had been, after all, broad daylight when the murderer entered Anna's condo.

Soon the 911 call became a focal point after EJ Rondano produced a transcript of the call and they all had a chance to go over it and listen to the tape a few times. There was something to the call. Cops hear hundreds of 911 calls throughout their careers. Two rules generally apply to 911 calls: The caller is frantic and more than willing to freely give out information; or the caller is trying to hide things.

In this 911 call, there seemed to be a bit of both.

"I saw a guy go into the apartment at 1-2-3 Harbor View. . . .Those were some of the first words uttered by the caller. "She lives in apartment 1-0-5?" the dispatcher had asked.

Those words were the first indication of where the attack had taken place. The road wasn't quite right and the number was wrong.

Dispatch was confused.

Then the caller yelled: *"ONE-OH-THREE HARBOR VIEW!"*

Before saying, *"One twenty three . . ."*

Dispatch asked for a name. The caller indicated she was speaking of a friend.

"I don't know her name, but she's my neighbor and she lives in apartment 1-0-5."

Friend or neighbor? Two different ways to describe

someone. And now dispatch had four different address numbers: 106, 123, 103, 105. Plus, the caller didn't know the woman's name. The caller had to be close by when the incident occurred—because she claimed to have heard yelling.

Then came the bombshell: "And the guy was in there . . . He *attacked* her."

The guy.

So the SPD set out to sit down with witnesses, anyone they could find, and play the tape to see if anyone recognized the voice of the 911 caller. If they could interview the 911 caller, lots of confusion could be cleared up.

"Nobody could recognize the voice," Holt explained later. "More than that, nobody knew of any problems Anna Lisa might have had. She was a very smart, well-respected girl. Everyone knew that she was with Nelson Sessler, so that wasn't a surprise to anyone, like maybe the relationship was very private."

Another theory that had to be considered, and looked into seriously, was the possibility that Anna Lisa, and even Nelson Sessler, if they were placed into the context of whom they worked for, were involved in any way in the drug trade. Both worked in some capacity for pharmaceutical companies. It was thought that they would have access—which they didn't—to serious narcotics. Enter Oxy-anything into the equation and big street money emerged. If someone was running a drug operation, all bets were off. Bloodshed and drug dealing went together like sand and sea. Even if someone *thought* Anna Lisa was bringing those exotic, hardcore drugs home, or her condo was somehow full of them and she had access to them, it could be a reason—a motive—for murder.

The case was only a few days old, but was already running just as cold as the weather, which had suddenly turned.

With temps in the high 30s, low 40s Fahrenheit, the breeze coming in from the Long Island Sound made it all that much more frosty, bringing those respectable late-fall temps down into the 20s. It was a stiff wind, as the local fishermen called it. The type of cold air that shreds through whatever clothing a person is wearing and settles straight into the bones.

Near five o'clock in the evening on November 10, the superintendent of the condo complex introduced Greg Holt to two landscapers who had been working around the complex on the day Anna was murdered. Holt was interested in this. The men were said to have seen something.

Through a translator (both men were Mexican and spoke only Spanish), Holt asked what had stopped them from talking when they were approached earlier. On the day of the murder, the men were asked if they knew anything. Both had said no.

"I'm a Mexican national and very scared of police," one of them said.

Just as Holt had expected. People had things to hide. It was one of the main reasons why it took so long to solve some cases.

Secrets.

"I was in the complex as part of a landscaping crew," the other man explained. "We [were] blowing and collecting leaves. Routine work around here. Near nine forty-five, I saw a guy outside of unit 105, sitting in a truck, as if waiting for someone."

"He was just sitting there?"

"Yeah. He was in a furniture delivery truck. Box truck. Double rear tires, hydraulic lift gate in the back—and the rear door was open and the lift was down. It was a white truck."

"Anything else?" Holt liked where this was going.

"Two men," he said next, indicating as such with two fingers. "They got out and they waited around the truck."

"What else?"

The translator said, "He knows nothing more."

As Holt continued poking around, his partner Tom McGinty was conducting interviews and beginning to work through a long list of people in and around Anna's world. Two other investigators contacted a man who was moving in above Anna in a condo unit he had not yet finished remodeling. He said he had seen Anna "from time to time," but he did not know her. She seemed pleasant enough, quiet, kept to herself, like most people in the complex. There was never any trouble or yelling or noise coming from Anna's.

"I did have a team of carpenters working on my unit that day," he explained.

"What were they doing?"

"I wasn't there. I had them there waiting for a delivery— a desk from Staples. They recall this because the desk wouldn't fit through the door, so we talked."

He gave the officers the names of his carpenters.

CHAPTER 17

ANNA LISA HAD a smile that invited those around her to fall under what was her hypnotic, genial, warm spell. They were drawn in by Anna's light and tender nature, her calm and humble demeanor. In terrific physical shape, Anna adored playing tennis and had played on company teams and local athletic clubs just about until the time of her death. If she spotted a child or someone who was having trouble with his or her game, there was Anna, up close and personal, willing to share what she knew without coming across as a braggart or someone showing off. Beyond tennis, Anna loved to ski. She was even a certified scuba diver. And yet it was her charm and gentle friendliness—two persistent qualities everyone who knew her described with a jovial spark—that set Anna apart.

At Anna's funeral in Michigan, the Raymundos handed out a brief brochure celebrating Anna's life and her indelible mark on the world. On the cover of the remembrance, there was Anna Lisa, smiling from ear to ear, her darkly rich black hair perfectly set up in a bun, but several carefully placed locks (bangs) were hanging down, showcasing her beauty and elegance.

"She wanted to be a CEO (chief executive officer) of a big

company," Dr. Renato Raymundo said of his daughter. Anna was . . . survived by her sister Bernadette, a structural engineer, and Renato Junior (RJ), a computer information technologist.

In a tribute to Anna, on the cover of the brochure, the Raymundos wrote that Anna was, before anything else: *a beautiful child of God.*

Her funeral was a Catholic ceremony. Anna's coffin was draped in the traditional gold blanket; the tall Easter candle at the front of the altar was lit and represented Anna's presumed resurrection with Christ. Mourners cried and exchanged hugs, leaning on one another for support and comfort during a time that seemed so surreal it was hard to consider it nothing else but a nightmare. This "generous" woman was "devoted to the pursuit of excellence in health care." Anna was someone who cared passionately and sincerely when it came to helping others. Despite dedicating herself to family, friends, and, above all, "her Savior, Jesus Christ," she had been murdered in her home. She was taken away so suddenly by an act of brutal violence. It was implausible to think that anyone would want to cause Anna harm. Why would someone take this wonderful, calm, caring person away from her family and friends? These questions and the attendant emotions were implicit on the faces of mourners: the astonishment, confusion, pain, loss, dread, and, finally, compassion.

"She lived her life to the fullest . . . ," Renato later said of his daughter. "It was very painful and disheartening as we waited . . . before we could—before she would be released from the morgue. It was with God's grace that our second daughter, Bernadette, and her husband . . . were able to fly [to Connecticut] right away from Michigan."

It was Bernadette and her husband who identified Anna at the morgue. They were sitting alone in a room with a video monitor that showed Anna's face, frozen in death, on the screen. Crying, shaking her head, Bernadette indicated yes, that's her sister. Renato and Susan couldn't do it. They couldn't stand the thought of their dead Anna becoming a lasting, final image etched into their minds—living the rest of their lives with that picture of dead Anna, representing the cruelty and pain she suffered in the moments of her death. It was excruciating for them to fathom seeing Anna like that.

The death of his daughter hit Renato especially hard and heavy. He had no idea the impact would be so detrimental, so substantial and abiding. Time, in effect, would not heal this wound, Renato surmised at first. "I suffered through unbearable grief, depression, and agony," he said. "So much so, that I could not function normally. I continued to have chest pains and needed medication. I started to question my faith and my God—why this had to happen to *us*. After all, we were devoted Christians."

There are so many questions of "why" within the wavy lines circling out from the ripple effect of one murder; these are questions that go on and on, unanswered, and haunt victims' families forever. It never ends: the pain, the sense of loss, abandonment, confusion. There is the need to know why their loved one had been taken so early—why are they alive and their child dead? Why did someone have that much hatred and evil inside him to take such a gifted, loving life?

For the next four months after burying his daughter, Renato would not attend mass. He would not go inside a church. He folded up into his shell. He didn't speak much. He didn't get much out of everyday activities. He became bitter and "turned away from God." He could not understand why God would allow such a hideous thing to happen to such a wonderful human being, one of God's own children.

"Our disbelief that this horrible event would ever befall our beloved and innocent Anna Lisa had caused me" to leave the church, Renato explained, looking back during those years after Anna's murder. "I gradually overcame this, with the help of our Almighty God and the spirit of Anna Lisa watching over us, and promised never to question God again."

Still, there were times when Renato "burst out crying" for no apparent reason. He soon found solace in visiting Anna at her grave every Sunday after mass, along with his wife, Susan. At the site, Anna's beloved parents would stand, look down, smile, cry, and "talk to her." They'd bring flowers. "We would tell her some news about the family and the progress of her murder case."

The word "progress," however, was not one the SPD would have used to describe the first week of the investigation. There just wasn't anything happening to excite detectives. A lead would come in and seem promising, but then it would fall to the wayside, placed in a stack of reports growing fatter as each day passed.

Anna's sister, Bernadette, had dropped off a tape of that last call Anna made to her parents in their Florida home on the morning she was murdered. Detective Tom McGinty sat down and listened to the tape. Anna sounded her cheerful self, saying she was checking in on her parents and would be working from home all day. Noting the time, 10:34 A.M., this gave the SPD a window now into a more exact time of the murder—and told them Anna had planned to be home all day.

The 911 call had been made near 12:30 P.M. From this new information, it seemed Anna had to have been murdered somewhere between ten-thirty and twelve-thirty, probably closer to twelve-thirty, or shortly before the 911 call was made. This could prove to be an important clue later on when the right information came in. It would also prove important when questioning potential suspects—easily ruling a person in or out.

Holt and McGinty learned from Sergeant Richard Colwell

on Monday, November 11, that a call had come into the station house over the weekend—and they might want to have a look at the report. It was telling at face value. A woman, Jennifer Campbell, who lived in Rochester, New York, had seen a story on her local news about Anna's murder. She called right away.

"I've known Anna for ten years," she told the officer she spoke with that weekend. "We were roommates at Harvard," Jennifer explained further. "Anna came to see me here in Rochester about one month ago. She spent the night. She was very upset about an ex-boyfriend and actually kept me up all night talking about him. She was scared. She said the guy just wouldn't 'take no for an answer.' He had been calling and calling her at home and work."

Obsession—maybe the number one motivating factor in this type of murder. Someone just doesn't get it. Cannot take being rejected. The anger builds and builds and then . . . boom!

An explosion of rage.

"He did show up at her work, too." Then, prompted by a question from the officer, Jennifer said, "Her current boyfriend, Nelson, he probably doesn't know about this guy."

As far as she knew, Jennifer explained, Anna had met the guy in Massachusetts about four years before her death, when she lived there while going to school. He still lived in that same area.

"You can ask around at her current job in New Jersey and find out his name—I know that she told several of her girlfriends there."

"Anything else?"

Jennifer seemed a bit hesitant. "There is one more thing."

"What is it?"

"This boyfriend, Anna told me, he had what Anna described as 'deviant sexual behavior.' That whenever they would engage in sexual activity, he would have to have some other, bizarre activity going on—that the sex was never 'normal.'" Jennifer said she did not know what, exactly, he liked done to him or what he needed "going on" around him in order to be stimulated, but it was weird.

As time passed, it was clear to the SPD that this case was turning into a caper, a whodunit of which they had no clue. There seemed to be so many possibilities. For example, a coworker of Anna's from New Jersey was interviewed. She claimed Anna was a member of Match.com and, going under the screen name "sweetheart_ny," would check her account while in the office in New Jersey. There was even one time when Anna had met a guy from her own building, but she was not into him. He was a painter, the woman said, a plumber or a carpenter.

Yan Vanderven took the info back to the major crimes offices and got to work. He logged into Match.com. Searched. Scrolled through screen after screen. Put in search terms, including "sweetheart_ny," but he came up short. Nothing. Anna was nowhere to be found on Match.com. The SPD would query the company and have them do a more substantial, in-house search; but so far, there was nothing relating to Anna Lisa on Match.com.

The other thought was, if Anna was on an Internet dating site, meeting strangers, anything was possible. There was no telling what Anna Lisa could have gotten mixed up in, or what type of nutbag she could have met. Meeting strangers from Internet dating sites, most cops agree, was a crapshoot of the most dangerous kind. One never knew what was going to happen. Cops had seen so much violence and rape and plain old-fashioned crime associated with Internet dating and meeting sites, it drove them mad that people—especially females by themselves—still met strangers online and then in person.

* * *

Greg Holt found those two carpenters working upstairs, above Anna's condo, who were hired to wait for the Staples delivery of a desk. This was probably the most promising lead of the new week, thus far. Maybe they had seen something or someone hanging around Anna's—maybe, in fact, one of these two was the killer.

"We arrived about nine," John Barton (pseudonym) told Holt. "We saw three . . . landscapers near the street blowing leaves when we arrived." That was solid info. It checked out. The carpenter said he and his partner went up to the condo on the second floor, turned on the television, and started watching TV while waiting for the Staples delivery.

He described the truck. The desk wouldn't fit, they all realized, so they worked at getting it to fit through the door. "We took off the door and leaned it against the neighbor's door."

That was the entrance into Anna's condo. It was 9:45 A.M. when they did this. Anna had called her parents within the hour. It was close to the time of the attack.

"What did you see, hear? Was anyone home in that condo next door?" Holt asked with anticipation.

"Nothing. I never heard anyone next door and I never heard a sound of any kind within that unit. I saw no one enter or leave, and I never saw anyone walking around that area other than the landscapers."

He never spoke to anyone else, either.

Holt took out a photo of Nelson Sessler. "You see him?"

John Barton studied the photo.

"No."

* * *

Near this same time, Tom McGinty was with Nelson Sessler, trying to squeeze additional information out of him. It felt as though Nelson was still guarded and didn't want to give up things, unless pressed hard. But as McGinty kept up pressure, Nelson yielded, and provided the SPD with several names of former boyfriends and friends of Anna's from the Shippan Racquet Club, a tennis facility, close to the condo, where Anna played.

Had she met a psycho while playing tennis? Perhaps he followed her home one day. It would fit with Anna opening the door and letting someone in—someone she knew.

"I know of a man from Canada or Massachusetts," Nelson said, "as well as a man from Long Island, who Anna described as 'bad,' for which I have no explanation why. That piano in her condo . . . that was given to her by a man who moved to Japan."

"His name?"

"Don't know."

"Who delivered the piano?"

"Have no idea."

"Mr. Sessler, did you and Anna have any wine in the days prior to her murder?"

This was something that interested McGinty and Holt. The SPD had found two wineglasses, dirty and used, inside the condo on the dining-room table, near Anna's piano, next to a half-drunk two-liter bottle of Coke. If Nelson hadn't drunk the wine with Anna, somebody else had been there.

"I recall maybe on Tuesday of that week, each of us having a glass of wine while playing a video game in the living room. I don't remember if we left the glasses on the table in front of the television in the living room or if we put them in the sink. We didn't finish the wine. But I don't recall how much of it was left in the bottle or the glasses."

One of the crime scene photos showed a broken wine bottle, which seemed to be empty because there was not a lot of wine spillage near it. There were shards of dark glass scattered on the white tile floor of the kitchen near a wine rack (inside the kitchen) and on the wood floor leading into the next room out of the kitchen. There was a violent struggle in this location, for certain. Exercise equipment and everyday items such as clothes, a necktie, sneakers, boxes, plants pulled out of their pots, and other things were scattered all over, as though two people were fighting for control of the other. Near where some of the glass wound up, on the jamb of the doorway leading into the kitchen, were smudges of blood, some of which contained prints, as if someone (it would turn out to be Anna) used the doorjamb as leverage. That blood spatter, which landed on the walls and dripped (also Anna's), went all the way around the curved wall, heading into the next room and the stairway leading upstairs. Not too far from there, maybe ten feet, was where cops found Anna with her right foot up on a box, a streak of blood across her heel and upper foot, and her left foot, bloodied and dirty, on the wood floor, the toes leaning on the stem of a plant. There was a ten-pound barbell about four feet northwest of Anna's foot on the wooden floor, blood spots all over it, and a nasty, coagulated halo of thick blood on the wooden floor, thick and silky, near that. It was absolutely obvious from this evidence that Anna's killer used the barbell to try and beat her to death. What was also clear, the more one studied these crime scene photos, was that although Anna's killer might have appeared to be strong, with the amount of struggle that went on, the SPD could not rule out that Anna's killer was a woman.

"She had a lot of friends down at the racquet club," Nelson reiterated for McGinty. "Most of them were females."

CHAPTER 18

NELSON SESSLER WAS beside himself with regret and self-resentment as Anna's death and the search for her killer consumed just about every waking hour since the madness began on November 8, 2002. He was upset about the way he had treated Anna and the fact that he could not make amends directly to her. Knowing Nelson was feeling down, in the week after Anna's death, a few friends from out of state visited him and stayed with him at his apartment. They were there for support, both moral and personal. Nelson was a good guy at heart. He'd made his mistakes, like so many others before him. What happened to Anna was something he could have never thought to be possible. Life had turned into a nightmare all during one seemingly normal ride home from work.

Sheila Davalloo, Nelson's ex-lover, was not about to abandon him now, no matter if they had broken up or not. Sheila wanted to be there for Nelson in any capacity she could—what true friend wouldn't? There was one night when Sheila and several of Nelson's coworkers from Purdue went over to Nelson's apartment with Brownie, the dog Sheila owned that Nelson loved so dearly, hoping the pooch would cheer him up. But Nelson wasn't around. He had left, so said his friends after Sheila and the others knocked on the door.

"He went up to visit his folks."

Nelson's parents lived in Binghamton, a near two-hundred-mile, three-plus-hour trek northwest of Stamford, into upstate New York, heading into the Adirondacks. Nelson must have thought it best to get up into those mountains and inhale some of that fresh air and just get the hell out of Dodge for a while. He wanted to clear his mind, take a deep breath, and be around family. Nelson had a brother and sister. He needed to see them.

Upon his arrival, Nelson was greeted with warmth and comfort. After saying hello to everyone and getting settled, his parents explained that, strangely enough, a "care package," as Nelson later described it, had arrived before he did: a box of cookies and a letter.

Both were from Sheila Davalloo.

For what Sheila had planned, this particular package should have contained an apple, with a note saying, *Take another bite . . . please . . . just one more.*

The real note—addressed to Nelson's parents—proclaimed how sorry Sheila was for the death of Anna Lisa. Of course, if there was anything she could do for Nelson or anyone in his family to make the load a bit lighter, she would bend over backward.

Anytime.

Anywhere.

Just say the word.

Looking at the note, Nelson thought, *This is a bit odd.*

But then, after reflecting on things, Nelson considered this to be Sheila's way of reaching out, extending a hand, offering her condolences, and perhaps being a friend. She had always talked to Nelson about being friends if they couldn't be lovers. Perhaps this was her way of initiating that new relationship?

"I thought it was very nice," Nelson said later, after his gut

feeling had told him something was up with the care package
and letter.

Oh, how the guy should have listened to his inner voice! It
would have saved him from what was about to be extraordinary circumstances, which would begin, after Nelson returned
home to Stamford, with Sheila calling him.

"And I started talking to her on the phone," Nelson said
later.

Just like that—the two were off and running once again.

Sheila told Nelson in a letter sometime later that while
they were seeing each other, he had said one of the most
"amazing" things anyone had ever said to her. It was back
when they had first started dating. It was the "nicest, kindest,
most amazing" suggestion, Sheila told him. They were sitting
around Sheila's condo, having an intimate moment. In all of
her vulnerability, Sheila opened up, saying, "I don't want to
have kids, Nelson."

"Why not?" Nelson quipped, puzzled by the revelation.

"My brother is so sick," Sheila replied. The indication was
that she wouldn't want to bring another person who needed
her undivided attention into the world; her brother was her top
priority.

"You need to have a sick child," Nelson suggested after
thinking about it.

"What?"

"Yes. Children who will help you clean up your act and
become more responsible."

Sheila thought about it. Her credit card spending had
gotten out of control. The debt she had amassed was immense. There were other parts of her life she needed help
with—especially relationships and choosing the right mate.
Nelson meant well: a needy child would help her figure out
what was most important in life.

It was "from that day on," Sheila said, explaining how

much the conversation had meant to her, that she had fallen in love with him. And yet her version of love ran the gamut of emotions. Sheila had been that "love you/hate you" type of woman who went up and down with the ebb and flow of a relationship, and never, ever felt secure within it. She'd obsess over silly things: wait by the phone, knuckles in her mouth, pacing, wondering what he was doing, whom he was with, where he was. Sheila had issues with love, issues with depression—the severe type that saddled her to bed at times. When, for example, Nelson Sessler was preparing to go back—fully—to Anna and end his affair with Sheila, he tried to let Sheila down slowly. However, she saw things quite differently. To her, what she and Nelson had was no simple fling. She was not just some woman he could have sex with and toss away like a used condom.

Sheila had written to Nelson near this time, claiming he had run away from her, without reason or warning: *as if I'm a hunter and you're a scared deer.*

She called that time for her "so sad." She was confused that there were no "final words" from Nelson back then—he just disappeared without explanation. No real, tried-and-true good-bye or explanation. As far as Sheila felt, she had no idea that she was being used as a bed partner, someone with whom Nelson was literally testing the waters. But later, as she thought about it and looked at the relationship through an entirely different point of view, Sheila realized Nelson had, back then, disposed of her like garbage. She was mystified—and angered—by how he could simply "toss people away when" he "no longer" had "any use" for them. For Sheila, Nelson was "more than a lover and a partner"—obviously, feelings Nelson never had for her. To Sheila, as odd and incestuous as it sounded, Nelson was "like a brother I never had."

What Sheila Davalloo meant was that she had always felt she had lost her brother to mental illness and had never benefited from having that loving, little brother to talk to and pal around with. And when Nelson ditched her in lieu of being exclusive to Anna Lisa, well, it brought all those feelings back up again. Didn't Nelson understand what he had done? Didn't he *see* it?

Thinking about it more deeply, the point Sheila came to, she later wrote, was that Nelson had never been "capable" of having a "nonsexual relationship" with a female. He'd have to always hop into bed and do the nasty at some point; it could never be about friendship, about companionship and intimacy. About pure, unconditional love.

It would always be about sex.

Apparently, however, with that letter and cookies sent to Nelson's parents in upstate New York, Sheila was ready to forgive, forget, and move on, being that true friend, even if Nelson could not be.

After Nelson and Sheila broke up for good somewhere during the 2002 summer, Sheila went to see Stamford licensed clinical social worker Fran Lourie, a referral from Purdue Pharma's health plan. Clinical social workers diagnose and treat mental, behavioral, and emotional issues. They sit and listen to clients talk about problems going on in their lives at the current time. They offer help in solving and coping with those problems.

Thirty-year-old, single female . . . came in for relationship problem, the clinical social worker wrote in her notes from that first meeting with Sheila.

"Tell me about yourself," Lourie asked after they sat down. "Your family history . . . et cetera."

"My mother is from the border of Italy and France. My father [is] from Iran. I have a twenty-two-year-old brother. My dad is very quiet, but emotional."

"How do you know that?" Lourie asked, interrupting.

Sheila looked down. "I just *know.*"

Sheila explained that her father was an academic. "He's taught and published." He was a smart guy who apparently held his cards—emotionally—close to the vest.

"Tell me about your mother, Sheila."

"She's emotional, too. Cries, but then it's over. She had worked in scientific lab research for thirty years. My dad is just waiting for her to retire."

After a bit more of this back-and-forth about Sheila's family situation, Lourie asked her new client why she was there. Why had Sheila Davalloo felt the need to enter into one-on-one social work at this moment in her life? Was there a specific episode that had spurred the visit?

"Boyfriend," Sheila said. She seemed stoic and unsentimental, as if reciting a list of things she's been thinking about lately. Her remarks didn't seem spontaneous. It was as though Sheila had made a list in her head of what to talk about and was now checking off each item. "I see him once every two weeks," she added. It was obviously not enough for her. She needed more out of the guy, but he was unwilling.

"What do you two do when you get together?"

"Same thing—movie, dinner, sex. He has a girlfriend."

"He does?"

"I didn't know about it when we started dating, about a year ago." From this statement, it wasn't difficult to determine that Sheila was disappointed. It came out as though she had been suckered into a relationship with an unavailable man—all of it based on and rooted in a lie—and then found herself not being able to give him up.

"How have things gone?" Lourie asked.

"Oh, I've been depressed. Christmas last year, for example, I lost ten pounds and cried constantly."

The social worker wondered why Sheila hadn't sought treatment then. Why now?

"I always thought therapy was silly," Sheila explained. "I believed I could deal with my problems on my own. But now I realize I need to talk."

Sizing up Sheila as her client began to feel more comfortable talking about her life, analyzing her, Lourie wrote, *Tearful at appropriate moments . . .*

Sheila seemed to be a normal, smart, career-minded woman who found herself mixed up with a guy she couldn't have all to herself. This wasn't the first or last time Fran Lourie would see this routine domestic situation.

"Might you tell him how you feel?" Lourie suggested.

"I would be more comfortable not telling Nelson how I feel."

"How does *he* feel about the relationship?"

"At first he said the relationship was 'flat'—that there were no ups or downs. He's opened me up to my needs, though. I'm more open with friends now because of him."

Lourie asked about Sheila's past relationships.

"Just two, but I ended those." So it would appear, according to what Sheila claimed to Fran Lourie, that this was the first time she had been dumped. "The first relationship was with a guy seven years older than me. He was ready for marriage and kids. I wasn't. I wanted college and grad school."

Lourie nodded her head in agreement. It seemed reasonable for a woman of Sheila's age at the time to want to achieve those goals.

"The second man?"

"Oh, geez," Sheila said, "he was this dry statistician with whom I shared *no* interests."

They talked some more about how those relationships went, and then Fran Lourie made her assessment, writing, *She feels lowered self-esteem as a result of current relationship and feels she NEEDS MORE.*

"Next week?" Lourie asked. The session had gone well.

Sheila seemed to be opening up, getting honest with herself (by the clinical social worker's assessment). More work was needed, sure, but Sheila was a highly educated woman; she could benefit remarkably from social work and therapy.

"Yes," Sheila said. "See you then."

CHAPTER 19

SHEILA DAVALLOO WENT back to see Fran Lourie on September 9, 2002, one week to the day after they had first met. It might have seemed odd that Sheila did not choose a social worker closer to her condo in Pleasantville, New York, but Lourie's office was near Purdue Pharma, and Purdue's insurance plan had made the referral.

Sheila had some news, she explained, sitting down in the social worker's office. She'd made some strides over the past week.

"Oh?"

"I told my boyfriend I don't want to see him anymore."

They discussed how "difficult it must have been" for Sheila to come to this decision and still have to see Nelson at work, especially on work-related projects. Sheila agreed it would be hard, but it was something she needed to do in order to feel better about herself.

Sheila sat and told Fran Lourie what she believed Lourie wanted to hear. She continued to spew a fantasy she was writing for the social worker as they talked, saying, "He e-mails and leaves messages, which I anxiously anticipate."

That was a lie.

One of several Sheila was telling.

Then, to play up her role, Sheila cried for Fran Lourie, staring into her lap, her shoulders bouncing slightly, tears streaming down her cheeks. It was all too much, Sheila said. She wasn't dealing with the situation as well as she thought she would or could.

"Tell me what's painful, Sheila?" Lourie encouraged.

"His positive qualities. That's what I'll miss. His sense of humor. The rapport we had. The fact that he alone understands my poetry . . . how much I really want to be with him."

This, of course, was only the tip of Sheila's actual, true behavioral iceberg—what was hidden underwater became an enormous chunk, including how Sheila Davalloo truly felt about Nelson Sessler. In fact, it was near this same time that Sheila did something many might assume was a bit desperate on her part—while many others would soon see it as it was: criminal and obsessive.

Sheila would listen to Nelson's calls on his voice mail at work in order to see what he was doing, where he was going, with whom he was speaking, and, most important, where his relationship with Anna Lisa was at that current moment. It was easy to get into his voice mail. Every Purdue employee, upon starting the job, was given a phone number and voice mailbox. A worker went into the account and set up a pin number. Treating the voice mail as simply there for work-related things, some employees—including Nelson—left the password that the account had been given upon its setup: 1-2-3. Nelson had never changed it. Sheila knew this, of course, because she had set up her own account once. Sneaking over to his desk one day, Sheila tried the pass code and just like that she was in.

Yet, if going into Nelson's account and listening to his private calls wasn't enough, there was a weekend when Sheila had learned when and where Nelson was flying off to. So she went ahead and made plans to fly not out of the same airport in state, but she chose a location in another state (Nevada), so she could purposely "run into" Nelson during a connecting flight. She even managed to book a seat somehow right next to Nelson. Then, seemingly "bumping into" him there at the airport and then inside the airplane, Sheila acted surprised, telling Nelson, "It must be destiny! Look at us."

With Sheila ostensibly opening up to Fran Lourie— however strewn with lies her revelations were—it appeared she was making progress. Here, only two sessions in, and Sheila had realized that despite how much she wanted to be with the guy, how much she loved him and thought they were perfect together, she was willing to leave him for the sake of her own good.

"There are things I have neglected telling him," Sheila continued to Lourie, "that weigh heavily on me."

Sheila and the clinical social worker spoke for quite some time about those issues and how Sheila could deal with them. This was a great moment, maybe a turning point, in Sheila's therapy, Fran Lourie believed—and it was only the second week.

Lourie had a suggestion for Sheila, a way for her to deal with those unresolved feelings. "I would like you to write Nelson a letter that *won't* be sent. You will bring it in here next session and we will discuss it. Can you do that, Sheila?"

"I think this will be helpful."

Full range of appropriate affect, Lourie wrote in her notes at the end of this second session.

The following week, September 20, 2002, Sheila arrived with some more encouraging news.

"He called and called, but I did not respond to one phone message," Sheila said as they got started.

More lies.

"Great, Sheila. Good start."

As Lourie listened, however, what became apparent was how Sheila was still very "obsessed" with many aspects of the relationship, along with not being able to give up on it. She was talking about things and it became clear to the social worker that Sheila Davalloo was still deeply involved in the emotional high she was getting from the relationship with Nelson Sessler, even if they were no longer officially seeing each other. Sheila was still fully engaged in what she could get out of the relationship, even though they never saw each other on an intimate level.

She is still very ambivalent, obsessing about his motivations for sending mail when she's out of the office, Fran Lourie wrote as Sheila talked her way through this third session.

According to Sheila, she wanted to "put up a front" for Nelson, and not "give him the satisfaction of knowing [she's] hurt."

"Why, Sheila?" Lourie asked, trying to get her client to open up about her feelings regarding still wanting to dance with Nelson, even though they had ended things.

"I'm angry, that's why."

"What makes you angry?"

"He told me that I needed to [feel] the experience of being left. . . ."

In other words, Nelson felt it his obligation to break up with Sheila so she could experience what it felt like to be dumped—according to Sheila, this was something she had never gone through because she had been the one to end relationships in her past.

"Let me ask you, Sheila, what would your father say about the predicament you find yourself in today?"

"Both my parents would be 'shocked.' It was always under-stood in my house, growing up and even now, that emotions were there, but not openly expressed. There was never any physical or verbal affection in my home."

"And how does that make you feel?"

"I definitely feel very close to my parents, nevertheless," Sheila added. "But I could never discuss emotional struggles with them. I'm stronger than my mother and wouldn't want to upset her in any way. My dad is just very quiet, but I think he would understand me."

In her notes, Fran Lourie wrote this question: *Her fantasy of him?* Sitting, listening to Sheila talk about her father, Lourie wondered whether this man Sheila was describing during her session was the actual person, or what Sheila had *wanted* him to be. Further along, she added that "weekdays are harder" for Sheila because she had contact with Nelson at work. Then the clinical social worker wrote about a short rant Sheila had gone on near the end of the session. Sheila was upset because *[Nelson] had a history of cheating on girlfriends.* Sheila was equally upset when: *She realized she was not the first.* Through this latest rant, Lourie began to see shades of perhaps Sheila not being entirely truthful. The social worker wrote, *She has difficulty in giving up the fantasy of him and what she felt was there.* Sheila's reason for not wanting to give up on Nelson was the idea that it would render the entire relationship, from day one as "meaningless": *Which [is something] she still does not believe.*

They agreed to meet in one week.

On September 30, 2002, Sheila Davalloo arrived at Fran Lourie's office and looked to be in better spirits. She had a glow about her. She wasn't beaming, by any means, but she didn't come into the office with her shoulders slumped, head to the floor, tears in her eyes.

"I've been less tearful and depressed," Sheila admitted as they began.

"How's it going? . . ."

"I've spoken to him on the phone—I called—and have seen him at work."

Part of her therapy was to speak to friends about what she was feeling. Sheila explained that it wasn't going so well in that regard.

"Why not?" Lourie wondered.

"Um, people at work, they tell me they're fed up with hearing about what they called an 'obsessive relationship.' So I've decided to get away from him for a while. I need to do that." Sheila added how she had been going down to North Carolina three days a week for work as part of being a manager for clinical trials. "Tuesdays, Wednesdays, and Thursdays. So I'm trying to convince my boss to allow me to stay down there for a month. There's a void, anyway, that I'm feeling that my friends here cannot fill."

"And what do you think that problem is?"

Sheila looked away. She went quiet for a time. Then, after a brief moment of reflection, gave a one-word answer: "Loneliness."

Sheila believed—or, rather, made Fran Lourie believe—that Sheila had no one. After Nelson, there was no one else who understood her, cared for her, loved her, made her feel alive, and took up that extra baggage of being involved with Sheila Davalloo. What was clear here, maybe in retrospect (because Fran Lourie never mentioned it in her notes at this time), was that with Sheila Davalloo, it was never about what others felt, what others did, what others gave to the world. With Sheila, it was only about her. Every part of Sheila's world revolved around how she felt, what she got, what she lost, what she could get.

It was never about anyone else.

Nelson Sessler, Sheila explained further, had validated her feelings and made her complete, as a person. Nelson was the only one, Sheila said, who had read her poetry, which had become an essential part of her life during those gloomy, dark days of parting with Nelson. She had thrown herself into expressing her feelings through writing poetry. She felt this was a major aspect of who she was as a human being—and she had shared it—this intimate, personal reflection—with only one man, Nelson.

"I need recognition and appreciation for that private part of myself revealed only through my poetry," Sheila explained, sounding more like a beatnik from San Francisco during the 1960s than a woman with a very high-paying, six-figure job, a beautiful condo, fine friends, a family that loved her—not to mention a huge secret, among many, she was keeping from her social worker.

"Nelson is the only person to whom I've read my poetry. I would never read it to my family or friends. It represents my creativity and innermost thoughts and feelings."

"And do you think, Sheila, that Nelson's appreciation of your poetry fueled your fantasy of what that relationship was?"

She thought about what Fran Lourie was proposing with the question. "Yes, I do."

"You can find other ways to fill that void, you know."

"How so?"

"Writer's groups, poetry classes."

This didn't seem to register with Sheila. Her focus was on Nelson. If she couldn't get his stamp on her poetry, she was crushed and could not show it to anyone else. She had given the keys of her creativity to Nelson and he shat upon it. She had opened her heart up to him and he spit on it. This deeply discouraged Sheila from wanting to show her poetry to anyone else, especially strangers in a critical setting, she said.

Lourie mentioned nothing about bringing that letter to Nelson that she suggested Sheila write, or Sheila reading from it, in her notes of this session. Either Sheila never did it, or they didn't discuss it. Either way, they scheduled another appointment, but Sheila mentioned she might be in North Carolina by then, so it was going to have to be tentative.

The social worker encouraged Sheila to call and think about a phone session if she felt the need to talk while she was away.

"I will, thanks."

If she thought therapy would help her cope with whatever was troubling her on the inside, Sheila Davalloo was kidding herself. A person cannot walk into a therapist's office and expect to get any help after half of what she has spewed out was nothing more than lies and made-up nonsense. Still, one would have to ask: Did Sheila Davalloo actually want help, to begin with? Why would she go to a social worker if she planned on lying to the woman?

Perhaps Sheila was nothing more than a pathological liar who could not help herself—and this fed that part of whatever demon inside her head needed nourishment. It seemed Sheila was working out problems that existed, for the most part, within a fantasy.

When Nelson—not Sheila (she had lied to her therapist about this fact, too)—severed those ties with her back in the summer of 2002, sexual or nonsexual as the relationship was then, Sheila later wrote to Nelson that this rejection greatly angered her. She admitted feeling grief, too, as if mourning the end of a marriage. But despite how desperate she was to get back with Nelson, trying everything she could to convince Nelson he was "the one," Sheila wrote, *I wish you the best of everything in life.* But then, odd as it came out, she followed that encouraging sentence with this: *Anger is a productive emotion that quickly subsides.*

Strange choice of words. Was Sheila trying to be poetic? Clever? If so, the thought was out of context, as though she had been thinking out loud.

Sheila then mentioned in the same letter how "blessed" she now felt for the time the two of them had had together. To cap off the letter, Sheila left Nelson a few departing poems, both of which were saccharine and adolescent. In one line, she wrote how her "soul" had transformed itself (after she and Nelson broke up) into a "blizzard of cries." Then, a few lines later, her broken heart had become a "torrent of tears," a common phrase that can be found with a simple search in a host of books.

Nelson Sessler had, apparently, shattered this woman and her belief in love, life, and what it took to sustain a healthy relationship.

Strangely enough, during this entire time that Sheila Davalloo was chasing Nelson Sessler, going to see a therapist, carrying on and on with friends and coworkers—both before and after Anna's brutal murder—inside her own home in Pleasantville, New York, Sheila Davalloo had the one thing she seemed to be looking for in Nelson: a companion, a lover, a life partner, a best friend.

Yes, throughout the entire time she was dating Nelson Sessler, and even as she began to work herself back into his good graces (and soon his bed) by sending that care package to his mother and father in New York and then calling Nelson to console him over losing Anna, Sheila's husband of a little over two years waited for his wife to come home at night.

Sheila Davalloo was a "happily married" woman.

ACT TWO

THE CONFLICT

CHAPTER 20

THEY WERE WALKING through the campus parking lot back to their cars after a movie. Paul Christos and Sheila Davalloo had been graduate-school friends for six months by then. It was only recently that they had been getting closer, having more intimate conversations. They were sharing more subtle, lustrous eye contact when alone, both provocative and meaningful, and a full-fledged feeling was growing between them that there was something else going on besides two friends from school going out together. There was a spark.

Chemistry.

On this night, after Sheila had gone over to her car to head home, as she began to drive away, she stopped. She got out. She walked up to Paul, who had just sat down in his vehicle and rolled the window down.

Paul wondered what Sheila wanted.

Without warning, Sheila kissed Paul. Not a peck on the cheek or a bump on the lips—but a long, affectionate lip-lock.

Now it was clear they were more than just friends.

"And from that point on," Paul explained later, "we just casually dated."

It was 1994. Valhalla, New York. Valhalla is just north of White Plains, south of Pleasantville, east of Tarrytown, west of

Greenwich, Connecticut. Valhalla has always had a reputation as an exclusive community, where the median income has historically been double whatever the state average was, same as the price of real estate. New York Medical College (NYMC) was founded in 1860 and for decades has been the go-to school in the nation for medical field degrees, having the distinction of being the largest private health-sciences university in the country.

Interestingly, 1994 was one of those inconspicuous years when it seemed that not too much happened, generally speaking. Yet, when an objective party looked at the year, several major crime stories emerged. There was a spate of high-profile crimes—the kind that makes those breaking-news reports so dramatic these days. There was the club attack on figure skater Nancy Kerrigan; Lorena Bobbitt was found not guilty under an insanity defense in the cringing mutilation charge of chopping off her husband's penis while he slept; the arrest of England's Fred West and his wife, after authorities began the excavation of Fred's Gloucester, England, home in search of bodies; and the crown jewel of all crime stories, the one setting the bar for bringing televised murder trials inside living rooms as entertainment: the O.J. Simpson trial.

As Paul Christos saw her during those early days after they first met and became fast friends, Sheila Davalloo was "a pretty girl, very impressionable, but also kind of . . . sheltered. She didn't have a lot of exposure to the normal kind of college life" most others had. "She wasn't over-Americanized. She was outgoing. She wrote a lot. She was friendly with everyone, her advisers [at school]. She came across as a normal person. . . . She was very intelligent. [She was] worldly in the sense that she spoke a few languages. I didn't know it, but Farsi was one. French and Italian, too, which I knew."

Paul and Sheila shared similar likes. Sheila, who had studied biochemistry at State University of New York (SUNY) at

Stony Brook (she enrolled at NYMC in search of her master's), adored going to the movies with Paul and sitting down and watching his favorite television series back then, *Star Trek*. They'd go camping with friends, or out to eat. They'd hang around campus, study, and talk. They'd go for walks. It was, by any standard, a normal college romance, perhaps with the potential to grow into something more serious.

Looking back on the relationship, Paul now believes that there were glimpses of a personality that Sheila might not have wanted people to believe she harbored. Sheila was born in Virginia. She moved to Iran with her parents when she was two years old and came back to the States when she was sixteen. Sheila's brother was actually born in Iran. They left that country, Sheila would say later, to get away from all the violence in the Middle East.

"I have a dark secret in my family," Sheila would tell Paul. She was serious about this, Paul recalled. It wasn't as if it was some sort of joke. "Ultimately, it's this secret that will break us up. We could never stay together."

"What are you talking about?"

"Trust me. It's a deep, dark family secret."

"What is it, Sheila? Come on!"

"I'll never tell you."

Watching her, listening to the tone of her voice when she talked about this dreaded "family secret," Paul remembered, "I could tell she was under a lot of stress about it."

It was real. Paul never doubted the authenticity.

They broke up once, Paul said, because of this secret and how it became such a burden on the relationship.

"She initiated the breakup."

Paul drove to Sheila's work after the breakup and had a chat with her. He couldn't just let one year of friendship and the romance die because of some silly secret. Whatever it was, Paul knew, he could deal with it.

"And we got back together again."

The secret kept coming up. Sheila would leave it alone for a time and then cough it back up when Paul least expected.

"Come on, what is it, Sheila?" Paul continued to ask. He understood everyone hides some part of himself, but anything could be talked through. They were a couple. They could get over this hurdle only if Sheila opened up and got honest. Paul knew Sheila had a mentally ill brother and wondered if maybe there was something there—something that the brother had done to her.

"No, I cannot tell you," she'd say adamantly. "Never."

"Come on, Sheila . . . what are you, married?" Paul asked one day, more jokingly than not. If she was, Paul surmised, it wouldn't be so unexpected. It happened in society today more than in decades past. He knew that. Cheating on a husband was not as taboo as it once was—what the hell was the big deal?

"No, no . . . nothing like that," Sheila insisted. She wasn't married.

Wow, this has to be serious, Paul thought. It became a wall in their relationship neither could get over. It was as though as long as there was this secret, the relationship couldn't move to the next level—and Paul was considering that someday, maybe, Sheila might be "the one." His wife. But the secret needed to be exposed.

He thought about it one night: *Something crazy in the family? Something with her parents? Maybe they're part of a cult?*

The bevy of emotions and thoughts Paul went through while dealing with this secret both saddled and baffled him.

Sheila wasn't a religious person, necessarily, Paul knew. But then, neither was he. Neither Sheila nor Paul ever talked much about religion. It just wasn't part of their relationship.

"I didn't know it then, but Sheila was raised Muslim," Paul

said, but that didn't mean anything to him. Paul didn't care. He'd embrace her religion, if that's what the issue was. He'd work things out. Neither of them ever thought cultural differences were an obstacle. They were in love. They enjoyed each other.

"What is it, Sheila?"

"Sorry, Paul. I cannot tell you."

CHAPTER 21

PAUL CHRISTOS HAD dreams, same as anyone. Like the high achiever he would become, Paul was a boy who studied harder than most in high school, banking on the investment of education as a means to get what he wanted out of life. He went to high school in White Plains, New York, not really knowing what he wanted to do later in life. So Paul ended up at the University of Rhode Island (URI) as a business administration major, thinking, *I can fall back on this after graduating.* It was a great major to use in various ways upon leaving school. A business degree could work in many different occupational situations.

After graduating in 1989 from URI, Paul became a landscaper, of all things; and after that, he found some security work. Business administration was clearly not what he had wanted to do. But then, as Paul was ruminating on life and the pursuit of his ultimate happiness, in 1992, he decided to pursue a master's degree in public health/epidemiology at NYMC. And if that wasn't enough, he soon added a master's in biostatistics as well.

Medical research and statistics would be Paul's focus and his life's work. He lived at home back then, in White Plains. When he graduated in 1995, Paul went to work for Strang

Cancer Prevention Center in New York City. Paul's line of work became dealing with cancer epidemiology, the idea of trying to figure out through genetics and statistics what makes colon, breast, and other cancers tick, essentially. Paul was designing studies that included looking into environmental, genetic, and lifestyle factors that might predict the cancer.

"All the stuff you hear on the news when they talk about different risk factors," Paul said.

Life was moving on a fast track. He loved his job. Strang was affiliated with Cornell Medical College, so Paul was also doing some teaching. He enjoyed the diversity of the work, the day-to-day routine of running the numbers, with the hope of coming up with that discovery ultimately helping people live longer, better lives, even perhaps cancer-free.

"You're contributing in some ways to the medical literature," Paul explained.

He had dated girls "on and off," but no relationship had gotten "all that serious" until Sheila Davalloo came along in 1994, as Paul was getting ready to graduate. A friendship with Sheila blossomed into romance. During that year, Paul had run a couple of study groups for NYMC to offset his tuition. Sheila had taken one of the study groups. She was pursuing a master's in public health in environmental health science.

"We were kind of at the same level," educationally and intellectually, Paul explained. "I never got the sense that she was interested in me, but then, after a while, it became clear."

It was that kiss in the parking lot of the campus theater that started things rolling. They were an item. They began seeing each other romantically from that day on.

Yet, that secret was always in the background like static, hanging there, unable to be squelched, beckoning both to bring it up every once in a while. Without getting over it, how were they ever going to make it to the next level of the relationship?

Sheila lived with her parents in Yorktown Heights, New York. Yorktown is one of those quintessential New England towns (even though New York is not really considered part of New England). The town was located in wealthy Westchester County, about thirty-five miles north of the city, somewhat farther north than White Plains. The Yorktown Heights section of Yorktown boasts a small population of between two thousand and ten thousand, depending on which census is referenced. The Heights is a community-oriented borough, with a 90 percent white demographic and a median income of $100,000. It's the perfect little place between Connecticut and Pennsylvania, just far enough away from the city, to raise a family. Housing prices are for the rich. People go to Yorktown and those small towns like it to get away from the hustle and bustle of big-city life. They migrate there to take in the fresh air, the breathtaking views of the mountains, and the idyllic setting. Sheila and her family fit right in. All—save for her brother—were high achievers who had made medicine and public health not only their life's work, but a vocation to get up in the morning and feel good about.

"Is Sheila home?" Paul asked. Although she encouraged him not to, he'd call her parents' house from time to time looking for her. Whenever he picked Sheila up or dropped her off, Paul was encouraged not to go in. He got the sense Sheila's parents did not like him.

"No." And then Sheila's mother hung up the phone.

This happened a lot. "They wouldn't put me through." Paul considered that they didn't approve of him dating Sheila. This was what he meant when he said Sheila wasn't Americanized. Her parents seemed to shelter her from the world, protect her.

One time, Paul called and asked for Sheila, and her mother said, "Why do you keep calling here? You're destroying *two* families!"

"What do you mean?"

She hung up.

Paul perceived that they didn't want Sheila dating him because of a cultural difference.

"But then she had always told me," Paul added, "that they didn't want her dating *anyone.*"

Paul and Sheila would meet at the park in Yorktown. Or back at Paul's parents' house in White Plains. They "hung out a lot." But never at her parents' house. Paul knew he was not welcome and he never pushed the issue. What could he do?

"I mean, it was pretty obvious that she didn't want me to meet her parents at that point and find out whatever dark secret was going on in the family," Paul recalled. "So I kind of fell into this 'I'll just meet her at the park a few blocks away' mode and allow the relationship to dictate what the next step would be."

"We can never be together," Sheila kept telling Paul.

But they continued dating. And this went on and on for nearly a year after that kiss.

Then, one day, Paul took a call that changed everything.

Indeed, that deep, dark family secret Sheila was trying to steer Paul away from was about to reveal itself.

Sheila couldn't hide from it any longer.

CHAPTER 22

"I NEED TO GO see my grandparents in New Jersey," Sheila told Paul one Thursday afternoon. They were on campus, planning their weekend. Paul liked to spend it with the woman he was falling for; Sheila generally always reciprocated that same feeling. They had been having sex for some time now—sex not being all that important to Sheila. She wasn't generally experienced and didn't seem to make it a priority in the relationship. Beyond that, besides the park, in the car, and maybe a hotel here and there, they didn't really have the privacy to have sex at will. Sheila lived with her parents; Paul with his. Additionally, from what Paul took away from the relationship thus far, Sheila viewed sex as nothing more than a *small* aspect of an evolving love affair.

"I'll be there all weekend," Sheila explained, meaning at her grandparents' home in New Jersey. She had done this before. She'd even told Paul where her grandparents lived, naming the exit off the Garden State Parkway, a major highway connecting New Jersey to upstate New York, Westchester County, and points beyond. Paul accepted that Sheila liked to visit her grandmother and grandfather. It was a nice thing she was doing. It said a lot to Paul about the type of person Sheila was—or, rather, the type of wife she might one day make.

It was the fall of 1995, just about a year—give or take—since that first kiss spawned a more serious relationship between them. Paul had already introduced Sheila to his parents. Despite a few bumps, things were moving along, getting serious.

Then, that one weekend Sheila went away, Paul took a call at home—and everything changed.

"Hi, yeah . . . I'm Sheila's husband," the man said in a thick Middle Eastern accent. "You're seeing my wife. . . ."

Paul could not believe it, literally. "Who is this?" Was it some sort of college prank? Were his and Sheila's mutual friends messing with him? Who would do such a thing?

The man explained he was Amir Balazar (pseudonym). "I am Sheila's husband."

Paul considered how the man could have acquired his phone number. He didn't believe what Amir said about being married to Sheila.

No way. Can't be.

"I want you to meet me at Lincoln Center in the city to talk about this," the man calling himself Sheila's husband said.

"Come on, who is this?" Paul asked. He was becoming slightly angry.

Could it be Sheila's brother?

"I want you to meet me in the city," Amir said.

"Okay. Let's meet." Paul figured he'd call the guy's bluff, and that would be the end of it. The joke would be on Paul: *"Ha, ha, ha. You got me!"*

Paul traveled into the city and found himself on that same afternoon sitting in a hotel lobby, a quaint little café near Lincoln Center, waiting for a man who claimed to be married to Sheila. He was feeling a bit odd about the whole thing. The more he sat and considered how the call had come in, the man's tone on the phone, perhaps this was a setup of some sort. But why? And by whom? To say the least, Paul was feeling all sorts of emotions as he sat waiting for Amir.

Soon enough, a man dressed nicely sat down with Paul and introduced himself as Amir Balazar, Sheila's husband. Amir was a small man, with bronze skin and dark black eyebrows. He had Middle Eastern features, for certain. He was balding, and his head was completely shaved over the top, shiny as a freshly waxed and buffed gym floor. There was a carefully groomed circle of white hair ringing around his head from ear to ear. He didn't seem upset or angry. He was rather calm, in fact. This was a demeanor Paul considered a bit strange for a guy who was saying Paul was dating (and banging) his wife. There was an odd shyness about Amir, too. But overall the guy wasn't intimidating or there for a fight of any kind. This much Paul could tell: Amir was there to talk, to explain himself, and to explain his situation to Sheila's lover.

"We've been having some problems lately," Amir admitted, not going into detail about his and Sheila's marriage. "We separated. She moved in with her parents up in Yorktown. But we're trying to work things out now."

In other words, *My wife and I are getting back together.*

Paul still didn't believe him.

No . . . no way.

Amir sensed Paul's incredulity. What else could he say to make Paul believe he was telling the truth? It seemed pretty obvious at this point. Here was a Middle Eastern man, sitting in a café with a stranger, admitting that his wife was cheating on him. The problem was that this guy—her lover—just wasn't getting it.

"Where do you think she is right now?" Amir finally asked.

That was easy. "She's at her grandparents' house in New Jersey," Paul said immediately.

"No, no, no," Amir said. "She's actually at our apartment in the city right now." Amir explained that he had two homes: one in the city, another in New Jersey. "Look," Amir then went on to explain compassionately, "Sheila is the kind of person who is very emotional. For instance, she'd see a bird on the side of the road with a broken wing and she'd go out of her way to try and help this bird. She's troubled. But I want to work things out with her."

Paul was taken aback by this pronouncement. Could it be? Could he be staring at Sheila's *husband*?

The secret?

"I don't believe you," Paul said.

Amir took a deep breath. "Okay. But if you come with me right now, we'll take a cab over there and you can see her car right outside the building."

It was broad daylight. Paul thought about it. He was becoming progressively more anxious as each moment passed. Things were getting strange. What was this guy up to? Maybe he was planning on going uptown and putting a good beating on Paul?

"Okay," Paul said, thinking about it. "Let's go."

Off they went.

The cab ride was short. And as the cabbie pulled down Amir's block, Amir pointed to a vehicle. And there was—or what appeared to be—Sheila's car, a white Volkswagen Golf.

Now, how many white Volkswagens were there in Manhattan at any given time?

Hundreds, perhaps.

But Paul's heart sank and his throat became parched when he saw that one hubcap on this particular white Volkswagen was missing. That missing hub was a trademark of Sheila's vehicle. It was as if while staring at the missing hubcap, a clear picture of what Paul had been involved in slowly came into focus. It suddenly all made sense. Paul had been duped! Fooled.

Damn . . . it's her. She's married.

They got out. The cab left.

"Come on, come on . . . ," Amir said. He had another plan,

obviously. He needed Paul to be absolutely certain. He couldn't allow Paul to leave with any doubt that Amir and Sheila were indeed married.

Truthfully, Paul still wasn't 100 percent sold. "I want to speak with her," Paul suggested as they entered the lobby of the apartment building.

"Yes, yes. Of course." Amir shook his head. That was his plan. Get Sheila on the phone and have her tell the guy this was no dream, no setup, no joke. For all this time, Paul had been messing around with another man's wife. And, maybe more important to the relationship Paul thought he'd had with Sheila, she had been lying to him.

The concierge dialed up Amir's number and handed the phone to Paul.

Sheila answered.

Paul was stunned. He couldn't believe it. Her voice, so remarkably clear.

Sheila . . .

Still, Paul questioned everything. In fact, he considered, *Maybe it isn't her?* He found his thoughts roaming. *Maybe I should ask her a few questions to make sure? You know, what did I say on this day? What did we do last week? What movie did we just see?*

And so, while standing in the lobby of Sheila and her husband's apartment building, Sheila on the other end of the line, Paul asked Sheila a few personal questions, because, as he later put it, he needed "to just make sure it was her."

He needed to confirm the obvious. Paul was a stats guy. A scientist, essentially. He wanted definitive proof.

And so Sheila spoon-fed it to him.

Paul was crushed. Here was that dark secret. He'd guessed it long ago, but Sheila had lied and blown it off, saying no way. She could have come clean then. Now this: a mess. Paul was standing in a foreign place with Sheila's husband. He felt like a damn fool.

Paul didn't recall leaving, because he was so disturbed by the news. He cannot remember how he and Amir parted. What he did remember was that he worked in the city then. And that he hailed a cab, gave the driver the address to his office, and told him to put the pedal to the metal and get the hell out of there. He needed to collect himself before returning home. Figure out what to do. *Man, what a blow . . . and then how it all came down.* That phone call. The meeting. Sheila admitting it.

"Shame" and "embarrassment" didn't even begin to describe his emotions on that day.

What the hell just happened? What has been going on? Paul sat in his office and realized all of the times Sheila said she was going to New Jersey to see her grandparents—well, she was likely going into the city or to Jersey to spend the weekend with Amir, her husband. She was sleeping with Amir and Paul. What did she think was going to come of it? How could she think she could keep a secret like this forever?

Paul was devastated. He had considered that this woman would someday be his wife.

After some time inside his Upper East Side office, Paul's phone rang.

Sheila . . .

"What!"

"Listen . . . I want to explain. Let's meet for coffee in the city."

Paul didn't know what to do. He felt blindsided and tricked. Did it have to come to this? How could she do this to them?

"Why?"

"I want to explain."

Maybe, Paul thought, he owed her that much. "Okay."

They met in a restaurant near Paul's office. Sheila looked different, like the secret was finally out. She could breathe now. By most accounts, during this period of her life, Sheila was a good-looking woman. She had long, curly, thick, rich black hair, tanned skin, a tiny space between her two upper-front and center teeth (like the girl on the television show *CSI*) that could be attractive, a few beauty marks on her face, which could be equally striking if a guy is into that sort of thing, a fair shape, and a unique, large smile. She looked Middle Eastern. And that look worked well for Sheila back then.

"It is the big secret," Sheila began. "I'm married. Yes. I'm sorry. But I'm unhappy, Paul." Sheila explained that they had lived in Italy for a time and Amir was never home. (Incidentally, she had first lied to Paul and told him she was Italian and French, before coming clean and admitting she was Iranian.) "He's older. I cannot relate to his friends."

Trapped. That was the image that came to mind for Paul as he listened. Sheila was saying she had been trapped inside this marriage. Like a prisoner.

And she wanted out.

Amir was seven years older. They had married on March 4, 1991. Sheila was now twenty-two years old; Amir was twenty-nine. For the past few years of the marriage, Sheila said, they had been acquaintances, roommates. Sheila could not relate to the guy on any level.

Paul sat listening, shaking his head, still in disbelief that she had lied to him all this time. Why not just come clean? How hard was that? They could have worked things out.

"It was an arranged marriage," Sheila said. "His parents were friends with my parents. Both are strict Iranians. That's what they believe. They didn't even want me to enroll in the master's program. I would stay in the apartment in Italy for days and days, depressed . . . not knowing what to do."

Years later, Paul would speak with Sheila's parents about Amir and this supposed "arranged" marriage. "And they told me that none of this was true. They did not arrange the marriage—and, in fact, they didn't even want Sheila to marry [Amir]. But she was very insistent about marrying him. Once they were married, however, her parents became very adamant about her staying with him."

Hence, Paul reflected differently on the phone call, when Sheila's mother told him he was breaking up two families.

Paul thought about what Sheila was telling him. It wasn't so much that Sheila was married, but that the marriage was arranged and she believed she couldn't get out of it.

Now that the secret is out, she's in a bad marriage that she wants out of. . . . Paul banged this possibility around in his head as they sat and talked it through on that day.

Paul was willing to help—and to stick around.

Sheila told Paul that Amir was the first man she had ever slept with. She was "repressed sexually," Paul said, and really "didn't have much experience." So the idea that she was stuck in this marriage with a man she didn't love—a man who was never around, according to her—was not so far-fetched.

Plus, Paul was in love. Love can do many things to the mind, especially when a young man is wrapped up in his work and his studies and his life seems to be going on a fast track toward a white-picket-fence future in suburban New York, maybe a few kids, and that climb up the vocational ladder.

"My family is opposed to a divorce," Sheila said, adding that it was going to be difficult for her to do, but she wanted and needed to do it. She could not stay locked up in a lifeless marriage. She'd been a prisoner for far too long already. Paul had helped her break out of her shell after they started officially dating. She had reason and purpose again.

"It seemed to bother her," Paul said later, "that she had gotten locked in this marriage with an older guy and had never been able to live the life of an American twenty-year-old . . . New Yorker."

As they sat together and talked it through after the Amir incident, Paul could see that Sheila was distraught, unhappy, and depressed about her situation. He sensed that she was sincere about wanting out of it as fast as she could.

So he decided to stand behind her. Support her through the divorce. And be there for her on the back end of it all.

"You decide what you want to do," Paul said as they prepared to leave.

"I want to divorce him."

CHAPTER 23

WHILE SHEILA DAVALLOO was in the midst of her "therapy" sessions with Fran Lourie during the fall of 2002, looking back on the relationship with Nelson Sessler, which she had supposedly let go of, Sheila was secretly coming undone. She was a mess. She later claimed to have been suffering from a severe addiction to pills, Vicodin and Valium, two "wonder" drugs that allowed her to function in a world that was imploding around her. And the cause of that addiction, which she kept hidden from her therapist, was Nelson Sessler and her desire to be with him. But those in her life at the time said Sheila did not come across as someone heavily involved with pills. And if she was abusing drugs as much as she later claimed, she did a damn good job of hiding it. As it turned out, this drug addiction—same as most of Sheila Davalloo's life—was one more lie in what was becoming a mounting list.

When asked later on about this time in her life, Sheila said she had not recalled ever being "obsessed" with Nelson Sessler—and that presumed obsession with Nelson was not why she found herself so depressed, withdrawn from life, and leaning on pills. It was something else, she said, not what people thought.

"I know maybe it was a *sexual* obsession," Sheila explained. But that was it. Her preoccupation was with the sex she'd had with Nelson—not with the man or with the relationship. Yet, on several occasions, Sheila used the word "obsessed" when talking about Nelson to two different therapists, never once claiming that the obsession was purely sexual.

"Pure 'obsession' would be inaccurate," she explained, trying to talk her way out of it. "I would not use the word because I don't think I'm obsessed. I never thought I was obsessed with him. In fact, I would get tired of Nelson very easily after a day with him. He's very unorganized. Very all over the place. I would get very tired of him *very* quickly."

Sheila claimed she only thought about Nelson "a lot" because she "worked with him very closely." She was forced to communicate and encounter him at Pharma.

When she later wrote to Nelson, however, Sheila expressed a theory about their relationship, explaining how it was something more than Nelson had realized. Even months after they broke up, Sheila was still consumed with Nelson and how he felt and thought about her. This was an issue that was becoming increasingly important to her: how Nelson viewed Sheila. It was one of the reasons why, after Anna Lisa was murdered, Sheila saw that tragedy as an opportunity to wiggle her way back into Nelson's life.

I've been worried sick about you, she wrote to Nelson. She then explained how she kept "going over" everything in her mind trying to "envision" what Nelson thought of her, not to mention all that he must have been going through. She was worried and focused on what he believed, even so many months after they had severed romantic contact. Sheila couldn't have Nelson think she was a bad person. This bothered her. So she relayed an anecdote to show, by example, how much of a moral human being she was. In this letter, Sheila brought up a day when she and Nelson went snowboarding with a group of people, some of whom were Nelson's family. There were photos depicting a happy couple on this day—two adults having a fun time out on the slopes together, enjoying each other's company amid friends and family.

As they walked the slopes, Sheila initiated a conversation with someone in the group and asked him "a concerned question" about the war. She was referring to the turmoil in Iraq and the despondency of Middle Eastern people, mostly the women and children, innocent victims, being killed every day. Sheila liked to play up the fact that she was Middle Eastern, when it seemed to suit her in a conversation or situation. Conversely, she had abandoned her heritage many times, denying that she was, in fact, Middle Eastern. When it served her needs, she used her race to get what she could out of those around her.

According to what Sheila later wrote to Nelson, as she and someone from the group walked the slopes, that person responded to her statement about the war and the natives dying by saying: *"Let them be killed. . . . There are too many people anyway."*

She described this conversation to Nelson because she knew it would sting him—that is, if he believed her. By then, it's safe to say Nelson didn't believe much of what Sheila Davalloo had to say, or particularly care about her thoughts. Nelson was in it for the good time. Problem was, Sheila just didn't get it.

That night, after her little chat on the slopes, Sheila told Nelson she went home and wept. There was a dark, heavy sadness enveloping her. She couldn't believe how callous people were, how uncaring and evil to say and suggest such a diabolical thing as ridding the world of people because there were "too many."

I remember bursting into tears . . . , she wrote Nelson. And then, perhaps reminding him, she explained how he had asked her on that same night, *"What's wrong?"*

Sheila told Nelson about the comment earlier that day and claimed to have thought about it all day long. It weighed on her emotions, she said. She couldn't get her mind off it, and it had basically ruined her day.

On that night, Nelson believed that it bothered her so deeply because she was from Iraq—a mistake, since her family hailed from Iran—and that maybe she was "sympathetic" because of being from the Middle East.

Years later, Sheila told Nelson how, "in reality," not only was she upset over the comment, but she wrote, *I can't stand the thought of anyone dead or even hurt. . . .* Then, in the same letter, she went on to make a point about something that would one day become utterly imperative to the investigation into Anna Lisa's murder—and a dangerous game Sheila was about to embroil Paul Christos in—writing, *You should know that I am afraid of blood.*

It was the fear of blood, she added in the same letter, that had steered her away from medical school. Quite an odd statement to include in the context of what she was writing to Nelson about—but then, as time went on, those who read the letter would understand this to be the core of who Sheila Davalloo truly was: a killer who believed she could talk her way out of whatever she wanted with a simple explanation.

CHAPTER 24

PAUL CHRISTOS DECIDED that staying with Sheila and continuing to love her was the right thing to do—a decision that might just cost him his life.

With her honed manipulation skills, Sheila convinced Paul she had been in a loveless marriage she believed she could not get out of. However, Paul and the love they shared between them was enough for her now to gain the courage to face Amir and demand a divorce.

True to her word, in early 1996, Sheila Davalloo moved her belongings out of the Manhattan apartment she shared with Amir and into a small apartment in the basement of a home in Valhalla, New York.

Amir was "pretty amenable," Paul explained later. "He actually helped her move."

Sheila was now close to Paul and school and her parents. She could begin the process of planning a future with Paul. She could start a new life.

Things appeared to be back on track.

None of that—the blue skies over the horizon, the thought of not having to be there every night for Amir, or finally having Paul just a phone call away—made Sheila feel any better. She was still "very depressed about the divorce," Paul later recalled, looking back. Especially the idea of what it would do to the relationship she had—as tenuous as it was already—with her parents.

"I have destroyed Amir's life," Sheila said to Paul in a fit of tears one night, curling up into a fetal ball. "He could never remarry and never have children now."

Oh, the power Sheila Davalloo saw herself as having. It would come out later, of course, but Sheila was exhibiting the behavior—in plain sight—of the total narcissist she was. It was never about anyone else but Sheila Davalloo. Life always revolved around the way she felt, what people thought of her, what people were doing to her and for her, and how she was perceived in the world. Sheila was crying, telling Paul she held the power of Amir's happiness in her hands, and it was tearing her apart to use that power to sting the poor man. He didn't deserve it. He was a nice guy—just not the man she wanted to be with.

"I have to divorce him, though," Sheila insisted.

And so she did—at least that's what she told Paul.

But, in actuality, Amir was the one to file for divorce and sue Sheila. In fact, Paul would find out later, Sheila never even showed up in court to finalize everything.

Regardless of who filed for divorce, as the fall of 1996 began, Sheila was a free woman. Now she could marry any man she pleased.

Paul and Sheila fell into a routine as 1997 came to pass. She lived in her basement apartment and now they had a space to hang out. Sheila was divorced. Their relationship was moving along, however strangely it had started. They'd get together with mutual friends at Sheila's and have dinner. They'd go out and do all the things couples do.

For Paul, although Sheila was torn up about the divorce,

this was a time when he actually felt like they were officially dating and the relationship was moving somewhere.

No more secrets . . . that Paul knew of, anyway.

"There was a time there, after her divorce, where she was really depressed," Paul recalled. "Visibly depressed."

Seriously concerned, Paul would ask, "What's wrong?" Sheila would sometimes stay in bed all day. She would not want to talk or eat.

"I've destroyed his life," she responded. Sheila couldn't get over how she'd ruined Amir's life by divorcing him. "He's very depressed. He's on medication. . . ."

Paul interpreted Sheila's behavior as a stage she had to go through in order to get over this particular chapter in her life. It would all pass one day. All Paul had to do was be patient and support her through it.

"She wanted to end the marriage, but it clearly upset her to do so," Paul said. "It seemed like genuine guilt over ruining somebody's life. She didn't want to stay with him, but she was feeling it."

That severe depression lasted several months, and then, just as Paul had anticipated, "she came out of it."

Their relationship took a normal track, according to Paul. He even met Sheila's parents. And they started to warm up to him, if ever so slightly and slowly. They spent Christmas, 1997, half at Sheila's parents' home and half at his. Whatever the standard trajectory of a relationship was, Paul and Sheila seemed to have found that groove.

Sheila graduated with her degree in 1998. By this time, Paul's parents and Sheila's parents were hooking up and having dinners together. By now, Sheila and Paul were talking engagement.

The two sets of parents "were both supportive of our plans," Paul recalled.

Paul never saw Sheila lean on drugs or alcohol to cope

with her problems. Even those anxiety medications she later said she became addicted to were not anywhere to be found in their relationship.

"Things were fairly normal," Paul recalled.

Sheila was into the sitcom *Friends,* and she liked to make a special night out of watching the show. She related to every-day problems and situations the group on the series dealt with. It was fantasy, sure, but the show gave Sheila that way out of her own world, if only for half an hour per week. She read ro-mance novels, of course. She liked to cook. She worked on her poetry and would often, contrary to what she later told Fran Lourie, show Paul her poems and ask his opinion. Paul wasn't a poetry scholar, by any means, but he thought she was pretty good with words and encouraged her to continue.

At night, before bed, Sheila liked to read dieting books and focused her extracurricular study mainly on health and body and how to stay trim and fit. She also studied flowers, painted, and drew pictures.

Sheila found a job in White Plains that she adored. She threw herself into it.

"She was determined," Paul said of Sheila and the jobs she had. "She liked to move up. She never liked to stay in one division at work. And she was kind of looking to get into the research side of things. Work was important to her."

The one thing Sheila did do as she became absorbed in the office environment was get involved with coworkers and their drama. She'd always come home with a story about this one or that one and how he or she was getting in the way of a promotion. She thrived on the competition and the cutthroat stories of corporate vixens and villains vying for the same jobs. It was as if this fed a part of Sheila's ego—providing nourishment it wasn't getting from anywhere else. What stim-ulation one person might get from movies or television shows, Sheila seemed to obtain from the stories she heard around the office.

And then Sheila came home one day and told Paul she decided to go on a trip with a coworker to France. "A bike tour" of the countryside, Sheila called it.

It seemed exciting and adventurous. It would do her some good, Paul figured.

"Great," Paul encouraged. He didn't see an issue. They were set to get married by 2000. They had been engaged for some time now. This would be a good way for Sheila to take a trip with a friend and get away for a while. She'd been through a lot. She could clear her head—and what better place to do it than the countryside of France.

A strange thing about Sheila during this time was how her brother, who had been diagnosed with schizophrenia, had never been told Sheila and Amir had divorced, nor that Sheila had been engaged to or even had started dating Paul. But one had to wonder if Sheila, too, had been touched mentally. Paul didn't know it until years later, but there was one incident involving Sheila and Amir that might have been a deal breaker for Paul, if he had known about it before they got married.

Amir had been in bed one morning inside one of their homes. He awoke to the smell of gas. Natural gas. It was like the kind used for cooking.

Jumping up from bed, Amir quickly put on a bathrobe and ran from the bedroom into the kitchen, quite alarmed by the depth and heaviness of the aroma.

He could hear the hiss of the gas burners—all of which had been turned on.

As he realized this, Amir bolted over to the door; and just then, he saw that Sheila was simply walking out. Later, Sheila admitted that she'd turned on the gas. She never said she was trying to kill Amir. It was a situation built around the idea that she had developed of "feeling trapped" in the marriage. Sheila had decided she wanted a life without Amir and thought she was "losing her mind." She played off this attempt on Amir's life as suffering from depression, not knowing what she was doing. She said she'd always had issues with harming the men in her life. She even went so far as to say she had a "problematic mental pattern . . . with men."

Heading into his marriage with Sheila, Paul Christos didn't know any of this. But, boy, he was about to find out firsthand—in a strangely violent, brutal, and bloody way— just how far Sheila Davalloo would go to get rid of the men in her life she didn't need any longer.

CHAPTER 25

SHEILA CAME HOME from France after that bike tour trip of the countryside with her coworker and Paul realized a change immediately. Something was wrong. Sheila seemed closed. Lost. Not really willing to share things, like she had done before the trip. On top of that, Paul felt Sheila's thoughts were preoccupied with things that did not involve him.

"She wasn't really happy to come home . . . ," Paul recalled. "She had been gone maybe a week, ten days. . . ."

Yet, within that time, Sheila had almost become a different person. It was instant. Sheila began having concerns about the marriage and Paul and continuing the relationship.

Second thoughts.

The truth was—although Paul would not find out until years later—that Sheila had met someone in France. A man. While on the bike trip, she had slept with him, Paul was told, and she had fallen for the guy.

"I was told later that Sheila had confided in a friend that she'd met a man in France, was attracted to him, and didn't know what to do with me. And her friend told her, 'What are you doing? You're home. You're getting married.' And then, I guess, it all kind of passed."

This was only one sign of Sheila's instability and emotional fragility, which Paul was a witness to during this period leading up to their wedding. There were plenty of other incidents that Paul could have viewed as red flags, if he had a magic looking glass or a crystal ball. For instance, when Sheila found out Paul had told his parents that she had been married to Amir while she and Paul were dating, Sheila flipped out.

"You betrayed me!" she screamed. "I cannot believe you *did* this." Then she became "hysterical," crying and yelling incoherently, finally locking herself in the bathroom, weeping uncontrollably.

An angry, manic high, then a deep low.

Paul found out soon enough that the fit was over the fact that Sheila felt ashamed and humiliated by the idea of "people knowing she was married and living separate from her husband." There had been "lots of pressure from her parents" to make that marriage work.

Sheila had a similar crying and screaming (manic) spell when she realized Paul had told his brother and sister-in-law that Sheila had been married before.

"How can you betray me like this, Paul?"

Then Paul went and told his parents Sheila had a mentally ill brother. Sheila went berserk, kicking and screaming and locking herself in the bathroom again, raging how she felt once again embarrassed and humiliated to the core—and it was all Paul's fault.

"There was a high level of secrecy in her life," Paul remembered, "about her parents, her Iranian background, and her brother."

The brother was a "family secret that was rarely discussed, and no one," Paul added, "outside her family, had ever met him. There was a lot of guilt and pain whenever she would discuss her brother's mental illness with me. When I would probe too deeply, she'd have fits of anger and crying."

In retrospect, this was all a small display of the true rage and violent nature Sheila Davalloo could dredge up at a moment's notice.

Not long after she came back from France and experienced that sudden moment of doubt, stemming from the overseas affair, Sheila refocused her attention on Paul and their upcoming nuptials. As January 2000 came, planning the wedding was Sheila's main course now. She didn't want a big wedding (same as with Amir). She wanted something small, intimate, not a lot of fanfare. The engagement had lasted a total of eighteen months. Paul and Sheila had known each other since 1994 and had dated for many of those years. All she wanted was for the wedding to be quick—get it over with and begin life together.

"Friends were saying before it happened, 'When are you two going to get engaged?'" Paul said. It would come up often as the years passed. Paul lived with his parents then, but he spent his weekends in Valhalla with Sheila.

They wound up having about "sixty to seventy" people at the May 28, 2000, wedding, Paul recalled. It was mostly friends and members of Paul's family. Sheila's family, although they didn't stage a large presence at the ceremony or reception, had actually kicked in and helped pay for it.

"Sheila's family had maybe one table. Sheila had just started working for Purdue Pharma, in Norwalk, Connecticut—and she had a table of friends from work at the wedding."

For whatever reason, Sheila Davalloo decided to keep her surname.

Before the wedding, Sheila had purchased a condo in Pleasantville, New York, which became their new home. Pleasantville is one of those Westchester County boroughs off the Saw Mill River Parkway, about thirty miles north of

Manhattan. As the name of the town suggests, Pleasantville appeals to the hardworking, highly educated, and on a fast track to be wealthy "New Yawker" looking for a suburban haven away from the city—but a locale that is still close enough to be able to jaunt downtown in a beat. John Cheeveresque all the way—that is Pleasantville. Pleasantville's website boasts a bucolic image, noting that the town is *synonymous with extraordinary neighborliness, volunteerism, tranquility and tolerance. . . .*

For people like Paul and Sheila, each climbing his and her way up the ladder at their respected jobs, both heading toward those big, six-figure-income numbers that suburbanites chase, Pleasantville was Emerald City. With about seven thousand residents, the town was small enough to feel tucked away in the country, and yet large enough where a resident didn't have to travel far to go shopping. There are rolling hills of green acreage, swanky parks, plenty of striking waterways, BMWs, Mercedes, Porsches, fine schools, and, to boot, the corporate home of *Reader's Digest*—a town seemingly ripped from the pages of a yuppie fairy tale.

That September, after settling quite amiably into their new town and home, Paul started a doctoral degree program in epidemiology at Columbia University on West 168th Street. Sheila allowed herself to fall into her work at Purdue and was soon transferred to the Stamford, Connecticut, building for a raise and promotion.

The life they had chased—and possibly dreamt of—was now coming to fruition. However, Paul and Sheila began to realize, as they became more successful in their careers, they had less time to spend together. Paul not only worked in the city, but he also taught classes at NYMC two nights a week as a second job.

Sheila would come home from work at night, curl up with a book or go online, and then fall asleep near eight-thirty or nine o'clock. By the time Paul wandered in, his wife was already sound asleep.

"We would have weekends together," Paul later recalled, "but Sheila had developed outside interests and [new] friends."

She joined a volleyball league and started to hang out with her new coworkers. Paul could not relate with any of it and was extremely busy with work and study. He might see one of her new friends at a restaurant or over at the house for a quick dinner; but other than that, he had minimal contact with Sheila's new life outside the home.

"We seemed to be living separate lives as my school commitments increased, but we were still close and reasonably happy together."

Or, rather, that was how Paul viewed the situation.

Sheila, on the other hand, was getting bored. And boredom in a relationship for Sheila Davalloo was never a good thing. It never led to anything productive. Sheila Davalloo had already proven what she liked to do when she got bored within a marriage and felt trapped. And with Paul, of course, that former behavior would not change. Sheila was out and about, surrounded by new people in Stamford, and now she had her eye on someone at her new workplace.

Nelson Sessler.

CHAPTER 26

ANYTIME PAUL MENTIONED Sheila's brother, she went off. This brother of hers became a sore spot in the marriage. She'd cry and be consumed with guilt for not being able to "do more" for "the brother," Paul recalled. Even during their wedding, the brother was mentioned (and protected) in a subtly strange way. Sheila had insisted that a prayer be said during the church service especially for her brother, who was supposedly suffering from a nasty bout of the stomach flu (the public story during the wedding). And as the marriage sluggishly marched forward, 2000 into 2001, Sheila and Paul were spending less time together, drifting apart. Sheila's brother eventually became the focal point upon which Sheila could pivot a plot—a storyline she had been dreaming up and carefully planning.

"Tell me about him," Paul would encourage Sheila. He wanted to help. He wanted to be there for his brother-in-law (who did not even know Paul existed). Paul wanted to assist Sheila any way he could and see if there was something he could do.

"She'd lose it and cry, and it was *clear* that there was a lot of *guilt* wrapped up with the brother somehow."

From what Paul gleaned, the brother had been doing okay

through high school; but after entering college, he had a major mental breakdown of some sort while Sheila was overseas.

Most people would not want to hide their mentally ill brother, Paul considered as time passed. Sure, there was a tarnishing blemish placed on the mentally ill, and society would rather not want to hear about it. However, family members wouldn't lock themselves in the bathroom and have a fit because a concerned spouse mentioned the brother and offered to help. It just didn't seem to Paul like it was an appropriate response to her brother's illness. There was something more to all of it.

"She was ashamed of her Iranian background, telling people she was French and Italian—it wasn't until years and years after we started dating that I figured out she was Iranian. She was ashamed of her brother. . . ."

There was another part of Sheila that became obvious as she and Paul continued to entertain guests, friends, and family at the condo. As Sheila would prepare the meal before guests arrived, she would get highly stressed while cooking. Nothing seemed to go right, and she'd react emotionally whenever this occurred. If Paul went out for her to grab a last-minute item at the supermarket and, God forbid, he came back with the wrong brand or item, watch out!

"What the hell have you done? It's wrong!"

She'd scream and yell and lock herself in the bathroom—only to come out after a few minutes, tail between her legs, staring at the carpet, apologizing.

"I'm so sorry, Paul. I didn't mean it."

Paul said Sheila suffered from hyperhidrosis (there was also a friend and a report corroborating this), a condition where a person sweats excessively and profusely at unpredictable times. Some sufferers of the condition might sweat in the mountains of Alaska in January. The temperature has nothing to do with it. The regulation of body temperature is somehow off.

Humid weather, Paul said, had a tendency to worsen her symptoms. Sheila would become very depressed and withdrawn.

"The condition would cause her to get upset a lot . . . and make her tired early in a workday and weaken her concentration." Especially severe for Sheila was "hand and foot sweating." She finally had an operation to correct it, but it didn't fix it entirely. What the surgery did do, according to Sheila, was make her cold more quickly and easily. Sheila, however, accepted this as a side effect she could live with, because overall the operation reduced her stress level.

"I never feel quite right," she'd tell Paul on certain days.

Paul wrote off most of how she was feeling as a side effect from the surgery, or an ill effect of the condition.

By November 2001, Sheila was more withdrawn from the marriage, as was Paul, he later admitted. They just didn't seem to have the time for each other; and when they did, there was coldness, a wall of some sort there between them, as if they didn't really know each other anymore.

"I want my brother to come over and visit," Sheila said one night.

Paul considered this to be a move in the right direction. Maybe she was opening up? Perhaps she was allowing him access into a part of her life she had not let anyone else into.

"Okay," Paul responded.

"But . . . he doesn't know we're married, you know that," Sheila said.

"And . . ."

Paul assumed Sheila was going to tell the brother and then the three of them could begin a relationship.

Sheila had another plan, though. Something, well, a bit more extreme.

CHAPTER 27

SHEILA'S PLAN WAS for Paul to leave on certain evenings and some weekends so she could pick up her brother and bring him over to the condo for a visit, or to spend the night. They discussed Paul sleeping at his parents' house and/or getting a hotel room. Sheila explained that they'd have to take all of the wedding photos and anything having to do with her and Paul's relationship and put it away before she took off and picked up her brother. That meant clearing the bathroom of Paul's toothbrush, shaving supplies, bodywash, antiperspirant, or anything else having to do with a man being around the house. The slightest thing could set the brother off, Paul was told. There'd be no reference to Paul in the condo. Sheila and Paul would strip it clean of Paul's memory or presence.

No "his" towels.

No books.

No smells.

Nothing.

It seemed pretty risky, not to mention punishing. Paul was made to feel like he didn't exist. He didn't matter. But then, what if Sheila got caught? How would she explain the big lie to her brother? Wouldn't it all backfire if he came over and found out she was married and nobody had told him?

Sheila didn't seem to think so.

Paul considered the idea.

"It'd be like once a month," Sheila explained, as if it was no biggie. "Then, depending on how it goes, maybe *twice* a month. He'd sleep over sometimes. And just visit for the day at others."

Paul rubbed his chin.

I'd have to stay at a hotel, Paul thought, explaining why later: "Because I didn't want my parents to know the specific frequency of me leaving the condo, and I was embarrassed about this."

Everyone has secrets.

Paul stayed at a local Marriott. It was annoying, sure. Having to leave his own home for the weekend and being told by his wife not to call or stop by unexpectedly. But as he continued to think about the situation, Paul considered that, in the larger scope of the marriage and his love for Sheila, he might be "helping Sheila spend some quality time with her sick brother." It was a *good* thing. And what the heck, someday soon, perhaps she'd come around and agree to introduce Paul to her brother.

"Please, Sheila, tell him about us . . . please . . . ," Paul would say as he packed for the weekend. He'd have to bring his printer, computer, clothes, everything he needed to function for a few days. He couldn't come back because he'd forgotten something. That wouldn't work.

"Okay," Sheila said. "When the time is right, I will. Paul, I promise."

Paul was actually working on his doctorate, so the time alone, inside a hotel room, became an unexpected gift to his studies. He found the silence and solitude ideal for working on his research and writing papers.

Still, the guy had a wife and a fairly nice condo in Emerald City that he had to turn around and walk away from once or twice (for now) a month. It must have been humbling and sobering, if not humiliating, for Paul to suck it up, essentially, and allow Sheila this major opportunity within the marriage.

But he did it.

The weeks and months passed as Paul and Sheila fell into a pattern of spending some weekends or weeknights apart, this as Sheila's brother apparently stayed at the condo. There were moments when Paul would question this. He'd come home to two empty wineglasses in the sink or a pair of men's trousers (he didn't recognize), much smaller in size than Sheila had explained her brother to be, left in the laundry room.

So Paul would ask Sheila about the wineglasses and pants.

"And she always had a quick answer, a quick comeback that I believed."

Paul would also find a way to explain it to himself.

"Maybe part of me wanted to find out about an affair so we could part ways," Paul later deduced.

With the hope of catching a glimpse of the brother (or, if she was cheating, Sheila's lover), Paul even left the condo one weekend and came back and parked down the block. Nothing ever came of it, however. Paul waited and didn't see anything, so he left and went back to his hotel room.

Maybe it's all in my mind. . . .

Still, if Paul had uncovered what Sheila was up to, he would have seen that this was one more manipulative pattern of Sheila Davalloo's—besides, that is, the fact that she was lying to Paul about her brother coming over. The other major lie in their lives around this period was a refinance deal on the condo Sheila had facilitated. Refinancing the condo would not have been such a bad thing for a wife to do for herself and her husband. What couple wouldn't like some extra money and a lower mortgage payment? But Sheila had secretly amassed—Paul found out later—a fortune in credit card debt.

How much? A whopping mound of paper debt to the tune of between $40,000 and $50,000, Paul thought. (It was actually more.) And when she did the refinance, Sheila packaged a major portion of that debt (but not all of it) into the new deal as a partial, quick payoff. Paul didn't pay much attention to the paperwork as he signed, and he didn't know what she was doing. He expected his wife to be up front and honest with him. If she was going to do something so drastic, so big, so long-lasting to their financial future, he expected she'd tell him beforehand.

What in the world was Sheila Davalloo buying that had amounted to such a substantial amount of money?

"You know, she bought a lot of clothes," Paul said, having a bit of trouble explaining where all the money went. "Her bills were really separate, so I really didn't know. A lot of the debt was incurred before we were married, and I didn't really read the mortgage refinance paperwork to realize what she was doing. . . . She bought a lot of expensive gifts for people and bought a lot of things for the condo."

Part of Paul's not paying much attention to the refinance centered on the fact that the condo had originally been purchased by Sheila's parents for her shortly before she and Paul were married. When they sat down to refinance on that day, Paul's name was actually placed on the deed—Sheila and her parents (a gesture Paul thought was generous and kind) were essentially giving him half of the property. Yet the mortgage had gone up close to $50,000—money Sheila had burned through as if she didn't have to pay it back. And Paul never suspected a thing.

CHAPTER 28

"THIS IS BULLSHIT, Paul," Sheila yelled one day. "You're never home."

They fought. Paul pleaded with his wife, noting how he was studying for his doctorate and working and teaching. If she could just hang on, life would calm down some after he got the degree.

Sheila would generally cave and say sorry for exploding. She was confused as to why she had such a short fuse. She claimed she wanted Paul to be there more.

Then, right after they began that whole deal of the brother coming over and Paul leaving for the weekend, Sheila brought up a situation that was going on at her Purdue Pharma office in Stamford. It was a topic, Paul soon realized, Sheila would relentlessly talk about to him and just about all of their close friends—a situation Sheila could not let go of, no matter how hard she tried. It was one that she would become more consumed with as time went on.

"There's this love triangle going on at work," Sheila told Paul one night. They were eating dinner. "The woman's name is Melissa, a friend of mine. She's having an affair with this guy, Jack Edward Evans, who is in a relationship with this other woman, Anna Lisa."

Anna.

Paul seemed interested at first. They were talking. Sheila was sharing part of her life with him. She seemed to be focused on Paul's opinion of the situation, what he thought, but more in the line of what he thought *as a man*. It became so important to Sheila—to the point of her being fixated on Paul's opinions, pushing him to answer her questions—that she acquire the right advice to give to Melissa back at work.

"Melissa knows that Jack is involved with Anna Lisa," Sheila said. "What should Melissa do, Paul?"

"I don't really know." Paul thought that perhaps Sheila would talk about this for a week or two and then drop it. He assumed that it would become something for her to do—something to keep her busy and then forget.

But she didn't. Instead, Sheila talked about this love triangle every day she was with Paul during this period. She'd describe the hot and steamy sex Melissa and Jack were having, how they'd meet up and sleep together. Melissa, Sheila said, was obsessed with Jack. She couldn't get enough of him. But Melissa was also very upset that Jack was still seeing Anna Lisa (who, in the love triangle story, was never given a last name).

"Why would Jack see two women?" Sheila would ask Paul, sometimes two or three times a week. "What is he *getting* out of it?" Sheila figured with Paul being a man, he'd have some insight.

"I don't know, Sheila. I have no idea."

By this time, near the beginning of 2002, Sheila and Paul were talking about this love triangle—Sheila bringing it up constantly—all the time. It was a continuous topic of their conversations.

"Why does Jack like one more than the other?" Sheila would ask.

"Why do you even care, Sheila?"

Sheila wouldn't answer. She'd play with the peas on her plate and fidget with her hair. Maybe take a sip of water. Then right back at it.

"They have sex all the time," Sheila would respond.

"Why is it that Melissa tells you *so* much about her sex life?" Paul asked one night. "Yet you, as you told me, tell her *nothing* about yours? Why are you so wrapped up in this love triangle, Sheila?"

"Oh, Paul. I've known you now for so long. What, ten years? We're boring people."

Their sex life then, Paul admitted, was "nonexistent."

Sheila was carrying on and on about this love triangle at her work. She'd tell anyone with ears about it. Friends were sick of it. Paul was tired of it. The guy at the local donut shop was probably sick of hearing about it, too.

One night, Sheila was talking to the husband of a good friend from work on the telephone. She started in about the affair, quite desperate for a man's point of view. She was now completely focused on what Jack was thinking about Melissa in relation to Anna. What was driving Jack to make the decisions he made? Sheila was consumed with this question of getting inside Jack's head.

"There's this woman named Melissa at work," Sheila explained. "She's having an affair with a man at work. He is seeing someone else—he has a girlfriend. But Melissa is in *love* with him. She knows he has someone else. What can Melissa do? Should she continue seeing the man and confront him about leaving the other woman? Damn, I don't know what to tell Melissa. Help me out here."

"Easy," her friend's husband said. "Tell Melissa to confront the man and make him stop seeing the other woman."

"What if he doesn't want to?"

"Melissa should not see him anymore, then."

As the love triangle became a more obsessive aspect of her daily life, Sheila developed and displayed a public hatred for Paul at times. They'd be out with friends dining or having a dinner party at their condo, and after Paul said something, Sheila would blurt out, "You're stupid! You know that, Paul. *Stupid.*"

Paul would give her a "nervous smile," one friend, who witnessed these humiliating, belittling outbursts from Sheila, recalled.

Part of those ill feelings Sheila harbored for Paul were no doubt based on the notion that as she and Paul went out with friends and had dinner parties at the condo, Sheila was laughing on the inside. Here she was pulling one over on Paul, and he had no clue what was going on. For one, her brother had never come over to the condo to sleep or visit. That was a ruse—an elaborate plan—Sheila had cooked up so she could have sex with her lover in the same bed she shared with Paul. Number two, that soap opera happening at work, involving Jack and Melissa and Anna Lisa, was actually a diagram of Sheila's love triangle: She was Melissa, of course; Jack was Nelson Sessler; Anna Lisa was, well, Anna Lisa Raymundo. Sheila was wrapped up in this game of obsession with Nelson, and Paul had no inkling. This was one of the reasons why Sheila considered Paul to be so "stupid" and naïve. Paul had been one of the top students in his class. He was studying for his doctorate. He was on track to land a very high-paying job in the world of cancer research. Yet, not only was his marriage crumbling around him, but his wife was cheating on him inside his own home, right under his nose while he went off to a hotel room for the weekend—weekends that were becoming more frequent as the spring thaw of 2002 melted away another Northeast winter. On top of all that, Sheila was asking Paul questions at dinner about the affair *she* was having and, in turn, getting advice from her own husband to use in that affair.

Absolutely mind-boggling.

Everything in Sheila's life was an invention at this point—carefully focused on Nelson Sessler and his relationship with Anna Lisa Raymundo. Sheila was lying to Paul, Nelson, and her coworkers about every aspect of her life. Those days when Paul found Sheila exhausted, in bed, sleeping for twelve hours, taking three-hour naps, wasn't because she had been depressed or had been experiencing difficulties from her sweating condition. Sheila was spent from running around with Nelson, taking weekend trips, going skiing, traveling to Boston, and having sex like a hormonal teenager—and still having to maintain the semblance of a marriage to Paul. She was constantly on her toes, having to cover one life up from the other. Nelson never knew about Paul. He'd be over and notice something in the condo that might indicate a man lived there and ask a question about it. Sheila would write it off with yet another lie.

"I'm divorced," she'd tell Nelson as they sipped wine and ate dinners and had sex in different positions all over Paul's house.

There was one day when Sheila called an old friend from a company she had once worked at in White Plains. The man later said he'd never had sex with Sheila, but they were close friends and stayed in touch even after Sheila got married and left the White Plains office for Purdue Pharma.

"Come out to Stamford with me," Sheila said. She wanted her friend to go rock climbing with her at an indoor facility.

"Yeah . . . yeah, sure."

The man later described Sheila as "a nice, average person who did her job and was liked by everyone. She was strong . . . tall and active. She played volleyball . . . and did a lot of swimming at the Y in White Plains." He was referring to the same period when Sheila was, at home, playing the role of the martyr, depressed, walking around with her head held low, sleeping all the time, not talking with or paying attention to Paul.

As they scaled the fake wall, Sheila started in about Melissa, Jack, and Anna Lisa. "Melissa calls me and cries and cries about Jack," Sheila told her friend as they prepared to climb.

Her friend rolled his eyes.

From there, Sheila carried "on and on" about the love triangle to the point where her friend became so bored and so uninterested in the saga that was Melissa's life, he tuned Sheila out and wondered why she was caught up so intimately in someone else's affairs. In fact, later, when he thought about it, the friend said that whenever they got together, the love triangle was all Sheila ever talked about. She wanted a male's perspective, some advice for Melissa regarding what she should do.

As the summer of 2002 approached, the two worlds of Melissa and Sheila, however, were becoming increasingly harder to deal with and conceal. Sheila needed Jack/Nelson to make a decision: Was it going to be her or Anna Lisa? There was an important component that Sheila didn't realize: Despite the ski trips, the weekends down to North Carolina, dinners, movies, sex in Boston and inside the condo, all those crazy photo-booth pictures of her and Nelson sitting and making zany faces, and then waiting for the long scroll print-out from the machine, walking hand in hand, with her head on his shoulder, as they pretended to be a couple at the mall, Nelson Sessler was simply *using* Sheila Davalloo. For Nelson, there never was much of a decision to make. He loved Anna Lisa; he lusted for Sheila. Nelson was planning on marrying Anna Lisa (so he later claimed). Sheila would never win that fight for Nelson's heart (and there's research available verifying that Sheila knew this and yet carried on, anyway, hoping she could win Nelson over at any cost).

That, my friends, is the description of a desperate woman who will go to any length to get her man—even murder.

CHAPTER 29

AS PAUL AND SHEILA were at home inside their Pleasantville condo one night, Sheila asked Paul to help her out with something. She explained how Melissa had gotten hold of "Jack's password for his voice mail." And, as the story went, Melissa had allowed Sheila to "listen to some of his calls."

Paul was stunned.

But also intrigued.

Sheila said Melissa would "track Jack's phone messages *daily*." Thus, every single day at work, at some point, Sheila would tap into Nelson's voice mail and check to see if Anna Lisa had called and what she had said.

What a disturbing breach of privacy.

Shaking his head in disbelief, perhaps looking up in the air (here we go again!), Paul found this a bit intrusive and exploitative, if not criminal. How far was Sheila going to become involved in this love triangle? Melissa was acting bizarrely. Now she was listening to people's voice mail messages?

What's next? Paul thought.

But then, as he considered it further, Paul decided to humor his wife.

"Okay, yeah. What would you like to know?"

"Melissa forwarded me a message from Jack's voice mail. I want you to listen to it and tell me what you think."

Sheila was determined to tap into what Nelson was thinking and what another male thought of the relationship between Nelson and Anna Lisa—all based on the tone and demeanor of this one message. Sheila wanted Paul to consider how Anna Lisa *sounded* on the voice mail: Was she in love? Was Jack in love with her? Were they an item? On the outs? It seemed preposterous to think that Paul could determine those intimate, personal details from a voice mail, but this was where Sheila had taken her little love triangle. She was truly grasping for any little bit of hope to hang on to in her lust and obsessive quest for Nelson Sessler. Sheila was desperate—a word that doesn't even begin to explain how manic and obsessed with Nelson she had become by this point—to hear from a man's point of view that Nelson didn't care about Anna Lisa, or that Anna Lisa didn't care about Nelson. The fantasy for Sheila was that Nelson would leave Anna Lisa and run into her arms. She held onto *any* bit of optimism. Any subtle look Nelson might have given her when they were together or in the office. Any word he said that might indicate he cared for her more than as a fling.

Anything.

Paul put his ear to the telephone. "Go ahead," he said. "Play it."

Sheila tapped into Nelson's voice mail and played the message: "'Hey, honey, it's Anna Lisa . . . was wondering when you're coming over. Buh-bye.'"

That was it.

"What do you want to know?" Paul asked, hanging up the phone.

"Her voice. What do you think of her *voice*?" Sheila was

frustrated, impatient. There had to be some clue, some indication in her voice as to how the relationship between them was going.

What a strange question. Paul considered by now that Sheila was living vicariously through Melissa, which was one of the reasons why she had become so obsessed with the love triangle.

"Why do you care so much about this love triangle, Sheila? Why does Melissa even *stay* with this guy?"

It all seemed so ridiculous to Paul. It had to be true.

"She stays in the sexual relationship because she is crazy about him and obsessed with him," Sheila explained.

Later, when Paul looked back on this period of his life with Sheila, he realized that people would question how he could possibly believe the stories Sheila was telling him and why he never saw through what was an obvious truth.

"Our marriage," Paul explained, "had become quite boring, both sexually and romantically, because of our work schedules and my doctoral program. So I believed the stories she was telling me."

It was easy, in other words, to accept what became their reality, their truth—it was too far-fetched to believe Sheila was making it all up. She came across so passionate and was so damn consumed with the love triangle. Paul sensed Sheila was getting a high from living through these people at her work—and it was keeping her busy.

But even more than that, Paul added, "Sheila would describe the details of the work triangle to mutual friends of ours, as well as to my parents, when we were all together."

So it was easy to buy into Sheila's lies. She was telling them to everyone.

During this period, Paul had gone to Stamford one day to meet Sheila at her office. As she was gathering up her things,

Sheila turned and said to Paul, who was standing by her side, "Come here . . . follow me."

How far was Sheila willing to go to perpetuate this lie?

Paul trailed behind his wife as she walked through cubicles and carpeted hallways inside Pharma, until finally coming upon a particular cubicle.

"See," Sheila said, "this is Melissa's desk."

Sheila then picked up a framed photo sitting on the desk. It was a picture of three women dressed in costumes for a Halloween party. She pointed to one of the girls in the middle of the photo.

"That's Melissa," Sheila said.

"Oh," Paul responded.

After that, Sheila took Paul to Anna Lisa's office and then proceeded to explain how Jack and Melissa had met.

"They were leaving a bar after happy hour one night . . . going to their cars"—sound familiar?—"and Melissa ran up to Jack and just kissed him."

Paul said he never put it together that she was using the same story of how he and Sheila had met because, "I don't think [then] that Sheila is Melissa. I'm caught up in the love triangle."

He believed his wife. He had no reason not to.

"What happened?" Paul asked, referring to the aftermath of the kiss.

"Melissa was embarrassed . . . but Jack said he was okay with it."

From there, Sheila further explained, "Melissa and Jack would occasionally go on dates, and one thing led to another. It wasn't until Melissa stumbled onto Jack's voice mail account at work that she found out about Anna Lisa."

Jack—er, Nelson—had been lying to Sheila also.

"Jack feels trapped by Anna Lisa," Sheila added, seemingly protecting Jack. "He doesn't really want to commit.

But Anna Lisa is pressuring him in some way. How do you think Anna Lisa sounds, Paul?"

"Well, Sheila, it sounds like Anna Lisa is giving him space. . . ."

When Sheila described Jack to Paul, she never talked about what it was Jack "did for Melissa" that had allowed her to become so enamored with the guy, but she had no trouble telling Paul how "Jack sometimes had a difficult time ejaculating. . . ."

In one breath, she'd talk about how Jack performed in bed; in another, she would say how Melissa liked it when Jack played the guitar for her.

And then, as this relationship involving Anna, Jack, and Melissa seemed to be the only thing Sheila ever talked about to Paul, things got even weirder. Sheila felt she could do no more within the capacity of the role she was playing in the triangle at work. There must be some other way that Sheila could find out if Jack was truly into Anna Lisa, or he was simply ditching Melissa because he was tired of her. It was then that Sheila, while rummaging through a closet inside the Pleasantville condo one night, came across something of Paul's that sparked an idea. Picking it up, staring at the box, Sheila devised a plan to find out just what was going on with Nelson and Anna Lisa. It was the beginning of a strange set of behaviors for Sheila that would ultimately lead to Anna Lisa's murder.

CHAPTER 30

PAUL HAD BEEN INTO the television series *The X-Files* back in the 1990s when the Fox series was at the height of its popularity. Later, when he had to explain why he had a pair of night vision goggles/binoculars in his house, Paul thought, *Who is going to believe this story?* But it was the truth. Back in 1994, Paul and a few buddies would head up to Pine Bush, New York, a familiar spot on the map for UFO watchers, and use the goggles to sit out there at night and look out for UFOs. It was a hobby, born out of his love for the television show *The X-Files*.

"I ordered them from a catalogue," Paul later explained. "Sheila actually even went with me [up to Pine Bush] once. . . ."

Thinking nothing of it, when Paul moved into the Pleasantville condo with Sheila, he had brought the goggles with him (along with other pieces of surveillance-type equipment he had once purchased during the years when he imagined he would someday join the FBI). These odds and ends were all thrown inside a box—the same way that so many folks collect "junk" over the course of their lives and just find it hard to part with. Paul tossed the stuff in the closet and forgot about it.

"Hey," Sheila said one night, "Melissa wants to spy on

Jack." In the love triangle story, Jack had never admitted openly to Melissa that he was seeing somebody else. "Whenever Melissa asks," Sheila explained, "Jack always denies." Jack presented himself as a single guy, but Sheila (or, rather, Melissa) had followed him and tapped into his voice mail and knew he was just about living with Anna Lisa, or at least sleeping at her home fairly regularly. She had never told Jack she knew this, however.

"What?" Paul said. This got his attention.

"Melissa wants to spy on Jack and see where he's going," Sheila said. "I want to help her. I need the night vision goggles."

"So you're going to go on a stakeout with Melissa to spy on Jack?"

"Can I use them?"

"Um, I guess. . . . Yeah, yeah, go ahead. I don't care."

Sheila was talking about committing a crime: stalking. Unless a person is a licensed private investigator, an individual cannot follow someone or sit outside his or her home and watch the house. It's a crime.

Paul got up off the couch and took out the goggles. "They're really good. You can see in the dark. If you really want to catch this guy cheating and see how much he's lying . . . ," Paul explained.

Sheila seemed excited by the comment.

Incredible to believe, but Paul was helping his wife spy on her lover, and he didn't even know it. Paul was thinking by this point in the love triangle, after hearing the story ad nauseam for so long, that Jack was kind of a "scumbag," running around with Melissa while lying to Anna Lisa and then turning around and lying to Melissa.

"Jack's not a nice guy, Sheila," Paul would tell his wife. "He's obviously seeing two different women." In fact, most of

Sheila's friends would say the same thing: "Jack's scum. . . . Melissa should get rid of him and move on."

That night, Sheila got dressed, grabbed the goggles, and headed out the door. She told Paul she was on her way to go meet Melissa and spy on Jack.

Paul went back to his reading, shaking his head. He couldn't believe it, but then he could. Here was his wife helping her friend spy on the friend's boyfriend. Things like that happen, Paul considered. It wasn't such a stretch to believe two women were getting together to spy on one of their lovers.

As Sheila went about her business of spying on Jack over a period of weeks, she would come home with stories explaining how "Jack almost caught us." In the affair narrative, it was always Melissa and Sheila together (and one could argue this is true), sitting in a car, watching Jack coming and going from what was Anna Lisa's condo. A few times, Sheila explained, they (Sheila and Melissa) thought maybe Jack had spotted them.

All this stalking was going on at the time after Nelson Sessler had broken it off with Sheila. Yet, Sheila was consumed with following Nelson and watching him. As this carried on, Sheila developed increasing paranoia about the situation, worried sick that Nelson had caught her in the act. So much so, one night after coming home from a stalking adventure, Sheila rustled Paul from what he was doing inside the condo.

"Come with me! Come with me," she pleaded frantically. Sheila was obviously worried about something.

Paul followed.

Sheila walked outside their condo and told Paul to stand in a certain spot. Then she got into her car, turned on the lights, and sat. After a moment, she rolled down the window and yelled, "Can you see me from where you are?"

"What?"

"If I'm coming at you with my headlights on, can you see me behind the wheel?" Sheila was reenacting an episode of stalking Nelson and him coming out of the condo toward her. She was worried he had seen her.

"I don't know. . . . It's hard to tell," Paul said.

"Well, what if Jack saw Melissa and me?" She was concerned about what was going to happen.

"Um, if Jack saw you, maybe he'll say something to you tomorrow at work." Paul walked back into the condo, throwing his hands in the air. "Whatever."

It wasn't long after Sheila let go of the stalking (which one could argue wasn't working for her because she was not obtaining the results she wanted) and focused her attention on something much more daring, risky, and sinister.

When anyone reading this steps back and looks at this escalating situation (from Sheila's end—because remember, according to Nelson, the relationship he had with Sheila was over by now), one sees the evolution of a psychopath intensifying her behavior. Here was a woman upping the need for stimulation, and becoming totally consumed with (and engrossed in) having to act on what was nothing more than a make-believe world she had created around herself. It seemed every time Sheila tried something new in order to get the desired result she wanted—and it didn't seem to fit into that growing, invented happily-ever-after tale she had for her and Nelson—or tried to fulfill the increasing amount of obsession she harbored for the guy, she kicked the situation into a higher gear.

"Melissa bought a lock pick set," Sheila told Paul one night as they sat home. They had more time together now because Nelson had left Sheila, so Sheila was forced to spend time at home.

"A what, Sheila?" Paul asked, somewhat surprised by this.

"Melissa wants to break into Anna Lisa's apartment during the day when she isn't home."

Commit a felony, to be exact—a freakin' B and E, no less.

"Why would she want to do *that*?" Paul asked. He was shocked and concerned by this.

"To look at pictures and get a sense of Jack's relationship with Anna Lisa."

Paul ran a hand through his hair and adjusted his glasses. *Wow,* he thought, *this thing has come pretty damn far.*

"That's crazy, Sheila. You're going to now break into somebody's apartment *just* to look at pictures?" Paul was angry. He warned Sheila that she could get arrested.

"Yes." Sheila walked over to a bag and took out the lock pick set. "See." She placed it on the table. Then she took it out and began "playing with it," Paul recalled, "on our front door . . . and then the patio door."

Paul took a look at it. He had never seen a lock pick set before. "Let me see . . . ," he asked. Sheila gave it to him and Paul tried it on the door.

("Just really, really out of curiosity," he explained later. "I never took it seriously that she would *ever* go through with it.")

The kit was cheap and didn't work.

Sheila took an angry turn. "Damn it," she said, frustrated. "It *doesn't* work."

They tried again a few more times and gave up.

Paul then watched as Sheila put the kit in one of their kitchen drawers.

"And I never heard about it after that incident."

* * *

After the lock-picking device failed for Sheila, she went to Paul and asked him about an eavesdropping device he had in the closet. Apparently, she had been rummaging through his things again, still not satisfied she'd exhausted every possible means of finding out what Jack was up to with Anna Lisa.

There was a time, as a much younger man, when Paul wanted to be a private detective and also perhaps even an FBI agent. So he ordered the device from the back of a magazine. This particular item was a "bugging device," as Paul later described it.

"Melissa wants to know if she can use your bugging device."

Will this ever stop?

"For what, Sheila?"

"She wants to put it inside Jack's office at work and listen to his conversations." Sheila had this pleading look about her, as if to say, *"This* one *last thing, Paul. Come on. Please."*

Paul walked over and took the device out of the box and showed Sheila how it worked, explaining how to turn it on and make sure it was hidden and so forth.

A few days later, Sheila returned the device, saying, "It didn't work, Paul."

"Okay. . . ." Paul had all but forgotten about it.

Sheila took out a second bugging device, which she had purchased from the same manufacturer. She had found a phone number and website on the back of Paul's device. She was very serious and determined, indeed, regardless of what Paul thought.

"This one was like a tape recorder that you would attach to the phone jack in the office," Paul said later. "It recorded incoming and outgoing conversations."

Some time passed. Sheila brought it back home and said it didn't work, either. Paul shook his head as he heard Sheila calling the manufacturer of the product to complain.

"What did they say?" Paul asked when she got off the phone.

"They said something about being inside a corporate building and it not working in those places."

Not long after this latest episode, Sheila gave up on the devices and focused her attention on something else.

CHAPTER 31

BY THE FALL, SHEILA was telling Paul that Melissa had sought counseling from a social worker "for help in dealing with her feelings for Jack." The situation, according to Sheila, had worsened for Melissa. "Why isn't Jack spending time with her?" Sheila would ask Paul, still demanding insight from his male perspective. "Why doesn't he open up to her more?"

Paul did not know how to respond anymore.

Then, what became a crushing blow to Sheila's hopes that Melissa and Jack (in reality, she and Nelson) might have a future, Sheila offered this: "He's spending more time with Anna Lisa." She even told Paul that Jack and Anna had taken a vacation together recently.

Was this it? Had Sheila heard enough?

The writing was clear, but Sheila wasn't apparently getting it—there was always that sliver of hope within her that Jack would turn around and realize it was Melissa who truly loved him the way he needed to be loved, and that he should drop Anna Lisa and run back into Melissa's arms.

The fantasy.

The obsession.

The fairy tale.

As the fall of 2002 passed, and her obsession with Nelson Sessler hit a peak, the reality that Sheila Davalloo could not (or would not) see through this thick fog of mania was how much she was at odds with herself regarding what to do. The guy wanted nothing to do with her anymore. He had made this point clear. Still, Sheila felt the need to make a decision, as if one existed and needed to be made: Should she carry on with her life with Paul, or continue to try and find a way to be with Nelson?

Sheila decided she had to do something. She was entirely occupied and wrapped up in a love triangle, which, truly, had only two sides left by this point: hers and theirs. She was totally immersed in this soap opera narrative, long after Nelson Sessler was done with her. For Nelson, he'd had a fling, sowed some oats, and was now back with Anna Lisa, running full steam ahead, perhaps prepared to go through with a wedding someday. Sheila, of course, came in contact with this scenario on a daily basis at work, with Nelson inside the office. She felt she couldn't get away from it.

Trapped.

Backed into a corner.

So, like she had in the past, Sheila Davalloo went to Paul for advice, couched, of course, as guidance for Melissa.

Paul had become so "sick and tired of these stories," he later said, "that I often recommended that Melissa [get with] Anna Lisa about Jack and work it out among the three of them."

Frustrated by the situation, Paul suggested to his wife that Melissa speak to Jack's girlfriend about the affair.

Get it out in the open. Get them talking about it. They were adults. They could handle it and discuss it with maturity.

"Confront her?" Sheila asked, perhaps surprised by Paul's proposal, maybe misunderstanding what Paul was trying to communicate: simply to go and talk to Anna Lisa.

"Yes," Paul said. He was beside himself with this narrative.

It was getting old. He was so sick of hearing about it every day. It was all Sheila talked about.

And so Sheila, unbeknownst to Paul, began planning a confrontation. Paul, of course, knew nothing about what Sheila was going to do and had suggested she only "go talk to Anna about it." And in all fairness to Paul, he never really suggested that Sheila go over to Anna Lisa's and bang on her door and tell her that her boyfriend was cheating on her with someone at work. He believed that in proposing a meeting between the two women, Sheila would finally drop the situation and move on with her life with him.

"You have to understand," Paul explained later with absolute sincerity, "in some eight years of knowing Sheila by then, I trusted what she said. It's funny. Sheila was always this very caring person. She would give rides to work for people, saying, 'Paul, this woman needs a ride to work. I don't know how to say no to her.' She'd drive her every day. She would never say no to people. She was always buying gifts."

There was never *any* indication whatsoever to Paul that Sheila was, at this same time (or at any time), planning the vicious murder of her love triangle rival.

But that's exactly what Sheila Davalloo was doing.

CHAPTER 32

THE MEMORY IS "vague," Paul later explained, but he recollects getting a telephone call from Sheila one morning. It *could* have been November 8, 2002, Paul was quick to point out—the day Anna Lisa was murdered. But he's just not certain about the date. It was unquestionably close enough to the date. (Plus, Sheila's cell phone records prove she called Paul at home on November 8, 2002, at 7:55 A.M.)

"Hey," Sheila said. Paul definitely remembers it was morning because he had just gotten out of the shower "early," which told him it was a workday.

"Yes, Sheila?"

"Melissa called me. . . . She's sitting outside Anna Lisa's apartment in her car and she wanted to know if she should go and knock on the door?"

"Yes!" Paul snapped. "Tell her to just knock on the door and get the affair out in the open." By now, Paul was "so bored with the story that [he] just wanted to hang up the phone and get ready for work." He didn't want to deal with it anymore. "If I thought about it more carefully, I probably wouldn't have said that, but, of course, I never suspected I was dealing with a sociopath. As well, I thought this was about *Melissa* (a woman I *didn't* know), and *not* Sheila. So I just said it so that the triangle would be out in the open and maybe these stories would go away."

Part of Paul telling Sheila that Melissa should speak with Anna Lisa was based on the idea that Paul believed "Anna Lisa would have a right to know" her boyfriend was stepping out on her. "I didn't know any of these people," Paul clarified. "I didn't know Melissa. I didn't know Anna Lisa. I really didn't know any of Sheila's friends at Purdue. So, after hearing all these stories, I always felt the woman Anna Lisa had a right to know her boyfriend was cheating on her. Just that somebody should tell her."

Had Sheila called her husband on the morning she murdered Anna Lisa? (Consider the 7:55 A.M. call that phone records later proved.) Sheila had checked into Purdue Pharma that same day at 8:09 A.M. Building records verify this. So she did not confront Anna Lisa right after calling Paul at 7:55 A.M. It wasn't until 10:53 A.M., on November 8, 2002, that Sheila was seen leaving Purdue Pharma, and the entrance and exit swipes from her security badge proved she left.

Sheila returned to work at 1:53 P.M. (The 911 call came in at 12:13 P.M.) The rest of the day was a "normal" workday for her. And according to a later memory, as Sheila herself explained to Nelson (recorded for police stealthily by Nelson in the months that followed Anna's murder), Sheila walked over to her former lover's desk at four o'clock that day and then left the building at 4:35 P.M.

Nelson's door was shut.

She knocked.

No answer.

Sheila turned around and walked back to her desk. She picked up the phone and called Nelson's voice mail: "Hey, it's me. . . . I wanted to say have a good weekend."

Nelson's soon-to-be fiancée was on the floor of her condo,

lying dead, surrounded by police. Blood all over the place. And Sheila was telling him to have a good weekend. Something she rarely, if ever, did after they broke up.

Talk about a psychopath.

After that, Sheila packed up her things and left work near five o'clock. She drove home to Pleasantville. She and Paul had a routine night. Sheila seemed fine. She wasn't manic or crazy out of her mind; she was rather calm and collected. She sat around, watched television, and then had little trouble going to bed.

The following day, November 9, Sheila and Paul weren't home for much of the day, but Sheila took a call in the afternoon. Someone from work had phoned and left a voice message.

"I have some bad news," the woman said. "There's some really bad news, Sheila." She did not elaborate any further.

Sheila claimed she couldn't get hold of the woman until the next day, Sunday.

"You know, you scared me," she told the woman, referring to the voice mail the previous day. "What's going on?"

"I thought it was one of [her] little jokes," Sheila told Nelson later, explaining this day, "to try and get me to call her back, because I wouldn't call her back during the day sometimes, and she was just so bored out of her mind."

After her friend explained the call was no joke, she told Sheila that Anna Lisa had been murdered. Sheila never talked about her reaction to this tragic news. And, suspicious enough, she never went to Paul (who was very familiar with the name Anna Lisa from the love triangle narrative) and told him Anna Lisa had been killed.

At some point that same weekend, Paul remembered after checking his credit card receipts later, he and Sheila had takeaway Chinese food at the condo. And Sheila spent a lot of time on the phone with a friend's brother from New Jersey (which phone records later backed up) helping him buy a car. She had even called several car dealerships for her friend's brother, inquiring about cars and prices.

For Sheila Davalloo, it was just one more weekend of her life.

Nothing different.

Nothing out of the ordinary.

"She seemed perfectly fine," Paul remembered. "She wasn't shaken up in *any* way."

Viewed from a clinical perspective, Sheila's behavior makes perfect sense. The source of her mania was gone: Anna Lisa. Sheila had gotten rid of the obstacle—in her twisted mind—preventing the fantasy from becoming a reality. It was as if a relief valve had been turned on for Sheila. She could breathe easier now. Anna Lisa was out of the way. Didn't matter that Nelson wanted nothing to do with her. She could figure that out later. The source of the complications between them—Anna Lisa—had vanished.

The only problem for Sheila, however, as she sat on the couch with Paul, perhaps even while they were eating that takeaway Chinese food, maybe slurping wet noodles, staring up every once in a while at her husband, feigning a smile, was that Sheila Davalloo likely realized right then and there that Paul was a second obstacle. If her plan after killing Anna Lisa was to come to completion the way in which she had fantasized all along, then what was Sheila supposed to do with Paul? (Sheila had hoped that she would be there now for Nelson as he began dealing with Anna's death, becoming for him the proverbial shoulder to cry on, and then his lover once again.) Carrying on an affair behind Paul's back—she had learned firsthand—had been hard work. She was exhausted all the time. Divorce, she had also felt, was too painful. It was too embarrassing and hard on the families involved.

So, Paul would have to go, Sheila decided. If she and Nelson were going to ride off together, there was no room for Paul on that white horse.

ACT THREE

THE DRAMATIC PREMISE

CHAPTER 33

AS THE END OF November 2002 approached, a mere three weeks or so into the investigation, it was beginning to look as if the SPD was going to have to sit back and wait for a break in Anna Lisa's case to come to them. Detective Greg Holt, working with Detective Tom McGinty, was certain Nelson Sessler knew something that could help. Nelson was still a potential candidate for a POI, so questioning him was walking that fine line of finding information and figuring the guy out. It appeared more and more that Nelson was not Anna's killer—both McGinty and Holt never really believed he was. But Nelson had information they needed—that much was churning inside Greg Holt and Tom McGinty.

The guy from Canada who seemed to have had a thing for Anna, long after she said she wasn't interested—a guy who was into strange sex, one friend of Anna's reportedly said—had seen something on the news about Anna's death and finally contacted the SPD.

He said he and Anna had broken up after he moved away. The long distance between them "did not work." They remained friends, however, communicating via e-mail, and both had discussed engagements to other partners. He said Anna seemed pretty certain she and Nelson, as of September 2002 (the last time he spoke to her), were set to be engaged and would be married soon.

The leads might have dried up, with the case running "cold as your freezer," Holt later said, but it did not stop the SPD from breaking it down, point by point, interview by interview. There were still many sleepless nights for investigators. There had to be an answer somewhere. Somebody held an important bit of info that would break the case open. They were certain of it.

Tom McGinty found a friend of Anna's she had worked with when Anna worked for Purdue Pharma.

"We just had dinner on that Tuesday, November fifth, before Anna's death," the friend explained. "We had a wonderful time, and there were no problems that I could see between Anna and Nelson."

"Was he at the dinner, too?"

"Yes."

McGinty asked about any previous boyfriends and how their time at Purdue had gone. Was there anything worth sharing?

There had been a boyfriend up at Harvard, where Anna went to school, who had "abused" Anna, the friend indicated. "She had a hard time dumping another guy and even had to leave, I remember, in the dark of night."

What about Purdue?

"Neither she nor I left Purdue," the friend told McGinty, "under happy circumstances."

"How do you mean?"

The friend accused the company of terrible things, adding how there were several lawsuits in the works.

That was about it.

* * *

Detective Greg Holt got ahold of some video surveillance from the Donut Delight up the street from Anna's condo. It was the coffee shop Nelson Sessler had claimed to be at on the morning of November 8, a routine stop along his daily work commute. It would be a good indication as to how truthful Nelson was if they could spot him in the clip.

Holt sat down and began watching.

There he was—Nelson Sessler, pulling up and purchasing his donut and coffee, just as he said he did, then leaving.

"And if you look," Holt recognized, pointing it out to a colleague as they watched, "he's wearing those same clothes he had on when we interviewed him."

Still, Holt and McGinty didn't know that Nelson Sessler was being untruthful with them by withholding information. Nelson still had not said a word about Sheila Davalloo and his fling. Apparently, he didn't see that it was important enough to share.

As the investigation continued, the focus seemed to be on Anna Lisa's romantic life before Nelson Sessler. Friends and former coworkers came forward to talk about Anna, painting the picture of a girl looking for love. Oftentimes, one friend noted, Anna was "falling hard and falling fast." But then an interesting piece of information came up. One of Anna's coworkers from the time she worked at Purdue told Tom McGinty that "Anna and Nelson had gone to see an ex-girlfriend of [his] about six months" before Anna's death. (That's the thing when a person becomes a murder victim: one's life is post- and premurder—this is how that person is remembered.) The reason they had gone to see the ex-girlfriend (the friend could not recall her name) was so Nelson "could see his dog, a dog he had owned with the ex-girlfriend, but had left the dog with her.

"Nelson and his ex were having problems," the former coworker explained to McGinty.

"Do you know what it was about?"

"She was unhappy with him dating [Anna Lisa]." Then the coworker spoke of another ex-girlfriend, adding, "She resembled Anna Lisa, and she had an eating disorder."

The things that came out during interviews—remarkable.

This same friend confirmed Anna was actively involved on Match.com. She had even met someone in her condo complex from Match.com, but "he was not good enough for her, because he was a salesman." His job was not adequate for what Anna was searching for in a mate.

This call and several additional interviews, along with something found during Anna Lisa's autopsy, had led the SPD to consider that a female could have murdered Anna. Just because the crime scene indicated a violent struggle, it didn't mean only a male could have manhandled Anna Lisa. According to one source, law enforcement uncovered two small burn marks—little dots—on Anna's body.

What could this possibly mean?

Perhaps Anna's killer controlled her with a stun gun, shocking her into submission first, before savagely attacking her with a knife?

It made sense. A knock on the door . . .

Anna answers.

Sheila explains who she is— *"Nelson's girlfriend, bee-otch! We need to talk."*

Anna somewhat recognizes Sheila, since they had worked in the same building for a short time.

Sheila walks in and . . . *boom!* Right there, in the foyer, as she's being escorted—or forcing her way in—Sheila jabs a stun gun into Anna's stomach and puts her down to the ground.

"She told me," Paul Christos later said, "that she bought a

stun gun for protection when she drove around bad parts of Stamford. . . ."

While dating Anna Lisa, Nelson Sessler had not lived in the best part of town with his two roommates.

"She claimed she lost it," Paul added, talking about the time period after Anna was murdered. "But on a separate occasion," he said, long after he had found out about the affair Sheila had with Nelson, "she admitted that she may have bought the stun gun for protection in case she ever confronted Anna Lisa about the affair."

So, before Anna's murder, Sheila Davalloo has a stun gun; after Anna's murder, Sheila doesn't have a stun gun. Cops learn Anna had two small burn marks on her body.

It doesn't take Sherlock Holmes to begin to point a finger.

None of this added up for Paul, simply because at the time he was certain Sheila was always talking about Melissa. There had been a weekend, back in 2001, just after Sheila had begun her affair with Nelson. Anna Lisa was working for Purdue Pharma then. She had not yet taken the job at Pharmacia in New Jersey. Paul was at Sheila's office, where he sometimes hung out on weekends while Sheila worked and he caught up on his school studies. It was a quiet place on the weekends.

"Come here, Paul," Sheila said.

They walked toward an office. When they arrived, Paul looked on the door and saw a nameplate: ANNA LISA RAY-MUNDO.

Sheila opened the door and showed Paul inside. "Come on, I want to show you something."

Sheila then pointed to a photo of Anna Lisa on the desk. As Paul could recall, Anna was standing on a dock, a building behind her. He thought maybe it was from a vacation Anna had gone on.

"You think she's pretty?" Sheila asked. She stared at the photo.

"Yeah, sure," Paul said.

They went back to what they were doing. Paul could not recall if Sheila said anything after that.

CHAPTER 34

PAUL CAME HOME one day in later November from work and Sheila approached him. He thought it was maybe November 22, two weeks after Anna's murder. But again, Paul wasn't certain of the exact date.

"Where were you?" Sheila asked.

"Work, school. Why? What's going on?"

"I cut my finger on a dog food can." Sheila showed Paul the wound.

It looked strange.

Paul had given in, and he and Sheila had purchased a schipperke in May 2002. The dog was a fluffy little black thing with pointy ears. Sheila named the dog Molly. Paul had resisted the purchase at first, but Sheila insisted they get the dog. One can only speculate that Nelson was talking to her about missing his pooch—a terrier—and, hoping to work her way back into Nelson's good graces, Sheila bought a dog and began sharing it with him. But then, in October, as the relationship between Sheila and Nelson suddenly fizzled, Sheila came up with the grand idea to get a second dog.

"Molly needs a playmate," Sheila pleaded.

"Okay, okay," Paul said against his better judgment.

So Sheila went out and bought a Boston terrier, Brownie—Nelson's favorite type of dog.

It was "a nasty-looking wound," Paul recalled, going back to the day he walked into the condo in late November and Sheila ran up to him displaying a cut on her hand. "But it wasn't actually bleeding in my presence. There was fatty tissue protruding from the scar. So I didn't know when the wound had happened." From looking at it, Paul could guess that the injury certainly hadn't happened right then, or even that day. There was a scar there that Paul reported seeing, which indicated it was an old wound that had either been reinjured, had healed improperly, or had become infected.

"What should I do?" Sheila asked.

Paul looked at it closely. "Well, you have to go to the emergency room and get stitches or something."

Sheila waited until the following day, so she claimed, and then went to a local walk-in medical clinic in Thornwood, New York. She then went home to tell Paul, "They couldn't help me."

What Paul didn't know was that Sheila had actually gone to a walk-in medical center the previous week to get the wound treated. It was a gash on her hand that Sheila acquired while murdering Anna Lisa, law enforcement believed.

"She obviously waited," Paul later speculated, "about two weeks to show this wound to me. And it looked that way. It appeared that the inner tissue was hanging out." It had healed improperly. "She must have had it covered up for the weeks in between, because I don't recall seeing it until that day she showed it to me. . . ."

Carla Hayley (pseudonym) had been friends with Anna Lisa since childhood, she said during a nighttime phone call with the SPD a few weeks after the homicide. "I don't know of any problems that she might have had, or of anyone who would want to hurt Anna."

It seemed like another lost call—information that meant nothing in the grand scheme of the investigation.

"I last spoke to Anna two weeks ago," Carla added. "Everything seemed fine. She would call and cry sometimes and get upset, but it was nothing major."

"Anything else?"

"Yeah, yeah . . . I was getting to that. It was last summer, Anna told me, when she came home one night and found makeup on Nelson's shirt. She said she confronted him about it, but 'he lied' to her. She knew he had a girlfriend in New Jersey that he would go to see."

Other friends were soon located by investigators. While putting together a picture of Anna's last few days, nothing of much significance came up. She played tennis. She went out for dinner. She spoke to friends. Everything seemed "normal." Anna was being Anna.

The only promising information would come sometime later when Tom McGinty interviewed another close friend of Anna's, who said she had been in contact in the days leading up to her death, and had even spoken to Anna on that morning.

The woman talked mostly about Anna's love life, which seemed to be ripe with insecurities and problems, mostly brought on by the men Anna chose. Other than a loving and caring relationship with a man on Long Island, which lasted one and a half years, Anna didn't have much luck when it came to romance. There was one guy who would forget her birthday and then try to make up for it by sending her flowers three or four days in a row. Anna didn't like that. She was "into him," the friend recalled, but "he would not commit enough to give [her] a ring," which was what Anna was looking for during those last few years of her life: a husband.

Some interesting insight into Anna's relationship with Nelson came out of this same interview. It wasn't as one-sided as it might have come across by talking to Anna's other friends. According to this woman, who had known Anna since 1995, when they met while teaching a class together, Anna had broken it off with Nelson several times "because he had not given her a ring yet. The last time she told me about this was two days before she was murdered."

Anna was "into Sessler's world," as the friend put it. But even so, she had no problem sending him home, kicking him out of her condo.

"When she would talk to him about marriage and a ring, and he would not commit, she would send him home. He'd leave sometimes for a month. Then she would take him back."

The other curious bit of info was that Anna, her friend relayed, had always been "very careful" when it came to "locking her door." Anna was also "security conscious," the friend stated.

"For some reason," the friend added, "she was scared. When she was alone, she would keep the lights on in her home, as well as her television. She would only turn off her light and television when Nelson was home with her."

Then a revelation of apparent significance: On the day Anna was murdered, this particular friend had spoken to her at about 10:05 A.M.

"How was she?" McGinty asked.

"She did not stay on the telephone as long as she usually did and hung up quickly."

"She say why?"

"I believe she either had another call or there was some-one at her door."

CHAPTER 35

"THE LONGER WE go, the colder this case gets," Greg Holt said, looking back on what was one of the most intense investigations he had ever been involved in. "There wasn't a *day* that went by—even if a new case came in—that at least one person in the squad was *not* working on this homicide."

Dedication.

That's how murders are solved.

As investigators studied the documents, going over Anna's case reports two and three times, looking to see if they had missed anything, the question became where to go next.

They traveled to New York City, and made plans to head to Canada.

"We interviewed some very substantial suits in Manhattan," Holt recalled, "that Anna Lisa had worked with—thinking that maybe there's a romantic connection that we don't know about. But it all turned into nothing. Every interview was nothing, nothing, nothing."

But then a promising lead came through; and Holt, McGinty, along with several in the BCI, believed they had locked onto something.

"The boat burglars," Holt called them. "This is our first *major,* hot lead."

Apparently, two guys had been looting the docks down near Anna Lisa's condo, stealing everything they could get their hands on. They were serial burglars, fairly good at what they did. Boat owners had been reporting valuables missing for months. These guys had been sneakily boarding high-end boats—cabin cruisers, sailboats, yachts—and knowing that all of the instrumentation aboard these types of vessels is made of brass, so as not to corrode in the salt and sun, they stripped the boats of it all, along with trunk loads of expensive fishing gear and radio equipment.

"We thought they were taking anything that wasn't tied down," Holt said. "But even if it was tied down, they'd rip it out!"

Thieves.

Boat after boat after boat.

Wiped clean.

The SPD took a call one day about a pair of shady-looking dudes hanging around a local restaurant, sitting in a car loaded with all sorts of fishing gear and boating stuff, which looked to have been jacked. The scene just didn't look right to the person calling it in, so she went with her instincts and figured something was up.

"I don't think they're fishermen," she said.

It seemed like an interesting lead.

CHAPTER 36

PAUL CHRISTOS HAD a meeting in Manhattan with several representatives from Pharmacia on November 13, 2002, to discuss a study he was conducting at Cornell. It was a clinical trial. They were testing a new cancer drug, always an exciting part of the job for Paul.

It was near noon. They were eating. All was going well. The atmosphere felt comfortable. The group from Pharmacia was very cordial and knowledgeable; they were people passionate about their work in every regard.

As the lunch wound down, Paul noticed a gloomy tone hovering over many in the group. It wasn't overtly obvious, but it was noticeable that something was heavy on their minds.

Paul asked if everything was all right.

"Yeah," one of the reps explained. "It's just that we're all going downtown tonight for a wake."

"Oh," Paul said. "Sorry to hear that."

"A colleague of ours was murdered last week."

It was a striking statement. *Murdered?* That was not something Paul heard every day from people he knew.

No one in the group mentioned the victim's name. She was known to Paul only as "a colleague."

While Paul headed home to Pleasantville later on that day, sitting in traffic, thinking back on his day, it occurred to him that he might know something about what he had heard back at lunch.

Wait a minute, Paul told himself. *Anna Lisa took a job at Pharmacia. Maybe Melissa did something to Anna Lisa?*

The thought lingered.

No. Couldn't be.

When Paul got home, after dinner—"In passing," he claimed—he asked Sheila about Melissa and Anna Lisa. By now, Sheila wasn't talking so much about the love triangle anymore. There had been a sudden lull in the narrative—at least inside Paul's house. There wasn't the intensity there had been. Sheila would mention it, but not in the same terms or passion as she had.

Of course, this makes sense, because Sheila had murdered Anna Lisa.

"Is Anna Lisa okay?" Paul asked Sheila. "I heard today at lunch that a Pharmacia employee was recently murdered." These were "random thoughts" Paul said he was sharing with his wife on that night. He wasn't taking it too seriously. Paul had remembered that, in the love triangle story, Sheila had once mentioned to him how Anna Lisa had changed jobs and was working for Pharmacia. Something within that statement and the lunch had clicked for him. He was wondering if Sheila knew anything.

Sheila seemed startled. "What?"

"Look, I just heard that a Pharmacia employee was murdered."

"Really?"

"Yes."

Then Paul thought about the feeling he'd had—that Melissa had done Anna harm. There's no way it could have happened like that. Not a chance. It was way too close. Too much of a coincidence.

It was the stuff that happens only in the movies.

Jokingly, however, Paul then said to Sheila, "I wonder if Melissa did something."

"No, cannot be, Paul," Sheila lied. "Anna Lisa's fine. She's living in New Jersey."

Sheila's reaction to this conversation, Paul later explained, "seemed calm and normal, so I didn't make the connection, and the conversation ended. I always wonder what would have happened if the Pharmacia reps had told me the name of their dead colleague that day. If they had said 'Anna Lisa' to me, I would have obviously asked Sheila about it that night and asked why she didn't tell me. I still doubt at that point, I would have figured out that Sheila was Melissa."

He paused.

"But who knows?"

As November progressed toward the Thanksgiving holiday, the tone and nature of the love triangle, from Sheila's point of view, had changed remarkably inside the Pleasantville condo. Sheila had become a bit passive and quieter where it pertained to Melissa and Jack's relationship and the entire "Jack, Melissa, Anna Lisa" narrative. There had definitely been a change in the dynamic. It was pleasing to Paul not to have to listen to this story night after night, but he was curious as to why all the talk about it had ended so abruptly.

And then one night, Sheila spoke briefly about what was going on. The way Paul remembered it, Sheila brought it up, saying, "Jack and Anna Lisa broke up."

"Oh?"

"Yeah. Now Melissa and Jack are together. Alone. Exclusively!"

"I'm surprised," Paul responded. "I'm surprised that Anna Lisa gave up that easily in terms of wanting to stay with Jack."

Sheila never talked to Paul about the details. She just shared that Jack and Anna Lisa had indeed called it quits, and Jack was now with Melissa exclusively. Sheila was certain of it. This was the reason she had stopped talking about the love triangle.

For Paul, he didn't press the point. Thanksgiving and Christmas were right around the corner. It had been over a year now since Sheila had brought the love triangle story into the home; to be done with it in any capacity was more than welcome. Maybe the breakup was a good thing: Perhaps Sheila would stop talking about it and move on.

What Paul didn't know, however, was that Sheila was preparing to move on, all right—it's just that her plans not only didn't include him, but she was devising a way to take Paul out of the picture entirely.

How?

By killing him, too.

CHAPTER 37

GREG HOLT AND Tom McGinty had developed a few promising leads in Anna's homicide. In the coming months, one of these leads would be known by its evidence label: #85 BAG W/FAUCET HANDLE. McGinty and Holt would not find this out for some time, but this was going to be one of the key pieces of evidence in the case the SPD would soon develop against Sheila Davalloo. Incidentally, hers was a name so closely connected to Anna Lisa and yet not anywhere near the SPD's radar at this point solely because Nelson Sessler had chosen not to say anything about Sheila.

This bag labeled FAUCET HANDLE contained the top, left-hand, hot-water knob from the vanity sink inside Anna's condo on the first floor—not far, actually, from where Anna's body was found. What was significant about this particular knob was that it had a small spot of blood on it.

Beyond that faucet handle, EJ Rondano had submitted scores of other evidence bags to be tested and checked for DNA. With this much blood spread throughout the condo, samples could be sent into the database to see if a hit came up. Could the SPD be so lucky? Law enforcement submits its evidence, including fingerprints, and weeks and maybe months go by and then, *bang,* a suspect.

Seemed more *CSI* or *Criminal Minds* than reality—but it did happen.

The boat burglars were soon brought in after that tip from a concerned citizen regarding a car full of what looked to be—and sure enough, turned out to be—stolen property from the nearby marina.

It just so happened that near this time, Detective Greg Holt had latched onto a report that a man had called in saying he knew a girl, a local to the Stamford dock area near Anna's condo, who had spoken to another man, who had claimed to have "killed a woman" in the condo complex within the marina area.

The guy, a "stone-cold" criminal named Gary Riley, had bragged to this woman about "watching the paper," where she "would see the story." This striking comment had been made near the time of Anna's homicide.

Holt tracked the guy down. Not Riley, but another guy who partied with Riley at a park across the street from the Czescik Marina, which just happened to be right down the block from Anna's condo. It was the very guy who had called into the SPD saying he knew a woman who knew a man who had killed the girl.

Finally here was a thread that might amount to something. Holt could picture a career criminal, a local doper, knocking on Anna's door, forcing himself into the condo, with the intent of robbing the place, and things getting out of hand.

Holt asked the guy how he knew the girl.

"Well, um, ah . . . ," he said, sniffling, scratching himself, "we party. . . . We get high once in a while and I occasionally turn a trick with her."

"What did she tell you?"

"We were smoking a joint one day there in the park. . . . She said she had just spoken to her friend, she called him Gary, and that . . . Well, she got scared when Gary told her he had killed a woman and that she should watch the papers for the story."

Holt had brought Yan Vanderven with him. He looked at Vanderven. This was beginning to feel good, like they were finally getting somewhere.

"Why did you call this in?" Holt wondered.

"Look, I felt like it was my duty. What was done to that girl wasn't right. I'm on probation. I need to remain anonymous here with this. I actually didn't think you would find me."

"Come on," Holt said.

"Right, I should have known you would. But I have no current cases pending here. I don't want anything from you. I just wanted to pass along the info."

In the days that followed, Holt took several calls from the same guy, who was freaking out that they'd use his name and this Gary Riley character would come after him.

Holt assured the source that his secrets were safe.

After some checking, Holt found out Gary Riley had a rap sheet as long as the Dead Sea Scrolls. The guy was trouble. He fed his habits by committing crimes in what was the typical drug narrative within the big city. And yet he also hung out in an exclusive section of Stamford, not the run-down, poverty-stricken neighborhoods.

This made sense to Holt, because good thieves hang out where the money is. They don't rob people in their backyards.

Gary Riley was not going to be a hard man to find. But any investigator worth his weight knows that the more he can dig up about a subject before he talks with him, the better prepared he will be to tell if the perp is lying or hiding something. The SPD needed to unravel this supposed confession by Mr. Riley as best it could before dragging him in.

CHAPTER 38

NELSON SESSLER WAS asked to come into the SPD and look at a few photographs found inside Anna's condo to see if he could identify any of the people. The visit was twofold: Detectives wanted Nelson to look at the photos, sure; but they also wanted to put a little pressure on him and ask a few more questions under the stealthy pretense that Nelson knew something he wasn't sharing.

Nelson looked pretty good, all considering. He stood tall. He was a good-looking guy who sometimes liked to wear that three-day stubble so popular today. Nelson couldn't get around that odd smugness he carried, like a shadow, Greg Holt said. The two of them did not get along. So it was up to McGinty, a cop whom Nelson had somewhat warmed up to, to speak with Nelson Sessler.

Nelson sat down and had no trouble telling McGinty who the people were in the photos. Those were good leads, McGinty explained, and they would follow up with those people by interviewing them.

Part of asking Nelson into the station house was to pick his brain a bit and figure out if he had anything new to offer. Since the homicide, the SPD, just days before this meeting with Nelson, had found out through Purdue Pharma security records that Nelson Sessler had swiped his ID badge to get into the building at 9:37:38 A.M. on November 8, 2002, and again at lunch to get from one area of the building to another (inside), and then to leave the building in the evening at 5:17:49.

Nelson Sessler had been at work all day, just as he had said.

"I wanted to ask you about an ex-girlfriend in New Jersey you might have had trouble with in the past, Mr. Sessler," McGinty said.

"Yeah . . . well, she lives in [Central Jersey]." He gave McGinty her name. "She was unstable, you know. She suffered from anorexia and bulimia." Nelson explained that the woman was a "national" figure in the sport she worked in. She was small, "four feet eleven inches, maybe one hundred pounds."

"You left your dog with this girlfriend, correct?"

"Yes," he said.

"You ever take Anna Lisa out to see the dog?"

Nelson thought about this. "No. Anna Lisa never met her."

They talked a bit more about when and why Anna left Purdue Pharma. McGinty confirmed what he had heard from other interviewees—that Anna was unhappy with management. Then they parted ways, with McGinty telling Nelson that if he thought of anything, he should call right away.

Here was one more chance, in a long line of opportunities for Nelson Sessler, to mention Sheila Davalloo, being that McGinty had queried specifically about one ex-girlfriend and seemed interested in her. Yet, Nelson failed to say anything about Sheila—a woman he was, at that moment, once again rekindling a former relationship with.

CHAPTER 39

DETECTIVES GREG HOLT AND Tom McGinty, along with two investigators from the Bridgeport Police Department (BPD), a neighboring town, had heard what sounded like a "Haitian female" calling into the *Connecticut Post* newspaper. The woman claimed she knew who killed Anna Lisa Raymundo. There was some sort of issue understanding the woman on the phone because of her thick accent, and the name she left with the newspaper had also been in question. But as soon as the SPD figured out the name, they looked up several people in the area and came up short. Holt and Vanderven took it one step further and tracked down a local reverend they believed might know the woman, but he listened to the tape and came up with another name altogether.

It turned out to be one more erroneous lead.

All of this could be funny. Or, rather, as a cop, one had to keep things positive and laugh once in a while, or an officer would simply go out of his or her mind. The reports from interviews alone during this period—just about a month into the investigation—numbered in the hundreds. The SPD had spoken to dozens upon dozens of people. They'd traveled all over the Northeast and were considering a trip to Canada. They'd get excited and then that exhilaration would dissolve.

A lead would come in; they'd run it down; it would turn out to be nothing. And throughout this entire time, all Nelson Sessler had to do was mention the name of Sheila Davalloo and this case was as good as solved.

No doubt about it.

Captain Richard Conklin sent out a press release before the Thanksgiving holiday, noting that the SPD was looking for the person who had made the 911 call "leading to the discovery of the body." The release also said detectives believed: *[The] person who made this call has information that could be crucial in helping to identify a suspect.* The release talked about how the police understood the importance of anonymity and the 911 caller might be in fear of coming forward "due to some personal conflict." But the SPD could assist the caller, "whatever the concerns." It would protect and assist them to "any extent possible by law."

The press release stated: *If this person is still not ready to come forward we are asking that they please contact detectives and initiate a dialogue.*

And so they waited.

Nothing happened—besides, perhaps, Sheila Davalloo, at home or work, seeing this plea from police come over the airwaves and wires, and laughing to herself about it all. Most likely, she figured she had pulled off the perfect murder.

CHAPTER 40

REGARDLESS OF HOW AN investigation is going, or where a detective thinks it might be headed, a law enforcement officer continues to press forward, many times in the face of frustration and angst—especially when the cop feels there is an answer out there somewhere.

Greg Holt and Yan Vanderven tracked down the woman who had made that call to a friend about Gary Riley. It wasn't hard to find her. She had been arrested and was sitting in a cell downstairs inside the SPD building. What at first seemed to be just another run-of-the-mill criminal out looking to trash-talk someone she knew on the street turned into something else entirely. And—boy, oh, boy—did this woman have a story to tell.

After Holt read the woman her Miranda rights, she admitted she had been a "smoking buddy" of Riley's, not his girlfriend. But not long after the homicide everyone on the block was talking about, she actually had spoken to a girl named Betty (pseudonym), who had claimed to be Gary Riley's fiancée.

"What did she tell you?" Holt asked.

"That Gary must have been involved in the murder."

"How so?" Holt followed, glancing over at Vanderven to get a feel for what he was thinking.

Not much yet.

"She was supposed to meet with him on the day" Anna was murdered. "But Gary had blood on him and she didn't want 'to deal with him.'"

Blood?

Maybe Holt and Vanderven should belly up a bit closer and listen.

"What time and where did all of this take place?"

"She called me from Shippan Avenue. But I finally saw her that day around, oh, about ten or ten-thirty at night. We met up in the south end. She was scared, man. She said Gary had told her that 'he killed the girl on Harbor Drive.' She explained how she looked at him and saw blood on his sneakers and pants leg."

"That it? Is that all she said?"

"She asked him why he had blood on him. He said, 'Because I stabbed someone.'"

Last she knew, Gary Riley was staying at the Stamford Inn. She had seen him there just a few days before she was dragged into the SPD. He was driving a Town Car.

"Let me ask you something," Holt said. "Do you believe what your girlfriend said about Mr. Riley?"

"Yes, I do. Riley is crazy. I believe he could do something like that. He's threatened her life before. He carries a gray switchblade type of a knife and I've seen him pull it out on her."

"How was she when you last saw her and she told you all this?"

"Scared . . . very scared. She smelled like booze. She was certain he did this [murder of Anna], because he had blood on his sneakers and pants."

"Where does Mr. Riley hang these days? Do you know?"

"Usually down at the Beacon Restaurant."

The Beacon was on Harbor Drive.

The SPD realized that the car containing all of the stolen property was Gary Riley's. Riley was hauled in under a warrant for burglary second degree and larceny third degree after a quick search of the locales Betty's friend had given them. He was finally found at the Super 8 motel in town.

Gary Riley had a knife on him, which the SPD confiscated, bagged, and shipped off to the lab.

"A mess, this guy," Holt explained.

"Yeah, yeah, that was my car—but this guy Jeff. . . . No, John, he stole it," the criminal explained. He was fidgety and scratched his arms and legs. He seemed nervous, but more so because he was talking to cops, not as though it was his general demeanor. "His name's John McBride. He took off with it." Riley knew he was busted. There was no getting out of the burglaries. They had too much on him.

Gary Riley sounded jumpy, but also "cooperative." He was interested in answering all the questions the SPD had for him. He said he wanted to help any way he could. The problem was, as Holt and later Tom McGinty listened to Riley, they hardly believed anything he said.

"Tell me about burglarizing those boats," Holt asked.

"Yeah, well, we were down there near those boats and all of a sudden we seen all these cops. I said, 'Shit, let's get out of here.' Then we realized that those cops—there was way too many of them—weren't there for us—it was something else."

Anna Lisa, Holt told himself. *Riley was down at the docks on the* day *and at the* moment *Anna Lisa was murdered.*

"Still, we got the hell out of there," Riley continued. "We piled all of the stuff we stole into my car and drove off. . . ."

On the day Riley had been picked up, the arresting officers had taken him down to the Yacht Haven East Marina area (near Anna's condo) to have him point out the many boats he and his partner had burgled. Yacht Haven is located directly on Harbor Drive, right near the complex where Anna's condo unit was located. Whereas, the Czescik Marina Park, from an earlier report/interview, was a ways down the same road, heading toward West Beach and Westcott Cove, on the opposite end of the neighborhood. From Czescik, there is no possible way to see Anna's condo unit or the complex. From the East Marina, there's a solid view of Anna's building.

"What happened to your car?" Holt asked as the interview with Riley continued.

"McBride took a look around, all the cops, all the stuff we had, so he got into my car and just took off!"

Riley wasn't about to call the cops on his friend, because it was his car that was loaded with stolen property.

As it turned out, McBride drove all that stuff to the neighboring town of Norwalk and pawned a lot of it off at a local shop that bought fishing gear. The SPD had run a check of all the local pawnshops and came back with a hit.

During his initial interview with cops after being picked up, Riley described McBride as an acquaintance he had just met. He kept calling him John McBride, though his name was later referenced as James as well. "He's a . . . black male, light-skinned, thin face, short hair—Afro style, but less than half an inch on the sides and about one inch on top. He's around forty years old. He goes about six foot one inch and about a hundred seventy pounds. He is usually clean-shaven. And he has this tumor on his neck behind his ear, but I don't recall which ear. It's small, but noticeably visible. He knows how to use a computer pretty well." After being asked if Riley noticed any marks on McBride's face, hands, or neck, Riley said no, "just that tumor."

As they were down at the docks with Riley on the day of his arrest, those officers brought Riley over to the docks directly behind Anna's condo at 123 Harbor Drive. The officer even walked Riley down to the docks in the rear of Anna's building.

"You ever enter any boats around here?"

"No."

"You ever been on these docks . . . in this area?"

"No."

They walked around the same general region. "Think about it," the cop pressed. It was easy not to believe Riley. He always seemed to be making things up as he went along. Several friends of his, whom the SPD interviewed, had said, "Riley loves to make up stories." Especially tales about himself.

"I could have been on these docks," Riley explained, "but I just don't remember. I usually walk around the docks that are generally higher up, more elevated than these here."

As Holt interviewed Riley, he got a sense they were likely not looking into the eyes of Anna's killer. The guy just wasn't that type of criminal. Riley was a lot of things, Holt knew for sure, but murderer was probably not one of them.

"Riley was holed up in a flophouse motel," Holt said later, "and told so many stories to his 'friends.' I think a lot of it was to get to share some dope, and a lot of it was to look big in front of them. They knew of the homicide, and that is why he could get away with the claims. He told so many different stories and versions that he became totally unbelievable. There was never any stock in his story that he was the perp in this case."

Holt asked if he killed Anna Lisa.

Riley said, "No way."

"Why did you lie then?"

"I was . . . I . . . I was just getting attention from fellow [criminals]."

The blood that had supposedly been seen on Riley's pants turned out to be ketchup.

"Interviewing him was hard, as he would change versions

and stories and 'truths' so often," Holt said. "Tommy [McGinty] never believed Riley at all—on anything."

Based on what Riley told them, the SPD went in search for James McBride, who could likely answer some questions about Riley and that day of Anna's murder. The SPD now knew that McBride and Riley were in the same neighborhood, at the same time, thieving merchandise from local boats. If they weren't directly involved in the murder, they might have seen something. Talking to both, trying to figure out who was telling the truth, would prove prudent in many different aspects of the investigation.

It *could* help.

Tom McGinty found one of McBride's former employers and went to talk to him. The guy was open and honest, as far as McGinty could tell. He spoke of how well McBride knew his job and the heavy equipment he operated.

"He was always polite and spoke well," McBride's boss said of him. "They called him 'Cosmo,'" his former boss added, "because his hair resembled the character Cosmo Kramer on the show *Seinfeld*. He's a good worker, and if he returns here this spring, I'd hire him back."

McGinty got an indication that McBride was from Florida. He'd had some unpaid motor vehicle tickets from the state that came back to bite him while he was working in Rhode Island. McBride's car was impounded after he was stopped.

Last time his boss saw McBride was November 5, 2002.

McGinty took a copy of McBride's Florida-issued driver's license.

Other reports came in that Gary Riley, in the days after Anna's murder, was out and about at the local bars "bragging" about being the SPD's number one suspect. One bartender said Riley had come in for a few drinks a day or two after the murder and told him that cops had dragged him in and questioned him for hours about Anna's murder.

It was becoming harder and harder to figure Gary Riley out. However, Holt and McGinty were about to get a piece of information from Riley that just might change the way they looked at things. Holt was beginning to feel that Anna's murder might not have appeared to be what it was.

"Most homicides are committed by males," Holt explained. And that was the premise the SPD worked under for the most part. For a cop, it made sense. Unless, that is, the crime scene utterly spoke of a female presence. "The interesting things to me were that Anna let the perp in during the day, when most people are at work—i.e., lunch with a girlfriend, or something like that," Holt added. "The fight took a long time to accomplish its mission. A male may have overpowered her much sooner."

As Holt looked over the autopsy report, studying it more closely, a feeling came over him.

"The disfiguring on the face," Holt remarked. Anna had been stabbed and beaten on the head and face. "And that," Holt concluded, "is very characteristic of a female perp."

CHAPTER 41

YAN VANDERVEN TOOK on the task of heading over to Anna's workplace to see if there was any new information to share. Sometimes, the more you ask the same questions, the better the answers start coming back.

Anna's office inside the New Jersey Pharmacia building had been sealed off since her murder. Vanderven brought EJ Rondano with him. They were prepared to go through the office to see what evidence had been left behind. Maybe there was an answer in a drawer somewhere, or in a notebook. On Anna's computer. In her Rolodex.

It was worth a second look.

As Rondano went through the small office space with two desks, which Anna had shared with another woman, Vanderven tried getting inside Anna's voice mail to retrieve her messages. But after several attempts, he couldn't figure out the pass code.

Finished with that, Vanderven found the woman Anna had shared her office with and sat down to talk.

The woman, who came across as a bit hostile and bitter, described Anna as "disorganized and naïve," adding, "She also seemed as if she felt she had control over everything, regardless if true or not."

"You ever meet her boyfriend, Mr. Sessler?"

"I have. I did not think he was a friendly person, in my opinion. She often spoke of her wish to marry him, and she was hoping that this Christmas he would give her a ring."

"She ever talk about fighting with him?"

"Just a few times. She called them 'big fights.' She was extremely upset. But I never saw any signs of physical injury—although, I don't think Anna would have *told* anyone if it did happen, anyway."

"When was the last fight? Do you recall?"

"Oh, yeah . . . it was just two days before she was murdered. There was also one fight they had right after Anna's sister got married. Apparently, Nelson had told Anna at some point that weekend of the wedding that she was fat and had to lose some weight. So shortly after the wedding, Anna then went on this serious workout regimen at the employee health center."

"She say anything to you about the other argument?"

"She did say that afterward she realized that maybe Nelson wasn't the right guy for her, which was an unusual comment from Anna." It was something the woman had not expected. She figured Anna was dedicated to Nelson.

They walked toward the office space the woman and Anna shared. EJ Rondano was just finishing up. They stood outside the doorway.

"She was very tired during those past few weeks before she [was murdered]," the woman explained, adding she had no idea why Anna had been so fatigued. Anna had never said anything about it.

"Anything else you can think of?"

The woman was a bit uneasy here. But it needed to be said, she believed. "Anna was a very provocative dresser, to the point of being inappropriate within the workplace. And I also believe she had a very private side of her that no one else but Anna knew about."

It seemed back to square one as the end of November gave way to December, getting closer to the 2002 Christmas season. A thought the SPD had was that perhaps Anna's killer had tossed the murder weapon into the water close to Anna's condo. With the chance of locating the murder weapon, Yan Vanderven met with the CSP dive team down at the Czescik Marina and then the docks in the rear of Anna's Harbor Drive condo.

Vanderven was preparing to go and interview a few of Anna's former friends from New York. He stopped by the marina to check in on any progress.

"Nothing," one of the divers told him.

"No?"

"Not a thing."

The dive team had spent most of the day searching both waterways and came up short.

Back at headquarters, along with Greg Holt, Vanderven started the interview by asking one of Anna's former friends what he knew about Anna and her dating habits. There had been constant feedback about a man everyone called "Big Tony" (pseudonym), whom Anna had once dated. This guy was supposedly connected in some way and had a falling-out with Anna. Lots of friends described hearing stories about him being "angry" and "abusive" and a good candidate for having had Anna killed.

Hit men, however, would never leave the type of mess found inside that crime scene.

It turned out Big Tony was anything but a menacing, vengeful guy. He was just some dude Anna had dated, and perhaps he was "mean to her," as a friend explained, but Big Tony had cheated on Anna and *she* ended it. It was hardly the situation investigators were prone to believe would cause a man to have his ex-girlfriend murdered.

An interesting aside came out of the interview, however.

"Anna's goal was to meet a man and get married," the friend explained to Holt and Vanderven. "She wanted to have children."

Holt was beginning to think Anna was indeed itching to become a wife and she thought Nelson was that guy. At least at one time.

Holt and Vanderven asked about Nelson and what Anna's friend thought of him.

"His reactions to Anna's murder were strange," the friend reported.

"How do you mean?"

"Right after she was murdered, he started saying, all of a sudden, that he and Anna were going to get married and that they had gone shopping for a wedding dress."

This was the first time the SPD had heard of Anna and Nelson actually discussing marriage together.

"Anna had helped Nelson get a promotion at Purdue recently."

"Anything else about Nelson?"

"Anna's parents didn't know he lived at her condo."

They chatted some more about Anna leaving Purdue for Pharmacia. Then: "She was a very demanding girlfriend. . . . She also knew of an ex-girlfriend of Nelson's that he was still in contact with. . . . Nelson is probably still intimate with her. He has a problem with commitment."

With whomever the SPD spoke, they'd generally play the 911 tape and ask if that person recognized the voice. If they could only find the 911 caller, maybe they could answer some questions.

"No, sorry" was what they heard over and over as they played the tape.

And then, when the progress of the investigation seemed bleak and going nowhere, a call came in. A tree service worker had been cutting limbs down by Palmer's Landing, a tiny little grass peninsula along Harbor Drive, not far from Anna's condo.

The caller said he had uncovered what he described as "a bloody sock" while walking through some brush.

The sergeant who took the call told him, "Don't touch it. Someone will be there soon."

"It's underneath some brush near the security gate into the complex."

When they arrived, the tree service worker pointed to the sock. "Right there."

It looked clean, except for what appeared to be a bloodstain.

During this time, investigators were busy tracking down Gary Riley's cell phone records, his whereabouts, his rap sheet, and anything else they could dig up on the guy. It was pretty obvious Gary Riley did not have anything to do with Anna's murder. However, it was, then, the only promising lead the SPD had to work with. And maybe Riley, in the end, would come up with something important.

Nobody working the case believed that more than Greg Holt.

While this was occurring, Tom McGinty was going through the motions of following up on Riley, taking a hair and saliva sample to send to the lab to be compared with any DNA found at the scene. That would rule the guy in or out, once and for all.

When McGinty interviewed Riley on that same day, he asked about his friend James McBride and what type of person he was. The thought was that maybe McBride had had something to do with Anna's murder.

Riley threw him under the bus. He talked about how badass McBride had said he was and how he liked to "fuck people up."

There *is* no honor among criminals.

On December 4, 2002, McGinty had Nelson Sessler come back into the station house. They wanted Sessler to sign a consent-to-search form so they could extract his DNA and take a hair sample. As they finished up with that, Nelson began talking. He apparently wanted to share a few things with McGinty he had recently thought of. Facts about Anna's life, Nelson thought, that could be important to the investigation.

McGinty was all ears.

"As I think about it," Sessler explained, "Anna used to like to walk around the condo clad only in a G-string. I'd tell her not to, you know, because people might see her. But she insisted that no one could see into the condo. She would even walk in front of the sliding glass doors dressed like that. When I told her not to, that people could see in, she'd say the hanging plants covered anyone's view from the docks or boats in the harbor."

The feeling from Nelson was that perhaps some nutcase had stalked Anna for a time, saw her in the G-string, and decided to attack her.

From there, he talked about a guy Anna knew who "might have done drugs." He added how he had checked her phone bill just recently and said, "There were several calls to someone in Queens, but I asked around and nobody knew who she was calling."

Once again, Nelson was giving up everything except Sheila Davalloo.

CHAPTER 42

IT WAS DECEMBER 8, 2002. Paul and Sheila had some friends over for a dinner party. By all accounts, it seemed like a nice night ahead. Entertaining friends was something both Paul and Sheila enjoyed, although Sheila often stressed over dinner and making sure everything was just right. Nevertheless, it gave them the opportunity to spend some time with people they didn't see much of. Part of this night was to include going to the Bronx Zoo to see the "Holiday Lights Show."

Sheila and her friend were sitting in the living room, talking before dinner. Sheila's friend looked down and noticed Sheila had a gash, somewhat healed over, about one to two inches long, on what she believed was Sheila's right hand. It appeared to have been a nasty wound at some point.

"Oh, Sheila, my goodness, what did you do?" her friend asked, pointing.

"Oh, that," Sheila said, dropping her hand, hiding it from view. "Nothing." Sheila changed the subject.

Her friend returned to it.

"It's nothing," Sheila said a little firmer. She changed the subject again.

The friend noticed Sheila kept turning her hand over and

staring into her palm, avoiding any exposure of the wound. She didn't want her friend to see it.

"I never received a straight answer from Sheila about it," the friend later told police.

As they prepared to leave the house for the zoo, Sheila became impatient as her friend dressed her three children in snowsuits, boots, and mittens. She actually got mad at her because it seemed to take forever.

"If you're mad, Sheila, because it's taking too much time, why don't you help me instead of just standing there!"

As the woman finished dressing her children, Sheila nuzzled her way over to her friend's husband and began asking him questions. The guy was a corrections officer (CO) in the state of New York, so Sheila believed he held some sort of insight into law enforcement tactics and the law.

"How do they find fingerprints?" Sheila asked.

The man was struck by this. It was such a strange question, out of context for the night.

"How do they distinguish them?" Sheila pressed. She seemed extremely interested in how one fingerprint was determined to be from one individual, while a separate print was determined to be from another.

The man didn't say much. He explained the differences in fingerprints on every person, which he had assumed every human being knew.

"But . . . are everybody's fingerprints on file?" Sheila wanted to know.

"If you never had a reason to be fingerprinted, then your fingerprints would not be on file," he said.

This seemed to calm Sheila down.

Tom McGinty and Greg Holt boarded a plane to Florida one day in January 2003. James McBride had been picked up on several misdemeanor charges and was being held. This was their chance to have a crack at him.

As they talked to McBride, Holt explained, it became utterly apparent the guy didn't have much to hide, or he didn't feel the need to talk in circles like his burgling partner, Riley.

"Yeah, yeah, I was down there on that day," McBride said, "ripping the boats with Riley. What can I say, you know."

They chatted for a time about the burglaries, McBride coming clean on everything. After that, Holt wound up taking DNA and hair samples from McBride.

"He was very cooperative," Holt remembered.

"I recall seeing the cops," McBride told them at one point, going back to the day of November 8, 2002. "Riley and I thought they were after us."

"No, they weren't after you. . . . We're looking into a homicide."

"I don't know nothing about a murder."

Leaving the interview, with not much more than the DNA and hair samples, which McBride gave freely, McGinty and Holt were hoping to locate Riley's Town Car, which McBride had said he had sold when he got to Florida. The car was now sitting in a junkyard, somewhere in the Sunshine State.

"So we decided we needed to go from junkyard to junkyard," Holt explained. Yet, as they began looking, stopping to talk to a local cop in an unmarked cruiser, asking him for directions through an open window, a car came up the back of where they were idling on the roadside and rammed the back of their vehicle.

McGinty and Holt were both hurt badly.

"It was a nightmare," Holt said.

When they got out of the hospital, McGinty and Holt spent the next four days, while nursing severe injuries, in the Miami area tracking down the Town Car.

With no information of any significance to bring back home, Holt and McGinty went back to Gary Riley.

"Riley is a consummate liar," Holt said. "This guy would lie about anything and everything. It's just part of his DNA to lie."

Still, something Riley had said bothered Holt. As he and McGinty got back home and settled down, beginning the process of healing, they talked about Riley one day.

"He said he saw somebody out there," Holt remarked. "Someone hanging around near Anna's condo."

This seemed significant: a possible person standing outside Anna's condo on the day she was murdered.

So McGinty and Holt went back to talk to Riley with the intention of bringing him out to the docks near Anna's condo.

"You said you saw someone—what house?" Holt asked Riley. "Come on, Gary, which unit did you see that person at?"

"The same house where all you cops were."

So they had Riley shackled and handcuffed and tossed him in the backseat of an unmarked car. As they came around the corner of Harbor Drive, near Anna's condo complex and unit, Holt said, "We're not going to tell you, but which house are you talking about here?"

"Take a right," Riley said from the backseat, directing them where to drive. "Go past the guard house."

Off they went in that direction.

"Stop. . . . Stop right here," Riley said as they rolled up in front of Anna Lisa's condo.

This got Greg Holt's attention. The guy knew Anna's condo. They had not told him which one it was.

"Right there, on the right," Riley said.

McGinty parked and they took Riley out of the car. They walked around a bit. Riley explained where the boats were that he and McBride had burgled, and where he and McBride took off from after seeing all the cops arrive. And as he was explaining this, for the first time since they started talking to him about Anna's murder, Riley said, "It was odd, you know, a red pickup truck with a ladder rack was parked right in front of that house." Being handcuffed from behind, Riley pointed with his head toward Anna's condo.

"No shit?" Holt said. "*What* house?" By now, they had walked away from Anna's condo unit.

"That house that I just pointed out to you."

"What else did you see?"

"There was a guy at the door, talking to a girl." Riley was referring to Anna Lisa's door and possibly Anna Lisa having a conversation with someone who had knocked on her door. "I couldn't really see her and couldn't hear what they were talking about."

So far, there was nothing new here. Riley hadn't said anything that interested Holt or McGinty.

Looking at Anna's condo unit from the front, a person would walk up a few stairs and come to two doors, just about side by side. These were Anna's and her neighbor's doors, connecting two town houses together. There's an area directly underneath the landing that one gets to by walking back down the steps that lead up to the landing, where the doors are located, just like with any porch area. The railings along the stairs had slats in them, shielding the underneath area of the landing.

As Riley was explaining how this guy was talking to Anna up on the porch, he dropped this bombshell on Holt and McGinty: "And there was this girl behind those slats."

"What?"

Riley explained how she was standing (or maybe crouching was probably more like it) underneath the porch. She was kind of hiding. It was as if she was getting ready to walk up the stairs toward Anna Lisa's or her neighbor's door, and then the man in the red truck came up, so she ducked underneath the porch to wait for him to leave.

She didn't want to be seen.

"Wait a minute," Holt said. "Gary, what are you talking about?"

"I saw a girl. I cannot describe her other than saying she was female and she had long black hair."

Sheila Davalloo.

CHAPTER 43

THE FREQUENCY AND so-called "visits" from Sheila's brother picked up again in January 2003. One might even be inclined to say they increased progressively.

"By January," Nelson Sessler later recalled in court, looking back on this time in his life, "I'd say, Sheila had invited me to go skiing on a ski trip, where she said she was meeting some friends, and, you know, did I want to do that? And I went with her...."

But on this particular ski trip (and others that would soon follow), there were no friends. It turned out to be just Sheila and Nelson—all, of course, by Sheila's manipulative design.

Still, Nelson Sessler was all in. Sheila had won him over. They were now seeing each other and sleeping together, merely two months after Anna was murdered. A friend of Sheila's later told police it was during this same period of "Jack and Melissa's relationship" when Melissa began to demand anal sex from Jack. And when Nelson slept over Paul and Sheila's condo, Melissa would "wake him up with a blow job each morning," the friend added, "because she really wanted to keep him."

So much for Sheila being sexually repressed. In fact, she seemed to learn fairly quickly what type of sex she enjoyed.

"I started sleeping with her again," Nelson said.

A gross understatement.

Sheila became Nelson's shoulder to cry on, Nelson later insisted. She was "consoling" him about losing Anna. They were sleeping together more now than they had in the past. The relationship had entered hyperspeed.

Exactly what Sheila had wanted all along.

"It seemed like once a week we'd go over to her house at some point in time to have dinner."

And sex.

For Nelson, he later said, his "whole focus" during this period (perhaps at those moments when he wasn't with Sheila having dinner and sex) was "to figure out . . . how Anna Lisa died. And I was, you know, very down on that. So Sheila was one of the few people that I knew in Stamford that actually, you know, was willing to talk about it. Most people sort of shunned me. . . . I didn't really have a lot of friends here to talk to about it."

Poor Nelson. The guy wanted to open up about losing Anna and talk about his feelings to someone, yet the only person he could find to listen was—lo and behold—his old mistress, Sheila Davalloo, the woman who had murdered Anna.

Yet, as Sheila slowly realized that all she had ever wanted was coming together right before her lusty eyes, there was one little problem in her life she could not deny or ignore.

Paul.

As Paul Christos sat back and watched what was going on in his marriage that winter, he realized "things were getting pretty bad." He could no longer deny there were serious problems between him and Sheila. A wall, truthfully, had emerged between them. They were roommates more than lovers or friends.

Moreover, the amount of time Sheila was now demanding

Paul leave the condo in lieu of her brother staying over was grinding on Paul's nerves. He was being asked to leave just about every other weekend, and sometimes during the week. But not only that, Sheila was making weird demands of Paul, apparently getting bolder and bolder.

"Take Molly with you," Sheila said one night. Paul was getting ready to leave on a Friday after work. Sheila wanted him to take the dog.

"Why?"

"Molly hates my brother."

The dog, Paul later said, did not take to males all that well, to begin with. It was some time before Molly even warmed up to Paul.

Paul wondered about Brownie. Why wasn't Sheila demanding he take Brownie, too? What in the hell was going on?

"Brownie can stay," Sheila responded. "She loves my brother." Brownie was a terrier, Nelson's favorite type of dog. "Brownie," Sheila explained to Paul as he gathered up Molly and her things, "even sleeps with my brother on some nights in the bed."

"You need to tell your brother about this marriage, Sheila," Paul demanded.

"Okay, Paul," Sheila responded. "Listen, I'm going to tell him on Valentine's Day that we got married, and that you are moving in with me here."

Sheila had a plan, she explained, to break the news to her brother.

Paul lit up slightly after hearing this. *Progress. Here we go. Yes!* By now, he was at his wit's end. He had ratcheted up the pressure on Sheila throughout January to tell her brother about them. He reminded her constantly. Sheila was getting a message that the wick was burning at both ends. Sooner or later, the powder keg was going to blow up or burn out.

"Beginning in early 2003," Paul recalled, "I was no longer

happy with the marriage, given the lack of affection between us and Sheila's extensive traveling on the weekends." Sheila told Paul that all those ski trips and weekends with Nelson to Boston and points beyond were places where she had to travel for work. "And the situation with her brother," of course.

They had grown apart throughout the three years they'd been married. Still, Paul always held on to some sort of hope that "things would eventually get better." On some days, he believed in the marriage, but he wanted it to end on others. He knew something had to give. They could not go on as they were for much longer.

Whereas Paul lived with a drowning marriage, day in and day out, feeling its effects drain him, he recalled Sheila not being the least bit fazed by what was going on inside the home.

"So there was never any pressure from *her* to improve things," Paul remembered.

Work and school were still feeding Paul's needs and keeping him busy. And maybe that's why he didn't see things as clearly as hindsight would later make them appear to be. On the other hand, whether Paul saw it or not, Sheila was being backed into a corner. As her relationship with Nelson rekindled and heated up (she had him all to herself, now that she had murdered Anna Lisa—and Nelson was responding to her desires), Paul wasn't just a thorn in her side. Rather, he was a dagger sticking out of her leg, tied to a ball and chain, constantly reminding Sheila that she was not going to be able to have it both ways forever.

By this point, Sheila was exhausted from running around with Nelson and trying to maintain a semblance of a marriage to Paul. She was once again taking three-hour naps, on top of sleeping eight straight hours at night. She attributed it all to her crazy work schedule of traveling so much, on top of a depression she claimed to be suffering from.

And Paul bought this, for the most part.

When she got up in the morning, Sheila liked to meditate.

"And she didn't like to be disturbed during it," Paul explained.

There was one weekend when Paul returned home to find all his clothes in one of the hallway closets.

"What's going on, Sheila? Why are my clothes—all of them!—in the other closet?"

With a straight face, Sheila responded, "My brother is trying them on."

What? No way, Paul thought. *He's so much heavier than I am.*

"Come on. I thought he's overweight?"

"Look, Paul . . . I moved them because he was playing with them, trying them on and stuff. I didn't want him to do that."

But Paul wasn't falling for these sorts of explanations any longer. The fact that Sheila washed the sheets before he returned to the condo, for instance, became a red flag. The wineglasses Paul frequently found in the sink, men's shirts and pants, which weren't his, in the laundry—it was adding up for Paul in his mind.

So Paul continued to tell Sheila that things needed to change. He could not—and would not—leave the condo every other weekend for much longer. There was going to come a time—in the very near future—when, Paul made it clear, he would refuse to pack up and leave.

"He needs to be told!" Paul would say angrily. "I'm growing tired of leaving the condo, Sheila!"

Sheila had a choice to make.

CHAPTER 44

THAT BLOODY SOCK found in the bushes by the tree expert turned out to be nothing. After being shipped to the lab, the results for bodily fluids came back negative. Whatever the stain on the sock was, it was not blood. So the sock was returned to the SPD and placed inside what was a growing number of boxes containing reports and bagged evidence.

The SPD came close in January—so damn close. Tom McGinty traveled to Westchester County to meet with a detective from the ID Unit of the Westchester County Police Department (WCPD) in Hawthorne—a town just south of Pleasantville, about two to three miles away from where Shéila and Paul lived.

Imagine that. . . .

McGinty was having the Hawthorne Police Department (HPD) look at a few latent prints collected from Anna Lisa's condo that had been checked back to "known persons in the New York database."

But that lead went nowhere.

How close.

And yet so far.

McGinty had been on Sheila Davalloo's doorstep, just about knocking, but the evidence spun him back around and put him on a fast track, along with Greg Holt and the rest of the SPD, back in Stamford, scratching their heads, wondering when and where this case was going to bust open.

Sheila was one of those women who did not shave her armpits or legs. This grooming decision to be "natural" is somewhat common in certain European countries. This cosmetic, hygienic chore, which most American women were accustomed to, just wasn't something, a former friend of Sheila's later said, that Sheila thought was for her. That is, until "Melissa became involved with Jack."

Then, of course, Sheila started shaving regularly.

In Early March 2003, Sheila was at work talking with a friend. They were chitchatting about typical work-related gossip when Sheila brought up the fact that a "Chinese woman had returned after being pregnant." Sheila mentioned how, just recently, "You know, Nelson asked me if I thought she was pretty!"

Sheila was taken aback by Nelson's question.

"What did you tell him?" her friend wondered.

"I said no!" Sheila snapped. "Then he told me he liked her."

It was the first time that the woman could ever recall Sheila using Nelson's name.

Sheila had slipped. She meant to couch the story under the love triangle umbrella of Jack, Melissa, and Anna, but she had lost her mojo in that regard.

This same coworker, a woman Sheila had known for nine years, when interviewed years later, talked about how, in October 2002, she was having dinner with Sheila, Paul, and her better half one night. As they ate, Sheila went on and on, talking about all the sex Jack and Melissa were having. She took it to the point where her dinner guests thought it was strange and felt embarrassed.

So Sheila changed the subject slightly and asked her friend's husband, "If you were Jack, would you leave Anna Lisa for Melissa?"

"Hell no," he said. "Why the hell would I leave when I have a nice girl at home and a whore on the side?"

As it were, throughout late November, December, January, and now well into February, the entire soap opera narrative had entirely disappeared from the workplace and at home with Paul. Sheila rarely mentioned it. Not even in passing. It was so obvious that Sheila had let it go that one friend asked her at work about it. Sheila had given no ending to the story. She had just stopped talking about it suddenly back in November.

"Anna Lisa got another job in New Jersey," Sheila said. "She bought a house there. Melissa and Jack are very happy now."

And that was the end of it.

"I told him," Sheila explained to Paul one night. "I told my brother about us."

Paul was struck by this revelation. It was the first week of March, and Sheila finally had come clean. Maybe there was hope for the marriage, after all.

"What did he say? How did he take it?" Paul wanted details. This was a major moment in their lives, a turning point. He had known Sheila for eight years now, and had never met her brother. Now she was claiming he knew about their marriage.

"He had a breakdown, Paul. He became emotionally unstable," Sheila continued. She sounded upset and, at the same time, sarcastic. "He now needs additional counseling." It was as if the attitude she gave Paul indicated: *"Hey, thanks a lot . . .*

for messing the guy up even more." Sheila added, "He also needs additional medication to calm him down."

Paul was speechless.

"I'm going to be meeting with him and his psychiatrist soon," Sheila lied.

A few days went by. Sheila approached Paul and told him she had gone to see her brother's psychiatrist with him.

"And . . . ?"

"The psychiatrist stated that I should spend two more nights with my brother over here in the condo."

Why, of course.

The dates Sheila demanded for this were March 17 and 18, 2003, a Monday and Tuesday.

"I'll explain to him what's going on then," Sheila told Paul. "He'll know that you're going to be here now and he'll be seeing you when he comes over."

The pressure cooker was whistling. Sheila needed to get Paul out of the picture before an explosion. The shame involved in another divorce was unbearable for Sheila. She could not admit defeat twice. Her ego would never allow this.

No, divorce was not an option.

Murder apparently was, however.

CHAPTER 45

TWO THINGS, PAUL later surmised, contributed to what he believed was Sheila's first attempt at killing him. All over the news near this time, Baltimore Orioles pitching prospect Steve Bechler had dropped to his knees during workouts in Fort Lauderdale, Florida. A short time afterward, Bechler died. He was twenty-three years old. *Sports Illustrated* and other major media outlets reported that Bechler was taking an over-the-counter supplement containing ephedrine, a very powerful stimulant. Preliminary autopsy findings indicated Bechler died from complications of heatstroke, which ultimately "caused multiple organ failure." Ephedrine was viewed as such a dangerous drug by sports officials that it had actually been banned by the National Collegiate Athletic Association, the National Football League, and the International Olympic Committee. Major League Baseball, however, allowed players to continue using it. It was soon determined it was actually the ephedrine that had contributed in a large part to Bechler's death. The media picked up on the story and ran with it.

As someone working within the drug industry, Sheila Davalloo watched the coverage with curiosity—although, it's clear now that she was watching this coverage not as a professional in the pharmaceutical field, but as a murderer looking for a clean way to kill someone.

For Sheila Davalloo, upon seeing the news about Bechler's death, a lightbulb went off.

Later, Sheila would claim Paul had been complaining of severe headaches during this period of the marriage, but nothing had worked to get rid of them.

"I never had any such headaches," Paul later recalled. "Perhaps she made that up."

Perhaps?

Sheila had always been "very much into health foods, organic foods, herbs . . . and over the years of our relationship," Paul added, "she always tried to get me to eat healthier."

One day in March, Sheila came home and approached Paul with an idea. "I have some vitamins and supplements here that would be good for you to take. I got them from my herbalist."

Paul looked at the bag. Sheila had placed several pills in a clear plastic bag. The pills were bright yellow. They weren't in a marked bottle or anything that might indicate what they were. Paul trusted Sheila was telling the truth.

"Herbs and supplements," Sheila lied.

"Oh."

Paul didn't think it was strange; by then, he had been used to Sheila being interested in alternative-medicine remedies. It would not be unlike her in any way to come home and announce some new natural remedy for getting rid of this or curing that.

"Look, you need to take between eight and ten of the pills, as per my herbalist," Sheila suggested.

Paul thought he was doing something naturally good for his body. Maybe it would lower his cholesterol, which he had been watching.

Anna Lisa Raymundo was a pharmaceutical research scientist from Michigan, living in Stamford, Connecticut, and working in New Jersey at the time of her death. The daughter of two doctors, Anna Lisa went to Stanford and Harvard, graduating at the top of her class.

The upscale condo in Stamford where Anna Lisa was stabbed to death on November 8, 2002. *(Courtesy Stamford Police Department)*

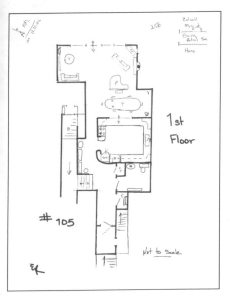

The first-floor layout of Anna Lisa's condo. *(Courtesy Stamford Police Department)*

The dumbbell found on the floor inside Anna Lisa's condo became a pivotal piece of evidence for investigators as they began to unravel this gruesome crime scene. *(Courtesy Stamford Police Department)*

The brutality of the attack was evident in the blood smears, smudges, and overturned furniture, proving there was a brutally violent struggle and that Anna Lisa fought for her life.
(Courtesy Stamford Police Department)

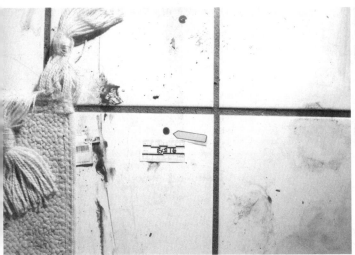

The murderer attacked Anna Lisa from the foyer area of the condo, and the struggle spread to the living room and beyond. *(Courtesy Stamford Police Department)*

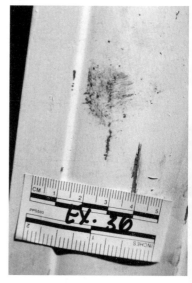

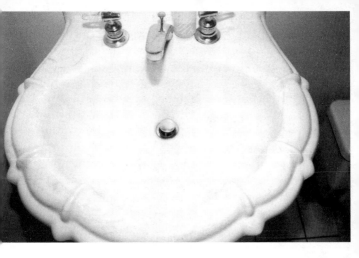

In the bathroom, CSI techs from the Connecticut State Police found blood on one of the faucet knobs. *(Courtesy Stamford Police Department)*

After this faucet handle was removed from the sink, it became one of the key pieces of evidence in the hunt for Anna Lisa's killer. *(Courtesy Stamford Police Department)*

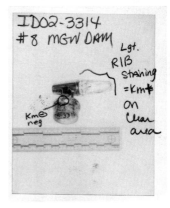

A Sharpie marking shows where one droplet of blood (not belonging to Anna Lisa) was found. *(Courtesy Stamford Police Department)*

Stamford Police Detective Greg Holt was instrumental in the hunt for Anna Lisa's killer. *(Courtesy Susan Orthwein)*

Stamford PD Captain Richard Conklin ran the murder investigation of Anna Lisa Raymundo from the Stamford Police Department. *(Courtesy the author)*

Westchester County Investigating Detective Alison Carpentier worked with Detective Holt to make the case against Sheila Davalloo for the murder of Anna Lisa Raymundo. *(Courtesy Alison Carpentier)*

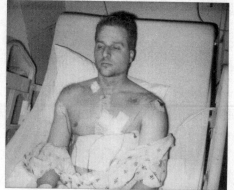

DD# 03-657

3/26/03   1130

At first no one suspected that the knife attack on Paul Christos in Pleasantville, New York, would be connected to the murder of Anna Lisa Raymundo. *(Courtesy Stamford Police Department)*

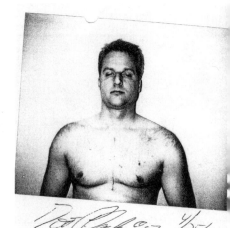

4/25/03
AT ADA SCHURE OFFICE   1250 Hrs

Weeks after the attack, Paul was again asked to display his wounds for police crime lab photographers. *(Courtesy Stamford Police Department)*

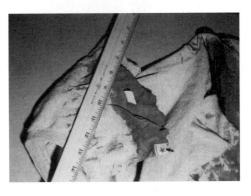

These bloody garments were found inside Paul and Sheila's Pleasantville condo after Sheila was charged with Paul's attack.

(Courtesy Stamford Police Department)

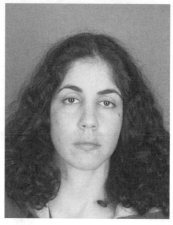

03-00266-01 (A)
DAVALLOO, Sheila Sara
Mugshot - Front

On March 26, 2003, four months after Anna Lisa's murder, Sheila Davalloo was arrested and charged with assaulting her husband, Paul Christos, in what she described as a "game" they were playing.
(Courtesy Stamford Police Department)

UP. YOU SHOULD KNOW I

SOLIDERS DYING IN IRAQ.

Two samples of Sheila Davalloo's handwriting.

This is the chair police confiscated after serving a search warrant on Paul and Sheila's condo.
(Courtesy Stamford Police Department)

These handcuffs were used to bind Paul to the chair—after which Sheila thrust a knife into his chest several times.
(Courtesy Stamford Police Department)

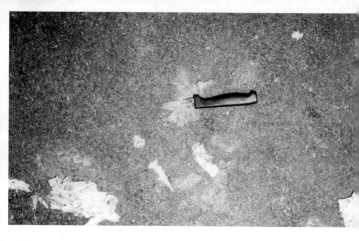

This is the paring knife, found on the ground outside the hospital, that Sheila used to attack Paul. *(Courtesy Stamford Police Department)*

Outside the medical center, Sheila Davalloo stabbed her husband again inside their vehicle. Paul bled on the curb before he was rushed to the emergency room. *(Courtesy Stamford Police Department)*

Detective Alison Carpentier questioned Sheila Davalloo extensively on the night Paul was stabbed. Throughout that interrogation, Alison believed there was more to Sheila Davalloo than just one crime. *(Courtesy Stamford Police Department)*

NYS DOCS

04G0449
DAVALLOO, SHEILA
5'8" 143lbs
DATE 05/17/2004

Sex - FEMALE   Race - WHITE   Hair - BROWN   Eyes - BROWN   DOB - 05/11/1969

While serving time for the attack on her husband, Sheila Davalloo was charged with the murder of Anna Lisa Raymundo. *(Courtesy Stamford Police Department)*

The murder of Anna Lisa Raymundo and attempted murder of Paul Christos grew out of an obsession Sheila Davalloo had for one man: Nelson Sessler. Here, Nelson and Sheila enjoy a lighthearted moment.

"Okay," Paul said. And so he took "about eight of them" right there in front of Sheila as she watched.

"I was up all night, with my heart racing and feeling queasy. . . ."

Paul's heart and blood pressure sped rapidly. He couldn't sleep. Couldn't even really think straight. His heart thumped violently in his chest as he stared at the ceiling.

After his body calmed down, Paul went to Sheila.

"Hey, I think those pills made me sick."

"I cannot understand why," Sheila said. She seemed sincerely worried.

A few days passed and Sheila approached Paul again one morning after breakfast.

"I went back to my herbalist and explained what happened. These," she said, handing Paul a different bag of pills, "were reformulated. . . . Take them."

Paul stared at the bag. He was nervous, but he trusted Sheila. They had problems, yeah, but he felt she was only trying to help. When it came down to it, what man would believe at this moment that his wife was actually trying to kill him?

"I am only taking five this time," Paul told her.

"All right," Sheila said.

Paul popped the pills with some water and headed out to the gym.

While on the treadmill, Paul's heart began that thumping, speeding pattern again. It felt as though his heart was going to explode.

"I felt queasy the rest of the day, with no appetite. We went to dinner later that night with my parents to celebrate my birthday . . . and I couldn't even eat my meal due to the queasiness and loss of appetite."

Paul went back to Sheila. "The pills made me sick again! I won't take them anymore."

"Whatever! I was just trying to help you, Paul."

Sheila dropped the subject of Paul taking pills, tossed the bag of extra pills into a kitchen drawer, and never approached him with the idea again. (Later, after cops were asked to go into the condo and search, a bag of what was determined to be Stacker 2 diet pills containing ephedra was found in one of the kitchen drawers.)

Sheila had tried to knock off her husband with ephedra (on his birthday, no less)—and she even admitted it to a close friend in no subtle way. One day after Paul had the reactions, she told the woman how "she had given Paul five ephedra pills, which she had taken home from work . . . and told him to take them all at once. After taking the pills, Paul became ill and . . . his heart was racing real fast."

Had Sheila admitted to her friend that she'd tried to induce a heart attack on Paul?

It would seem so.

When the Stacker 2 option didn't turn out the way she had planned, Sheila realized she needed to come up with another way. Something more effective and fail-safe—maybe a way that allowed her to have more control over the situation. Overdosing Paul with ephedra had backfired.

Looking at the situation in retrospect, however, it did not altogether scare Paul or get him thinking that his wife was up to something sinister. So Sheila had failed without suffering any consequences of that failure—which effectively gave her the green light to try again.

Sheila went back to the drawing board. And this new plan she had designed, which involved a knife and a "game," was foolproof, she unquestionably believed.

It *was* going to work.

CHAPTER 46

ON MONDAY, MARCH 17, and Tuesday, March 18, Paul rented a room at the Marriott in Tarrytown, New York, not too far from the Pleasantville condo he shared with Sheila. Paul was feeling much better physically after that aborted attempt to better his health—the one that nearly resulted in a heart attack. By leaving the condo for two days, Paul felt it was the space Sheila needed to break the news of their marriage to her brother. Paul felt a bit gratified, as if he had won the final round. He wasn't beating his chest with his fists; but still, the man felt comfortable and resolute in the fact that he had convinced Sheila to finally do *something*—and she was apparently listening. Sheila was going to tell her brother and now maybe they could get back on track with the marriage and start living again.

If nothing changed at all—worst-case scenario—at least, then, Paul wouldn't have to leave the condo anymore.

On that Wednesday, Paul returned home. He and Sheila talked. He made it clear to Sheila straight away "that [he] was no longer leaving the condo on weekends." He and Sheila had a discussion and there was to be no more weekend getaways for Paul at the local Marriott or his parents' house. He was staying home from now on. No further discussion.

Sheila was aware of this and agreed. Paul was fully prepared not to back down.

There was no way for Sheila to get around scamming her husband any longer while her lover came over and they had sex and dinners and acted like a happy couple. Hell, Nelson Sessler even walked Paul and Sheila's dogs through the neighborhood on some of the weekends and days he spent at the condo. ("I met individuals in her neighborhood," Nelson later commented, "even before Anna Lisa died, while walking the dog[s], and no one mentioned that she had been married.") If Sheila wanted to continue the fairy tale, she was going to have to get rid of Paul soon.

The only problem was that Sheila was forced to make this decision quickly. And as far as Nelson still believed, Sheila had been divorced twice and lived alone.

Meanwhile, Nelson was visiting a friend in Rochester, New York, a solid eight-hour drive heading from Stamford northwest toward Buffalo and the Great Lakes region—another eight hours back. He would be driving right by Pleasantville on his way home that coming weekend—he would be away from March 21, Friday, through March 23, Sunday. Sheila knew this, but Nelson had no intention of stopping at Sheila's and seeing her. It was a long drive. Instead, Nelson planned a pit stop in Syracuse to see his sister and then in Binghamton to see his parents, both of which were on the way home as well.

Sheila didn't have to worry about covering for herself on Friday night, March 21, because Nelson had told her he wasn't leaving Rochester until early in the morning on March 23, Sunday. Even if he surprised her with a visit, there was no way it was going to be on Friday or Saturday.

Nevertheless, what Paul and Nelson didn't know was that Sheila had been planning on seeing Nelson that weekend. Her goal was to have Nelson over for dinner on Sunday night.

Sheila figured Nelson would be heading past the Pleasantville area, toward Stamford, and she could call him and get him over there for a little grub and rub.

However, Paul was not leaving. This much was set in stone.

Sheila went to Paul on Saturday, March 22, and initiated her latest murder plan: "Paul, I want to play this game. . . . It involves a blindfold, being tied up . . . that sort of thing."

Paul was stunned.

Maybe things *were* changing?

"The game was not at all sexual," Paul explained. "I'd be happy to tell you if it was. I know everyone wants to believe it was, but it was not the case." There wasn't even the "intention" that the game would have a so-called "happy ending."

It was "not even remotely" there, Paul claimed.

People would find this hard to believe—especially law enforcement—after all was said and done. Many would ask: Why would Paul play the game if there was no sexual payoff? Paul explained how, for him, the following day was going to be stressful and busy at school. "And I always found Sheila to be restless . . . and I always felt like I wasn't giving her enough attention."

In defense of Paul, when the context of the situation and this so-called "game" is analyzed, two things become clearly obvious: One, Sheila was getting all the sex she wanted from Nelson at the time, some of it very kinky, according to her, and she had not been sleeping with Paul sexually anymore. Two, the game, as Paul and Sheila later described it, was designed (from Sheila's point of view) for one purpose and one purpose only: to kill Paul.

They were in the kitchen on that Saturday afternoon. Sheila said, "Listen, I heard about it at work—I want to play this game, Paul. Come on."

"A game?" Paul was curious. Their relationship wasn't at this stage. "Explain it to me, Sheila."

Sheila said Paul would lie on the floor on his back. His hands would be handcuffed behind him to the legs of a chair so he couldn't move around.

"You'd be blindfolded and then have to guess what certain items were that I place on your face and body."

Then Paul would do the same to her.

There was nothing sexual about it, Paul insisted.

Part of Paul wanted to pacify Sheila and play into her impatience. Paul had recently bought a treadmill and explained to Sheila that day how he was planning on putting it in the spare bedroom.

Sheila had been complaining that it was going to be an "eyesore."

Paul said he didn't care what she thought. He was putting it up.

"Oh, that's okay, Paul, don't worry," she responded somewhat jokingly. "I don't intend to keep you around much longer, anyway."

"What?"

Sheila saw the receipt for the treadmill on the table. "Oh," she said, "look, it's returnable within thirty days!"

Paul stared at her.

"I'm kidding. I'm kidding, Paul."

She wasn't.

They couldn't play the game that Saturday evening because they were headed out the door to Sheila's parents' house for dinner. The Davalloos had purchased a new home. They invited their daughter and her husband over to check it out. Sheila knew this when she suggested the game. She had no intention of playing it that night. All she wanted to do was plant the seed.

"She seemed distant from me," Paul remembered about that Saturday night.

Sheila had other things on her mind.

At one point after dinner, Paul got up and went into the living room. He wasn't feeling all that social. He turned on CNN.

Sheila gave him a glaring look. "She was angry. It was becoming a pattern. Whenever we went out with friends, she really didn't want me around." Paul sensed it: the things she said, the looks, that bad energy emanating from Sheila like an odor.

"I was always in the way," Paul recalled. "Clearly, I was becoming more and more of an impediment to her. She was picking on the littlest things."

Near this time, Sheila had gone to Paul and asked: "Look, Jack is taking a job in the UK. Should Melissa quit her job and go with him?"

Paul hadn't heard much about Jack and Melissa lately. "I don't know, Sheila. She could take some time off . . . think about it. . . . I don't know!"

The next day, March 23, Sunday, Paul met with some of his fellow students in the city early in the morning to go over a few things for an upcoming class.

Paul arrived back home at the condo, near noon. Sheila approached him, saying, "Let's go see your mother."

She insisted, actually.

It was a strange request—one that Paul hadn't heard much from Sheila lately.

"Okay," Paul said. It actually sounded like a nice, normal thing to do.

So they took a ride over to Paul's mother's house in White Plains and had a visit with her near one o'clock. They sipped tea and ate sandwiches. Chitchatted about mundane, everyday things mothers and sons and daughters-in-law discuss. Paul's mother mentioned the Academy Awards slated to air that same night on television. "Why don't the two of you stay and watch it with me?"

"No . . . no," Sheila piped in urgently. "We need to go."

They said their good-byes and, after an hour or so, were on their way back home to Pleasantville.

When they got home, somewhere near two-thirty in the afternoon, Paul walked the dogs. He brought them back into the house and continued playing with them in the spare bedroom. It was a lazy Sunday.

Sheila came into the room soon after and said: "Let's play the game?"

She was ready.

It was closing in on four o'clock now.

Paul hadn't thought about it since she had mentioned the game the previous afternoon. He surmised that Sheila had forgotten about it.

"I thought this was a bizarre game, but I figured that Sheila . . . was interested."

What the hell, Paul considered as Sheila stood before him, suggesting they play the game. *Why not humor the woman.* He had a major project due for school the following day, so he wasn't giving the game much thought, Paul said. Another day, another insidious request or comment made by Sheila. Paul was kind of used to this sort of unpredictable behavior of Sheila's by then. He never quite knew what to expect from her. Perhaps the game, on top of her speaking with her brother, was her way of saying she was interested in at least working on things.

Inside the spare bedroom was a desk Paul used for work, along with a wooden chair, which had a horizontal wooden beam at the base, like most chairs, connecting the legs. The idea was to handcuff the person playing the game inside the beam of the chair so he or she couldn't move freely or remove the blindfold.

Sheila placed a pillow on the floor. She explained that the pillow was for the player's head, so he didn't get hurt.

"I'll go first," Sheila said. She took out a pair of panty hose. "We'll use these for a blindfold."

Later this detail would seem sexy. Erotic. *Fifty Shades of Grey*-like.

But Paul kept insisting that it was not intended to be sexual in any way. After all, they had been sleeping in separate rooms by then. They were both fully clothed. Paul wore green khaki shorts and a gray/blue T-shirt. Sheila was fully dressed in jeans and a T-shirt. There was never any discussion about stripping down naked. The game was set up simply to guess what those regular, everyday household items were that were being rubbed on the bound player's body. What the game might lead to, Paul never speculated.

"It was just a game."

Sheila got down on the floor. Paul went over to the closet and took out a pair of handcuffs he'd had since high school and his days wanting to be an FBI agent. Hobby stuff, like the night vision goggles. Then he reached down and handcuffed Sheila's hands in between the horizontal bar on the wooden chair.

Sheila couldn't move around much.

Paul then placed the panty hose over her head until they reached her eyes.

"Can you see?"

"No," Sheila said.

The first item Paul placed on Sheila was one of the dogs.

"Who is it?" he asked.

Sheila couldn't tell.

Looking around the room, Paul grabbed a camera.

Sheila couldn't guess it.

A box.

She nailed it.

But after only a short period of time, Sheila didn't want to continue. She said, "Let's stop. Let's switch."

"Okay," Paul responded.

Then he uncuffed Sheila's hands.

Sheila tore off the panty hose.

"Your turn!"

CHAPTER 47

SHEILA DAVALLOO is a narcissist. When her life is examined, a pattern of behavior centering all on one person—Sheila—becomes inexplicably evident. For example, Sheila wrote a letter to Nelson Sessler in the years after her life of murder was exposed. She was desperate to explain to Nelson how badly people had simply misunderstood her and her intentions. She had never hurt anyone. Not ever. It was all a terrible mistake. It was a great confusion that would one day be explained and proven false.

First off, in a bid to try and manipulate Nelson into coming to see her (they weren't talking then), she said a lot would go "unsaid" in the letter because, well: *I would only be able to convey [it] to you in person.*

From that one point, Sheila hinged the remainder of her bizarre attempt to explain herself. She went on to say how "sorry" she was that Nelson was unaware of the fact that she was incapable "of hurting anyone." So she was now going to explain to Nelson how it was simply impossible. In fact, she wrote, earlier on that same day she had written the letter, Sheila had cried when she heard the news that two celebrities had passed away. It had made her sad. She felt for their families.

Beyond that, Sheila was especially "upset" when people "were hurt" and soldiers died in Iraq. It "choked" her up to think about what the families must go through after learning of a loved one's death. She related to this by placing her brother in the position of the person who was killed and then thinking how she would feel.

Sheila's handwriting is something to take note of. It is nothing short of perfect. Not good, but flawless. It's like staring at a specific font a computer has generated. She could write letters after letters, without any margins or lines on the page, straight and methodical, in this highly stylized penmanship of hers, which is so clear and precise that any recipient is inclined to think she *had* used a computer. Beyond the perfection of the letters, what emerges is how calm the hand is writing out the words. One would have to have a perfectly steady hand, along with an abundance of composure within, to achieve the precision Sheila does in these letters.[1]

As bizarre as it sounded (and looked) on the page, Sheila wrote about a "method" she had developed for "getting rid of flies" that did not involve killing them. She was trying to point out to Nelson that being the fragile, sensitive, caring person she was, she couldn't possibly even hurt a fly. She considered how "smart" a fly was for being caught inside a house, but was able to find a window and a way out, only to be stuck between the glass and the outside world. This might

[1] Go to the photo section of the book, where I've placed a few very small sections of Sheila's writing, as much as "fair use" laws would allow without her consent. Page after page of this same carefully plotted, equally spaced, perfect printing—this occurred after the woman had committed two savagely brutal and violent, deadly crimes. That speaks of a sociopath—one who can kill and then not have an ounce of guilt in her DNA, not even to disrupt her hands.

have been Sheila's cute way of projecting a metaphor. The fly had made it that far, but it could not break free, Sheila proposed as some sort of deep reflection. This bothered her, she seemed to say. She described how after she was able to calm the fly (or bug) down, she would then place a glass over it, capturing it. When the bug went toward the bottom of the glass, she would place a tissue paper over the top (lid), caging the creature into the glass, and then open the window and allow it to go free—unharmed, of course.

She explained to Nelson that, "truth be told," she had never liked him hunting. She actually hated that he killed animals with a gun.

But, in all of her hubris and madness, Sheila had saved the most embarrassing, perhaps most idiotic statement, for the end of the paragraph—a long section all about death, within what was a three-page letter.

Sheila had the nerve to describe how she "believed" if a person was "hurt or killed . . . intentionally," the death or pain created by that person's demise produced "an imbalance in the universe," along with "a lot of bad karma." This was the reason, she added, why she had always been so staunchly opposed to and against war—as though Nelson was asking (which he wasn't).

Imagine that. All the pain, suffering, and murder—it was too much for Sheila Davalloo's soul to take.

Concluding this thought, she further explained how "too much" of this bad karma in the world had the potential to cause and lead to "many more 9/11's" throughout her "lifetime."

Ah, the deep reflections of a woman who could not stand to hurt a simple fly. And yet, as Paul Christos was about to find out firsthand, this was also the same woman who was about to do her best to kill him in a terribly violent manner.

CHAPTER 48

"YOU READY, PAUL?" Sheila asked.

It was Paul's turn to be handcuffed and blindfolded.

His hands were bound behind his head, handcuffed through that same chair beam. Paul was on his back now, lying on the floor. His head was resting on the pillow so he wouldn't—*ahem*—hurt himself.

Paul could hear fine. He could not see. He listened as Sheila left the room.

She began with the dogs.

Easy stuff.

Then she rubbed a printer cartridge on Paul.

A Spider-Man figurine.

A calculator.

Then a shampoo bottle.

Each time she went to fetch a new item, Sheila left the room and came back in ample time. Paul could hear her roaming throughout the house.

"I heard her move into the . . . bathroom, various places in the house," Paul later recalled.

There was one item Paul had trouble guessing—a candle.

Sheila placed it on the side of Paul's face, moving it back and forth, slowly.

Still, he could not tell what it was.

"We seemed to be having fun playing the game," Paul said later. "Sheila appeared happy and calm. I was actually enjoying it."

Then Paul thought he heard Sheila in the kitchen, rummaging. She was foraging through cabinets and drawers, obviously looking for the next item she had in mind.

"You're better at this than me," Sheila said. She sounded hostile, at least the way Sheila later described her feelings. She was becoming consumed with "pent-up hostility" because she believed that Paul was "patronizing" her and treating her like her brother should be treated. Sheila claimed she was becoming upset because Paul was doing better than she was in the game.

"It's not fair," Sheila said, referring to how good Paul was at the game.

Make no mistake, Sheila Davalloo had one purpose in playing this game: to remove a scab from a wound.

When she came back into the bedroom after leaving again, Sheila said, "Paul . . . I have one last item here for you to guess."

"Okay," Paul said. He was ready.

Sheila straddled Paul. Her legs fell off to his sides, his legs underneath her crotch area. She placed that same candle near Paul's face, close to his mouth.

Paul could smell the wax.

And as this was happening, Sheila later claimed, she "saw" a "dark figure," which had been following her around since before Thanksgiving 2002—and, right then, that dark "figure was going toward [a] knife and picked up the knife. . . ."

Then, "within a split second," Paul recalled, he felt a

tremendous wallop, a startling and thunderous, powerful "blow to [his] chest." It was as if someone had dropped a twenty-pound weight on him. Paul had no idea what was happening. It was such a powerful blow, in fact, Paul remembered the desk near them actually shaking.

"Three seconds passed," Paul recalled.

Sheila screamed.

Then came another sudden thrust, a substantial thump to Paul's chest again. It felt as though the weight of a pallet of bricks, heavy and sudden, had landed on his chest.

Two more seconds passed.

"Oh, my . . . ," Sheila said, finally speaking. She sounded as if she was in a panic. "I think I hurt you. You're bleeding."

Paul was losing his breath. "Winded" was the way he characterized the next moments; "out of it."

Then Paul began to sweat.

Profusely.

"It was a mistake," Sheila said. "An accident."

Something had happened, Paul thought. He still couldn't see. He had no idea what was going on.

"Remove the blindfold. . . . Sheila, come on."

"It was an accident."

"Sheila, what happened?" Paul asked. The moment was becoming more frantic as time passed.

"Um . . . well, I think something fell on you. I think the candle hurt you."

Paul could sense his body changing. His heart was reacting to whatever had happened.

"Okay, don't panic, Sheila. Take. The. Blindfold. Off."

Sheila removed the panty hose.

Paul could see now.

Next, Sheila got up and started to look around the room.

("*Acting* as if she was in a panic," Paul later surmised.)

"I can't find the handcuff keys," Sheila claimed. There was

a tremendous amount of stress in her voice. She sounded manic.

"Okay, please help me break the chair so I can at least slide off the beam of the chair," Paul suggested. He still did not have any clue as to what had happened.

Blood was oozing from his chest, however, soaking his shirt.

The dogs were in the room "all over [Paul] and the blood," Sheila commented later.

Paul needed to break free. He wanted to stand up and try to figure out what had happened and, more important, what to do next.

His breath was shorter. More winded. He was sweating more copiously.

Bullets.

Something was wrong—terribly, terribly wrong. His body was responding to whatever trauma had occurred.

But Paul had no idea what it was.

Sheila put pressure on the chair leg and broke it.

"God job," Paul said. "Okay . . . that was good." It was as if he had to tell Sheila how to respond, how to act, what to do next. It was like she couldn't think on her own.

Or didn't want to.

"What do I do? What do I do? What do I do?" Sheila asked.

As Paul listened, he felt she was acting, as if her emotions and actions were not real. It was all too obvious to Paul, even as he sat there, bleeding and losing his breath.

"I'm still handcuffed at this point, but the chair is out of the picture," Paul recalled.

He hadn't stood up yet. Instead, Paul rolled over onto his side. He realized then that most of the pain—it was beginning to thump harder and harder and hurt more and more—was localized to his chest area.

Next, Paul's entire chest began to throb in pain. He also felt pain in his back, chest-high location. It wasn't limited pain, in any one particular area. No, it was all over.

Sheila left the room and returned with a glass of juice.

"Drink that, Paul, drink it."

"Call 911, Sheila . . . right now. Call an ambulance."

Paul looked down.

Blood.

"Help me, Sheila . . . ," Paul pleaded. "Call 911 . . . *please*. . . . Get an ambulance over here fast."

CHAPTER 49

IT WAS BETWEEN 4:00 and 5:00 P.M. Nelson Sessler had visited friends in Rochester, family in Syracuse and Binghamton, and was now heading back home toward the I-84 Freeway connector, on his way to Newburgh, New York, and all points beyond via the Newburgh–Beacon Bridge—a bridge that would dump Nelson into the Pleasantville/White Plains area of New York.

Nelson played guitar and had been in a band at one time. He had once written a song using lyrics from a poem Sheila had given him. He played the song at a club. Sheila was there. She was pissed off, a friend said later, because Nelson had changed some of the words from the poem in his song.

Sheila liked nothing more than sitting around and watching Nelson play his guitar. There are photos during this period depicting quite a happy couple spending time in Boston and skiing and just hanging out and having fun. In one photograph, Sheila is smiling from ear to ear, happily content, sitting on Nelson's knee. Nelson has a beer in his hand and is making a zany face. One would not know by looking at this photo that Sheila had a husband at home, and, more disturbing, she had murdered a woman—her rival in a love triangle—just mere weeks before the photo had been taken. Sheila appears to be a young woman in love, spending time with her mate.

As Nelson no doubt listened to the radio while driving down the highway on his way home, he had no idea what was happening at the condo where he had spent so much time lately, bedding down with Sheila. And yet, as Nelson drove, Sheila was frantically dealing with a situation at home that was spiraling out of control—while dealing with a husband dying from stab wounds she had inflicted, preparing to invite her lover over for dinner on that same night.

CHAPTER 50

PAUL WAS FADING. He knew now he was bleeding. He felt a tremendous amount of throbbing pain—one thousand toothaches—in his chest and back, the sweat, being fed by a growing fever, beading down his forehead.

Paul watched as Sheila searched for her phone.

She found it.

"My husband's been hurt. . . ." Paul heard Sheila speaking into her cell phone. He assumed she had a 911 operator on the other end of the line. "We were playing a game. He's bleeding. He's having trouble breathing." Paul then heard Sheila give the address to the condo. Sheila was running back and forth, in and out of the room, pacing.

"Please hurry. . . . Please hurry." Paul heard his wife say this several times.

The problem for Paul was that there wasn't anyone on the other end of that line. Sheila had never dialed 911. It was a staged call. And, boy, was she *some* actress! Paul later described Sheila in this moment, explaining how her voice sounded as if she was "panting . . . scared in a startled—in a startled way, [while] talking on the phone."

So now they waited for an ambulance that was not coming.

"I need to see the wound," Paul said. "Go get the mirror from the bathroom and hold it up so I can see. . . ."

He was breathless, still lying on the floor on his side.

Sheila did what she was told.

Looking into the mirror, Paul was confused.

"I didn't see any depth to [the wounds]. [They] looked more like scrapes," he reflected later. "So I didn't suspect anything at that point."

Paul still believed something had fallen on him and that was how he had been injured. He had no idea Sheila had stabbed him repeatedly in the chest, with the intent of killing him.

"I thought maybe she had fallen on me . . . or she had some kind of seizure. I couldn't really understand what was going on with the . . . the strength of the blow." The wallop had felt so powerful and sudden and heavy.

Paul stared at the candle on the floor before him. In and out of a slight daze—as he was losing blood and sweating and breathing heavily, gasping for air—the thought came to Paul that maybe there had been a wire inside the candle. As the candle fell on him, perhaps that wire inside it punctured his chest.

"It really didn't make any sense."

Nowhere in there, of course, was the notion that his wife was waiting for him to die. Or, even worse, that she had stabbed him!

Paul was losing a battle with a body reacting to being traumatized by knife wounds, though. He didn't feel he had the energy to move.

Some time passed.

"Where is the ambulance? What's taking so long?" Paul asked. "Call again, Sheila. . . ."

Sheila picked up the phone—Paul saw her do this—and made it appear as if she was once again dialing 911.

She wasn't.

Paul listened as Sheila seemed to speak to someone on the other end of the line.

"Let me talk to the operator," Paul said. "Put the phone up to my ear. . . ."

"The operator doesn't want to speak to you," Sheila responded. "She just wants you to lie down flat. . . . There are two ambulances out. . . . There's a delay of some sort. Two ambulances are on other calls, Paul. One is a stroke case. . . . The other . . ." She stopped short. "It's going to be about twenty-five minutes, they said."

This is bullshit, Paul thought. And although he was confused about what was going on, he was upset that no one was responding to Sheila's call. Why wasn't the call being bounced to another ambulance company? Was this some sort of joke?

Paul was fading . . . fast.

"Where's the key to the handcuffs?" During this crisis, Paul actually was embarrassed. He had a sudden anxious moment where he saw the ambulance showing up and there he was bound by a set of handcuffs, with panty hose on the floor. He and his wife claiming to be playing some sort of game that wasn't sexual.

Right.

Sheila was on the phone with 911, she said. Plus, she didn't know where the handcuff key was.

"Let me talk to the operator. . . ."

"You can't, Paul. She wants you to just *stay calm.*"

Paul was in pain—lots and lots of pain.

Shit, I've got a punctured lung, he thought.

There was a little bit of blood on the carpet, Paul noticed.

"She said"—Sheila added, still apparently on the phone with the 911 operator—"that your sense of time is probably off because you're hurt."

Sheila eventually hung up with the operator. She left the room and came back with some NyQuil.

"Take this," Sheila said.

"No, I don't want NyQuil, Sheila."

Paul was able to jostle one of his hands out of one side of the handcuffs and break free that side, while the cuffs dangled from the other hand.

Then he stood up best he could and found his way over to a futon in the same room, plopping himself down onto it, sitting upright.

At this point, Sheila left the room perhaps—Paul thought—to go out and try to find a neighbor or someone who might be able to help him. The motivating idea was that Paul needed to get to a hospital quickly or he was not going to make it.

So Paul waited.

Then he stood and walked into the living room before falling down onto the couch there.

Sheila was still inside the house.

"Okay," Sheila said, "I'm going now to the [local walk-in clinic] to see if I can find someone." She also said something about locating a neighbor.

Five minutes went by and Sheila returned.

No way she could have gone to the docs and come back in that amount of time, Paul thought. His sense of time was definitely not off in any way.

"But you must understand, I am disorientated at that point," Paul recalled.

Exactly what Sheila had planned and prepared for.

Sheila then curled up behind Paul on the couch and put her arms around him as if to snuggle.

"You're so brave, Paul. I love you. I love you."

"You know, Sheila, things haven't been all that good between us. We've really got to work on things."

"I know, Paul, I know."

Paul was restless. He sat up.

"Nothing I do helps you," Sheila said.

"I'm not good, Sheila," Paul said with a lethargic whisper. He was dizzy and breathing heavily. He was still sweating.

Sheila got up and walked away. Then she came back.

"I found the key," she said.

What Paul didn't know then was that when Sheila had gone outside supposedly to go to the doctor's and/or find a neighbor, she had made another call.

This one was for real.

CHAPTER 51

NELSON SESSLER WAS near the connector pointing him to the Newburgh–Beacon Bridge. He was driving by himself. Listening to music. Watching the traffic pass by.

And then his cell phone rang.

Nelson looked down and saw that it was Sheila.

"Hello?"

"Hey . . . you want to come over for dinner tonight?" Sheila asked. She was standing outside her Pleasantville condo.

Paul, of course, was inside.

Dying.

"Yeah, yeah . . . sounds great," Nelson said. "It's actually right on my way back home. I'll be passing through there later on."

When asked by police in the weeks to come, Nelson never said he spoke to Sheila earlier that day and asked her if he could come over. Sheila, however, claimed differently, saying: "I called Nelson . . . because he was supposed to come over that evening. He called me earlier to say that he was on his way and would stop by. I had thought I would send Paul to his parents' again and Nelson would come over. . . . [But] after the stabbing, I went outside with the phone and called Nelson and told him *not* to come over."

This statement is simply not true. Phone records prove as much.

Whatever the case, Nelson was still far from Sheila's condo. It would take him a few hours to get to Pleasantville from where he was.

Sheila told Nelson, in fact, that his timing couldn't have been better. The time frame for when he was arriving in the area would work out well for her. She had a few errands she needed to complete—one of which included finishing the job of killing her husband.

CHAPTER 52

NEAR THE TIME of the attack on Paul, Sheila later claimed (for the first time ever), she was having "visions"—actual psychotic sightings of various beings. There was one time, near Thanksgiving 2002, when Sheila insisted she was standing by the window in her Pleasantville condo living room. She was staring blankly out the windowpane when, out of nowhere, "this dark figure" appeared before her.

Sheila was startled. She watched as this dark figure "picked up a book and ripp[ed] it up" in front of her. It was as clear to her as if someone was projecting a film.

As she came out of the spell, Sheila looked down.

There was the book, torn in two, in her hands.

"I thought I was losing my mind," she said later.

It was then that Sheila decided she needed to begin meditating each morning to clear those demons from her thoughts at the start of each day.

As far as Paul and hurting him, Sheila wasn't "really angry at Paul," she later explained to her psychiatrist. She was referring to, of course, that day in March 2003 when she stuck that paring knife into Paul's chest several times while playing "the game." The thing about this revelation, however, was that Sheila failed to note that as they waited for an ambulance that was never coming, she was preparing to stick her husband again—and kill him, once and for all.

"Paul was as sweet as pie," Sheila recalled during that same session.

What truly pissed her off that day, Sheila claimed, was that inside her mind, as Paul guessed those objects she had rubbed up against him, she grew angrier and angrier each time Paul guessed right. This rage was internalized and growing all because she couldn't stand the idea that Paul was beating her at the game. According to Sheila's skewed excuse, it was a brewing combination of Paul winning the game and that "dark figure" Sheila claimed had been following her around taking over her thoughts.

Nothing more.

That was the reason, she told her therapist, she had stabbed Paul repeatedly.

It wasn't because of Nelson. Or because of wanting Paul out of the way. It was rage brought on by Paul winning the game.

After she stabbed Paul, Sheila concluded to her doctor, "I froze. I have a knife in my hand and Paul is squirming. I was scared."

The implication she gave was that she had no idea how Paul had been stabbed—or by whom. It was as if that dark figure, strong enough to tear a book in two with her bare hands, had come out and decided to kill Paul.

Sheila had no control.

But Sheila and—oh yeah—that affair she was having with Nelson, and that murder she'd committed already, that had nothing to do with it.

CHAPTER 53

BACK INSIDE THE Pleasantville condo, Paul and Sheila sat in the living room on the couch "waiting" for what Paul believed was an ambulance on its way—however late it was running. Time was running out for Paul Christos. What he didn't know was that one of the knife wounds Sheila had delivered "nicked the head of the lateral to the left descending artery" going into his heart. Left untreated, Paul was going to die. He was losing blood and breath and feeling the effects of that particular wound.

Dizziness. Shock.

And soon: unconsciousness.

Then death.

Sheila looked on, undoubtedly, anticipating her husband's demise, patiently waiting for it to take place. She would later claim she was out of it and fading in between the presence of that dark figure and reality. From Paul's account, however, this woman was calm, cool, and collected, even rubbing his back at one point while whispering "I love you" in his ear. Moreover, as Paul thought about it later, he began to see that Sheila had suggested they go see his mother earlier that same day so he could have one last visit with her before Sheila killed him. How diabolical and evil was that? Bringing the guy over to his mother's so he could see her before she would soon hear of his death?

"I love you," Sheila said, holding Paul up on the couch. This happened after Paul told his wife that it felt better to sit up. He could breathe more easily.

Paul contemplated the idea of demanding that Sheila take him to the hospital in one of their cars. But he weighed it against the notion that as soon as they left, the ambulance would pull in.

Then, without thinking about it any further, Paul said to screw it: "Let's go!"

He stood.

Sheila said, "Put on your jacket."

What a strange request!

"But I figured that she was embarrassed if anyone would see what happened . . . all that blood on my shirt." By now, the front of Paul's shirt was fairly saturated with a patch of his own blood running from his chest down to the end of his shirt near his waist. It was dark and tacky.

Sheila helped Paul put on his jacket and shoes.

"I'll be right back," Sheila said.

Paul waited.

"And she actually went down and got my car," Paul recalled, "and brought it to the front entrance of the condo."

Paul had no indication that his wife had tried killing him and was planning, at that moment, to make her next move to finish him off. The things she did made Paul feel as if she wanted to help. Paul hadn't seen a knife. He was still under the impression that the candle had cut him somehow.

Sheila helped Paul into his car. She drove, obviously. They discussed where the best place would be and both agreed on the Westchester Medical Center, a set of medical buildings both of them were familiar with, having gone to graduate school there. Moreover, Sheila's brother had been a patient in the psychiatric unit of the center, and Sheila's mother had even worked as an operating nurse at one of the facilities for the past eighteen years.

Paul got into the backseat. He sat up, leaning his head and body against the door and window.

"Go!"

Sheila took off and drove toward the back exit of the condo complex, not a frequently used route to get onto the main road, but one that Sheila, Paul considered, used from time to time.

"It was an unusual way to go . . . winding roads . . . ," Paul remembered.

Especially odd when the driver was supposedly in a hurry to get to a hospital.

Where is she going? Paul wondered.

After getting onto the road toward the medical center, Sheila pulled over and got out of the car.

Paul didn't understand what was going on.

Sheila opened the back door. "Lay down. . . . Please lay down. You'll feel better maybe, if you lay down flat."

"No, I feel better sitting up. . . . Just go!"

This is taking too long. I cannot believe how long this is taking. I'll drive to the hospital if I have to, Paul thought. He felt he could easily drive the car himself.

What in the world was Sheila doing? Time was not on their side. The center was maybe a six- or seven-minute ride on a good day.

"I'll drive, Sheila," Paul blurted out angrily.

"No, you cannot drive."

Sheila hopped back into the driver's seat and took off— this time going the proper way, toward the medical center.

As she drove, Sheila kept staring at Paul through the car's rearview mirror. ("She was hoping that I passed out," Paul later speculated.) Paul became concerned with Sheila not keeping her eyes on the road. She was swerving all over the place. He kept telling her, "Keep your eyes on the road. . . . Stop looking back at me. Keep your eyes where you're driving."

Sheila approached the medical center on Walker Road in Valhalla, New York, just off Grasslands Road and the Saw Mill River Parkway. She pulled into the Behavioral Health Center (BHC) portion of the lot. There are several lots, actually, encompassing what is a large facility with different buildings. The emergency room portion of the center, however, was well marked. It was clear where to drive and drop someone off at the ER.

But this was not where Sheila headed as she pulled in.

Paul wondered why she was driving toward the BHC in the back.

Maybe she knows where she's going. . . .

The parking lot was rather empty and unattended, since it was a Sunday. There were no guards on duty. Things seemed pretty slow.

Sheila pulled around toward the back of the parking lot. It felt to Paul in that moment as if she was driving away from the entrance.

Paul asked, "Is that the emergency room?" And as they drove farther away from it, he thought: *Maybe we can just walk to the ER. . . . Perhaps she doesn't know exactly where the ER entrance is.*

"I think so," Sheila said, continuing on toward the back of the parking lot (away from everything, where there was no one around), and then parking the vehicle not in a white-lined parking spot, but "kind of like near the edge of the parking lot."

Paul still considered that maybe they were going to walk from the car to the building's entrance; Sheila knew more than he did about entering the facility. Certainly, the last thing on his mind was that Sheila was actually biding her time, hoping he would pass out and eventually die.

Paul had no idea, but Sheila had taken with her the knife that she had used back at the condo to stab him with. She had it in the front seat by her side.

Sheila turned off the ignition and dropped the keys on the floor by her feet.

Purposely, Paul thought in passing as he watched her. *Weird. Why is she doing that?*

Paul shuffled a bit to try and get out of the car. His mind was focused on the ER entrance and getting some help. His foot, however, became lodged behind the passenger seat and he had trouble maneuvering himself out of the vehicle. His energy level was low, of course; now Paul was even dizzier and entirely winded. Still, as he watched Sheila get out of the car, he believed she was coming around to his side to help him out.

Sheila, though, had other things on her mind.

"Help me out here," Paul said.

Sheila walked over. Approached her husband. Not saying a word.

Paul watched as she reached down to, what he thought, dislodge his stuck foot so he could get up on his feet and exit the car—that is, until he looked Sheila in the face.

She had an "angry" pinch to her face, Paul recalled. She had seemed "normal" and "fine" up to that point while driving the car. But now?

Sheila Davalloo was a woman on a mission.

Had the dark figure returned?

Not a chance.

Sheila knew *exactly* what she was doing.

Within a split second, just as Paul realized something was wrong with the way Sheila looked, she lunged at him forcefully.

He felt something slice into him.

("A sharp jab in the chest.")

"Sheila . . . what's going on?" Paul pleaded.

He looked up and saw that Sheila was recoiling.

Resetting was probably a better way to describe this action.

Then Paul saw the knife—for the first time—clenched in Sheila's hand like a villain in a horror film.

Sheila was preparing to stab him again.

Paul looked on as Sheila backed her way out of the car. What he didn't see was that Sheila had lifted the knife up above her shoulder to prepare her delivery of what she hoped would be the final blow.

CHAPTER 54

SHEILA DAVALLOO WENT to a private school as a child growing up in Virginia. She was brought up in the Muslim faith. If asked about her childhood, Sheila would say she walked and talked "earlier than most children," although she never gave any specifics. "Adolescent, behavioral problems," as Sheila termed them, began when she was five years old, and continued until she was thirteen. Part of this, she claimed, was because of her upbringing, which Sheila routinely described as trouble-free and rather normal; yet the "frequent arguments" around the house with her parents she witnessed and took part in affected her immensely. Sheila liked to lie to her parents and rarely did what she was told. She even called herself "self-centered and willful" during this period.

Her history is devoid of any incidents of childhood violence, a doctor analyzing Sheila for psychotic disorders later wrote, *fire setting, bizarre behaviors, or significant mental health problems that required any professional attention.*

Depending upon who is asked, though, there are two camps of opinion regarding Sheila's mental health. Another doctor, one in Sheila's corner, said, "She cannot adequately control intrapsychic forces and has demonstrated self-defeating periods of emotional, cognitive, and behavioral dysfunction."

"Intrapsychic forces" are, basically, inner conflicts within the personality: *An emotional clash of opposing impulses within oneself, of the id versus the ego or the ego versus the superego,* according to *Mosby's Medical Dictionary.*

In the years after Sheila found herself facing the slow hand of justice, that same doctor said, she showed "signs of identity disturbance, being impulse ridden, unstable in love relations, and she can become intensely volatile and angry."

Interestingly, in looking at Sheila's behaviors during this period when she carefully planned and executed the murder of Anna Lisa and then planned and carried out a premeditated attack on Paul, her doctor claimed Sheila "did not fully know what she was doing was wrong, because her mind was poisoned with fragmented psychotic precepts."

He went on to claim Sheila felt "overly sensitive and often misunderstood." He said she had a "depressive disorder"; and although she had not shown any sign of a psychotic disorder while with him, Sheila was at risk of "psychotic episodes when under sustained periods of distress."

Other psychologists who interviewed Sheila during this period would later argue that this analysis was nonsense. It was a careful design by Sheila, after being caught with the canary in her mouth, to explain away her crimes. And Sheila's history growing up pretty much sums up and backs up the opposing analysis. There was no history in Sheila's background to support that "dark figure" contention on her part. The dark figure came into the picture only when Sheila found herself facing time in prison.

She invented it, in other words, when she needed it.

When Sheila entered the ninth grade, she began attending public schools. She never dated "as an adolescent." This type of socializing was forbidden by her parents. And within what was a volatile relationship Sheila had with her parents, for as long as she could recall, she always found a way to make things worse by bickering and fighting with them as she matured into a young adult. After one such argument with her parents, which turned into a meltdown by Sheila when she was fourteen, she took what she believed was an overdose of Tylenol. But Sheila never intended to kill herself; the incident was described later by her doctor as being "partially motivated by her attention-getting needs."

By the time she was sixteen years of age, Sheila was living with her family in California. Those years she talked about as being inconsequential. Nothing much of anything happened. Sheila got along with her brother and, as had been the case since she could recall, fought aggressively with her parents over just about everything.

After she turned seventeen, Sheila moved with her parents to where work had taken the Davalloos: Westchester County.

It was while Sheila was overseas, after she married Amir, that her brother developed psychiatric problems and was placed in medical care for mental-health issues. This followed a pattern, Sheila claimed, of a "family history . . . of heroin abuse and undiagnosed psychiatric problems"—and yet none of this had any effect on her. It was no one in her immediate family. There were "issues" Sheila had with her brother while growing up, she claimed, but she refused to talk about them in any detail.

Sheila repeatedly denied ever being sexually abused.

In short, despite some authority issues with her parents, Sheila Davalloo grew up in a respectable, happy family with money, and she never talked about having any difficulties or emotional problems in school or at home that would result in the dramatic "depressive disorder" and personality conflict she later described.

CHAPTER 55

IT WAS A SURREAL moment for Paul. If not for the shiny knife blade he now saw with his own eyes, Paul would not have believed what was happening. In that moment, that one split second of lucidity, as Sheila prepared to stab him again, Paul figured out that the wounds on his chest he had sustained back at the condo were, in fact, stab wounds. His wife had stabbed him! It suddenly all made sense to Paul. A moment of clarity came at a time when Sheila was trying to finish him off.

So Paul put up his hands to fight back, thinking, *My wife is trying to kill me!*

"What are you doing?" Paul said reactively. "Oh, my God. You're trying to kill me! What are you doing, Sheila? Stop!"

The moment was chaotic. A fight had ensued between a terribly injured man and his wife.

A fight to the death.

Paul got his bearings and "somehow," he said, "I pushed my way out of the car."

He stood in the parking lot. Sheila was in front of him, holding the knife.

Instinctively, Paul grabbed Sheila by the wrists. Then he put one hand over the blade.

The sharp steel stung his palm like an electric shock, slicing into his skin.

Coldly, in an unfamiliar voice, Sheila said: "You're taking me away from my brother. I cannot let you do that. I love my brother. I love my brother."

"That's not true, Sheila. I'm not taking you away from your brother. What are you *talking* about?"

There were several kids off in the distance playing basketball. They did not seem to notice what was going on. Paul put an eye on them, however.

"You've been pressuring me a lot about not wanting to leave the condo," Sheila said, apparently trying to explain herself, then adding, "I'm sick, and I'm taking my brother's medication."

Paul held on to the knife blade. He pleaded with her. "Let go of the knife, Sheila."

Paul was not going to die here in this parking lot, with the damn emergency room in sight, so close to being helped.

Not a chance.

They worked their way over to a grassy area, the edge of the lot. Blood was now pouring plentifully out of Paul from the latest wound he sustained in the car. His shirt was soaked and sticking to his skin, the open wounds throbbing as blood pumped out of them.

"Look," Sheila said angrily, "you're taking me away from my brother, and I *cannot* let you do that."

Paul was baffled by this statement when he considered it later. Even at that point, Sheila still maintained the lie: her brother.

("She could have easily said it was Nelson at that moment," Paul reflected. It was clear to Paul that Sheila was not in some sort of psychotic haze; she knew what she was saying.)

"Let go of the knife, Sheila. . . ."

Paul looked down at his shirt and saw all the blood.

Clearly, I don't have much time, he thought. Then: *What do people in the movies do in this situation?*

That thought led to another thought and an action.

Paul head-butted Sheila. She fell back a bit, but the blow did not faze her in the least.

"Help me, Paul . . . ," Sheila said.

Sheila let go of the knife.

Paul held it now in his hand. He looked at the knife, then at Sheila.

She stared at him.

"I'm sorry, Sheila, but I'm going to have to kill *you* now," Paul said.

CHAPTER 56

WHEN SHE LATER discussed her life leading up to these two defining moments—committing murder (which Sheila would never concede) and attacking her husband with the intent of killing him—Sheila said she was in "a steady decline in overall functioning." She had become "excessively moody and depressed." She blamed Paul for working a lot and teaching and not being around, which had, in turn, according to her, caused Sheila to suffer "even more stress." Then there were manic, impulsive moments, she admitted, when she'd jet off to see a friend in California or "embark on excessive-spending sprees."

All of it, Sheila said, trying her best to get out of the predicament she found herself in at the time, led to a time in her life when she could not be held responsible for her actions. It was someone else. Another mind altogether.

It was that dark figure.

In other words, it appeared that it was the stress of life that everyone goes through—life's realities—that caused Sheila Davalloo to commit two horribly violent acts, which, when boiled right down to it, were carried out in order to get a man—or, rather, what Sheila Davalloo *wanted* as the end result, getting a new lover.

Paul had always believed Sheila's debt was somewhere near $40,000 to $50,000. However, she had accumulated $20,000 in debt during 2002 alone, on top of an additional $40,000 she had on the books already going into that year. When Sheila refinanced the condo, she said she "satisfied the first set of her debts of approximately sixty thousand dollars. . . ."

And this was a woman who made a six-figure income at the time.

In speaking of Nelson, Sheila noted how even though she believed Nelson was a player and had been, according to her memory, "typically involved with a number of women," she "threw herself at him." She even admitted that Nelson was not really into her and was likely using her for sex, but she "began to fall in love with him." And so, what was she supposed to do? Just let him go?

Point, in fact, Sheila Davalloo was a manipulator. There can be no argument about this fact. As she sat and spoke to her psychologist later (long after both of those violent incidents she had perpetrated and had been involved in), Sheila played every role she believed would allow her a reprieve from having to acknowledge that she committed such terrible crimes. She cried and got angry. She came across as depressed, withdrawn, staring off into space. She "behaved in an apprehensive manner during the [forensic] interview." She claimed to have been suffering from an "ongoing" bout with severe anxiety. There was an incident, she added, which had occurred at the hospital where she was being interviewed, when she "freaked out and needed oral administration of psychotropic medication." In this case, the drug was Ativan.[2]

---

[2] The generic lorazepam, as it is more commonly called, is a "high-potency" antianxiety drug. A controlled substance, the drug is designed to calm people down.

It was during this same period that Sheila reported she was feeling impulses to wash her hands repeatedly because of "obsessive thoughts revolving around contamination."

Sheila had never seen a psychiatric doctor before 2002. She'd never had any trouble whatsoever with having a disorder of the mind or showed zero signs of obsessive-compulsive disorder (OCD). It was as if she had developed these disorders after murdering Anna Lisa and attacking Paul.

Furthermore, during this same interview, Sheila's doctor, after asking her several questions, wrote this note: *There were no concrete delusions or hallucinations admitted to.*

Where had that dark figure gone?

When she later discussed for a second time the book being ripped in two by the dark figure, Sheila described it as "going into a trancelike mental state." During these episodes, "everything in her visual field [became] black and white." She claimed to have had partial memory loss during this time.

When she comes out of these dissociative-like states, the doctor wrote, *she observes the results of her actions but does not remember how it all took place.*

Some would call this "volcanic rage"—a mind state that murderers need to enter in order to commit the crime—although they are well aware of what's going on around them. Another disorder that might explain Sheila's behavior (but certainly not excuse it in any way), which all her therapists missed, is called intermittent explosive disorder (IED). The Mayo Clinic describes it this way: *Intermittent explosive disorder involves repeated episodes of impulsive, aggressive, violent behavior or angry verbal outbursts in which you react grossly out of proportion to the situation. Road rage, domestic abuse, throwing or breaking objects, or other temper tantrums may be signs. . . . People with intermittent explosive disorder may attack others and their possessions, causing bodily injury and property damage. . . .*[3]

Now, add to that IED armchair diagnosis the fact that Sheila could unquestionably be considered a clinical sociopath and narcissist and there is one hell of a time bomb moving through life in search of an ignition for her fuse.

From all the evidence left behind, there is no doubt Sheila carefully and methodically planned and carried out Anna's murder and the attack on Paul—all because she wanted to be with a man. In fact, one could go all the way back to the summer of 2002, before she murdered Anna Lisa, and see clear signs of a sound person planning a murder—not a sick, twisted woman in a "dark" state. Sheila was with a friend and her friend's husband one day.

"You know where I can buy a stun gun?" Sheila asked the friend's husband.

"They're illegal, Sheila," the husband had said.

"So you have no idea where I can get one?"

"You can buy one from the back of a magazine. . . . Try *Soldier of Fortune*. I believe it's legal in California. When I lived there, I had a roommate who owned one."

Some time went by. They all got together again. Sheila explained how she had gone to California on a trip to see a friend.

"I bought a stun gun while I was there," Sheila bragged.

[3] For more information about this disorder, treatment options, and references to study it in more depth, go to: http://www.mayoclinic.com/health/intermittent-explosive-disorder/DS00730.

CHAPTER 57

"PLEASE DON'T," Sheila pleaded.

It had been a sarcastic remark: "I'm sorry, Sheila, but I'm going to have to kill *you* now." Paul had said it because he wanted to scare Sheila and let her know the "game" she was playing, it was all over. She was not going to kill him—at least not on this day. He had fought back and had won.

Paul stepped backward, about twenty feet, away from Sheila, putting distance between them. There was a pile of red building bricks behind him. Two piles, actually, close together.

Looking into the pile of bricks, Paul found a deep crack and placed the knife in between, allowing it to fall so as not to be accessible by either of them.

"I just wanted to get rid of the knife. . . . At this point, I'm thinking she's crazy, like out of her mind. I'm still . . . as crazy as it sounds, I am still protective of her somewhat. I just knew I needed to get this knife away from the both of us."

Sheila watched Paul ditch the knife. She said, "Good . . . good, Paul. . . . You got rid of the knife."

Paul didn't know what she meant. Was Sheila assuming he was covering up for her? That this was all going to go away?

But Sheila then rushed Paul and grabbed onto him.

"Paul . . . please stay with me. Please. Stay. With. Me. Talk to me. Talk to me, Paul."

"I gotta go get help, Sheila."

"Please stay. . . ."

Paul yelled over to the kids playing basketball. "Help me. . . . Help!" Paul needed medical attention quickly. Sheila wasn't making any move to get him to the ER. "Help me!"

The kids looked toward Paul and Sheila and stopped dribbling, but they did not seem to hear what he had said, or they didn't want to get involved.

Sheila had a good grip on Paul. She wasn't letting go. Paul was trying to get away from her, but he had trouble.

Then Paul took a swing at his wife.

He missed.

But it was enough to brush Sheila off him.

He had broken free.

Sheila must have fallen as Paul pushed away from her, because she was on the ground, now grabbing desperately and aggressively at his jacket.

Paul ran. Up ahead, about two hundred yards away, was the entrance to the BHC, where Sheila's brother used to stay when he had his moments.

Paul saw two people standing out front.

"Hey!" he yelled. "Help me. . . . I've been stabbed!"

Both people turned and saw him.

CHAPTER 58

SHEILA CAME RUNNING up behind Paul as he approached the two people standing in front of the building—one of whom was a medical resident.

Sheila must have heard what Paul had said, because she shouted, "No . . . that's not true. He attacked . . . *me!*"

By now, Paul couldn't stand. He was actually sitting on the curb out in front of the medical center. Spent. Barely able to lift his arms. Move his feet.

Sheila looked toward him. "He needs help," she said to the two people, suddenly dropping her lie of Paul attacking her.

"Please call 911," Paul said. He was out of breath. "Please . . ."

The medical resident used his cell phone to dial up someone from the hospital.

Sheila, at that point, took off.

A few moments went by. As Paul was talking to the two people now attending to him, Sheila pulled up in the car.

Getting out, Paul said she "still appeared somewhat irrational." He thought he heard her say, "He attacked me."

Sheila walked up close and personal to Paul. In a near

whisper, she said, "Don't you say anything or I will get into trouble." Addressing the two people standing there, Sheila said, "I can take him to the emergency room. Let him come with me."

"No . . . there's an ambulance coming. . . . He can stay right here."

One of the guys walked over to the car and grabbed the keys out of the ignition so Sheila couldn't take off in it.

Sheila sat down next to Paul. "You cannot say what happened or I'll get in trouble."

"Go away. Get away from me. Just leave. Leave the area."

After the concerned citizen made the call, the scene quickly filled in with police, an ambulance, and EMTs. Paul was placed in the back of the ambulance and prepared for a ride to the ER—finally. As EMTs did this, an on-scene cop hopped into the ambulance (standard policy in a case like this) and asked Paul what was going on.

Paul explained best he could, realizing the hastiness of the moment, even telling the officer where they could recover the knife.

Sheila was then taken into custody by another patrolman, who soon arrived, and was put into the backseat of a cruiser.

Paul was losing his battle, however. He was rushed to the ER. Inside the ambulance, he asked the EMT: "Am I going to die?"

The EMT did not answer.

After ER doctors hooked Paul up to an echocardiogram, they decided that closing the wounds with some stitches wasn't going to be enough. There had been one wound to an artery connecting to his heart and it had the potential to kill him.

"Is there someone you'd like us to call for you?" a nurse asked.

"My mother," Paul said. "But please don't call her . . . until my father gets home."

After a bit of discussion among doctors, it was decided that Paul needed open-heart surgery right away. It could not wait.

CHAPTER 59

WHEN PAUL CHRISTOS woke up postsurgery, he could not believe who was there, standing bedside, staring down at him.

Am I dreaming? Hallucinating?

It was Sheila's mother standing over Paul, looking down at him.

This must be some sort of plot to get rid of me!

As he stared at her, Paul said, he was thinking, "I'm wondering if I had stumbled on to some international terrorist cell or something and they all got together to get rid of me. Now here's Sheila's mother to finish me off!"

Mrs. Davalloo, however, was "actually concerned."

"What happened to you, Paul?" she asked.

Right then, another nurse came over and said, "You cannot be here . . . only immediate family members."

Mrs. Davalloo left.

Paul was doing pretty well, all considering. He was in and out of it while in recovery, but also fairly stabilized, seeing as he'd had open-heart surgery. Here was a healthy thirty-two-year-old man who would probably come out of it all okay in the end. It was a good thing Paul had fought the way he did. Any additional time and he would have likely had a heart attack.

While waiting to hear on his long-term prognosis after that initial evaluation by doctors, a Westchester County police officer walked into the room to speak with Paul.

"Can you answer a few questions, Mr. Christos?"

Paul thought he could.

It was 6:23 P.M. as Paul gave the best statement he could at the time about what had just happened. The first thing he said was "She blindfolded and handcuffed me to the chair."

As Paul talked his way through what turned out to be a one-page report, the one line the officer was looking for came near the end: *"I realized she was trying to kill me."*

It was enough to arrest Sheila Davalloo on charges of aggravated assault and bring her into the Westchester County PD for questioning.

CHAPTER 60

NELSON PULLED UP to the Pleasantville condo not long after Paul gave that incriminating statement about Sheila to police back inside the hospital. Noticing some action going on near Sheila's condo, Nelson parked his vehicle close to the front door. As he took the keys from the ignition, he saw cops swarming around Sheila's place.

What in the world?

Nelson walked up to the door. A uniformed officer stopped him.

"What's going on?" Nelson asked.

"There's been a domestic dispute, sir."

Nelson and the cop discussed the name of the woman who lived there, who Nelson was in relation to her, and why he was there.

Dinner with Sheila Davalloo?

Not tonight.

As he thought about it, however, domestic disputes generally involved a husband and wife, boyfriend and girlfriend. Nelson was puzzled in that regard.

"Somebody went to the hospital—one of them was stabbed," the cop told Nelson. "Her husband."

Husband?

Nelson thought Sheila had been twice divorced. It didn't make sense.

After speaking with the cop a bit more, Nelson took off toward his home in Stamford.

"That evening," he explained later, "I was thinking that . . . she had some altercation with a divorced husband. An ex-husband had come back."

Nelson had no idea that within forty-eight hours, police would be knocking on his door, wondering why he never came forward and said he'd been having an affair with Sheila Davalloo. Yes, Nelson Sessler was going to have a lot of explaining to do in the near future.

On that following Monday, Nelson was at his office, keeping busy, when two coworkers approached him. One of them held a piece of paper.

"You see this?"

"What?" Nelson asked, taking what looked to be a newspaper article.

He read it: Sheila Davalloo had stabbed her husband.

"I'm flabbergasted," Nelson said about his reaction at that moment. "From this article, [I understand] that she had stabbed her husband—and it sounded like a current husband."

Later, on the witness stand (under oath), Nelson claimed right after talking to those coworkers he went for the phone and dialed up the SPD (the day after Paul was stabbed). "And so I called the Stamford Police Department," Nelson testified, "and the individual who I spoke with before there, an officer. And I told him that he should look into Sheila Davalloo."

The fact that Sheila had invited Nelson over for dinner on the night she stabbed her husband made Nelson believe there was "some kind of [a] setup" going on. Had Sheila invited him over so he could help her kill Paul?

What he meant, clearly, by that "look into Sheila Davalloo"

comment was that he now viewed Sheila as a person of interest in Anna Lisa's murder.

Questions arise, however, regarding this contention Nelson later made in court. Why didn't he explain to the Westchester County Police Department patrolman he spoke to on Sheila's doorstep that night, for example, that he had been intimate with Sheila? Or, at the least, demand to speak with a WCPD detective? Why not call his contact at the SPD right away? Why (if he actually did) wait an entire day to make that supposed call? (No report of Nelson's "call" on that day to the SPD exists.)

"That is the *first* time I have ever heard that!" Detective Greg Holt said later. "Tommy [McGinty] and I were the only ones speaking to Nelson. . . . If we had a lead like that, we would have run with it immediately *and* found out about Sessler and Davalloo *before* Westchester [came to us]."

Frightened now of what he had done—or not done, rather—Nelson still did not admit that he'd been having relations with Sheila both before and after Anna's murder.

After hanging up with the SPD, Nelson claimed he made another call.

This time, it was to his lawyer. They spoke for quite a long time. Nelson spilled everything.

The advice his lawyer gave him?

"Don't talk to the police anymore."

ACT FOUR

THE CLIMAX

CHAPTER 61

DETECTIVE ALISON CARPENTIER was working the four-to-twelve shift on Sunday, March 23, 2003, when a call about "a man who had been stabbed . . . and is heading into surgery at Westchester Medical Center" came over the radio.

The detective hit the lights on her unmarked cruiser and dashed off to the scene.

Carpentier is a tall, attractive, and engaging middle-aged woman, with long black hair and a very thick, very noticeable, Long Island, New York, accent. Carpentier pulled up to the medical center just before six-thirty, walked by a cruiser parked out front with its lights on, leaned down, and looked inside.

Sheila was in the backseat.

"Suspect?" Carpentier asked the patrolman watching over Sheila.

"Yup."

"Take her back to headquarters," Carpentier said. By this time, Carpentier had been given a brief account of the circumstances surrounding Sheila's apprehension and what had happened to Paul. "Don't talk to her. . . . Don't say anything to her. . . . Just bring her back to headquarters."

"Right."

Carpentier watched as the patrolman drove away with Sheila in the backseat. The seasoned detective thought: *Another routine domestic disturbance.*

Indeed. Cops saw it all the time. Husband and wife fight. The neighbor calls the cops. The wife or husband wants to press charges. But then, he or she drops the case after thinking about it. They go home and have make-up sex. Six months later, they're fighting again. Carpentier believed she'd take a walk around the crime scene, develop some evidence, and then she'd question Paul. After that, she would go back to the station and interview Sheila, fill out the paperwork, and let the courts figure the rest out from there. Of course, Detective Carpentier had no idea that by stepping into this situation between Paul and Sheila, she was also getting involved in a brutal, unsolved homicide in Connecticut—one for which Carpentier would soon hold a very important key.

Before heading into the hospital to speak with Paul, Carpentier walked the crime scene and checked things out. The car itself had blood all over the backseat area, where Paul had sat, and also a good amount on the door. The curb out in front of the center had some of Paul's blood stained on the tar. It looked like someone had spilled a can of dark red paint. Over by where they had fought, one of Paul's shoes had been found.

Things got out of hand, Carpentier told herself. *There was a dispute and the wife acted out.*

She'd seen this sort of thing time and again. People who supposedly loved each other could be more vicious than those who supposedly hated each other. When veteran cops are asked, they will admit that it never ceases to amaze them what human beings will do to each other in the confines of their own homes under the umbrella of "love."

As Carpentier walked around the scene with a patrolman

and evidence technicians, an officer came out of the center and said, "They're rushing him into surgery. She got him in the heart."

Carpentier had seen the knife. It struck her that the blade was so short, maybe three to four inches long.

Still, it was clear from what doctors discovered after evaluating and working on Paul that had Sheila directed the knife just a smidgen to the left or right, north or south, it could have penetrated Paul's heart directly and killed him within moments. This beckoned Paul to later ask himself: *Didn't Sheila realize that she'd be the number one suspect? I mean, did she think she could kill me, stuff me in the closet, and then have dinner with Nelson inside the condo that same night?*

Apparently, she did.

Outside, Carpentier took a closer look at the knife, now inside a plastic evidence bag: "Man, to get him in the heart, she really had to use all of her might. The blade is *so* short."

This was the first red flag for Detective Alison Carpentier as she began investigating what looked to be nothing more than a routine domestic argument that had become violent and bloody.

CHAPTER 62

ALISON CARPENTIER IS one of those no-nonsense cops. She hardly took any crap from anyone. Born and raised in Valley Stream, Long Island, Carpentier was street-tough and suburban-smart woman, learning the ropes from her years of simply doing the job in one of the busiest, if not roughest, intersections of highway in the Northeast: the Long Island Expressway, the Bronx River Parkway, I-95, and the Henry Hudson Parkway, with several other tributaries and highways connecting to those. There was always something going on out there. It's a heavily populated, always busy, set of roadways connecting Manhattan with Long Island and Connecticut and New Jersey. Anything is possible at any time of the day. Calls come in of men masturbating in their vehicles while driving; women providing oral sex to drivers; people snorting coke off the dashboard; kids drinking and bouncing off the guardrails; drivers texting and talking; and the list of transgressions goes on and on.

There were no cops in Alison's family. The job was a vocation she felt would offer "something different" every day she went to work. The thought of slumming it in a cubicle farm or behind a desk all day—in and out, like a robot—did not appeal to Carpentier. She thrived on action and adventure and solving a new problem every day.

"Going into work and not knowing what to expect," Carpentier remarked. That's what she liked about the idea of becoming a cop.

Alison's mother was not so thrilled with her daughter becoming a cop. When she expressed her desire to join the police force, Alison was a twenty-two-year-old woman, with very little experience, who weighed a mere 110 pounds and stood five feet ten inches.

"Please don't do this," Alison's mother said.

"Ma . . ."

When the test results came in, and Alison held the envelope in her hand, her mother said, "In a way, I hope you fail. In another way, I hope you don't."

Alison knew her mother was supporting her.

The young, aspiring cadet had scored a perfect 100 on the exam and entered the Westchester County Police force after the police academy. Passing that test meant any police department in the county could call on her. Alison wanted the WCPD because they had a drug task force and a "mob squad," investigative unit.

She got it. Her first job was patrol.

For the next ten years, Carpentier drove the Henry Hudson Parkway and the Bronx River Parkway. One night early into her career, when she was traveling down the parkway, a young girl, bound and tied up, came hobbling out of the woods. She had been beaten and brutalized and savagely raped, not five minutes before Carpentier saw her.

"She wasn't even from New York," Carpentier recalled. "She was up here from the South, going to school. I think she'd been here a week or two."

They caught the guy later that same night, solely because the girl had given to Carpentier such a detailed description, right there on the scene. The girl had been jogging alone. The guy followed her. When she jogged down a path that was out of view, he attacked.

The lesson Carpentier learned: Expect anything at any time.

CHAPTER 63

SOMETHING DIDN'T SMELL right to Carpentier as she began thinking about Paul and Sheila. The detective was trying to figure out how an intelligent, learned person like Sheila Davalloo, who took home six figures, could not only act so stupidly, but wind up in the predicament she was in, and not have any explanation for it. There had to be more to it all, Carpentier sensed from the get-go. Why would Sheila want to kill her husband, as Paul had reported to the WCPD?

Carpentier is one of those officers never satisfied with a case until it is looked at closely and all the questions banging around her head are answered. She doesn't accept what is generally the norm: Most cases are what they seem, and are nothing else. Carpentier is one of those hungry cops, motivated by her instincts. During her ten years on patrol, Carpentier had done two years of undercover drug work, where she learned how to rely on her gut. It was throughout that time she began a long run of nominations by the lieutenants to become part of the WCPD's detective's unit (DU). However, Carpentier had been passed up on eight consecutive occasions, earning Alison the nickname of "the Susan Lucci of the DU's list." This was a nod to actress Susan Lucci who had been nominated for an Emmy for her work on the soap opera *All My Children* for nearly two decades before she actually won one. (Incidentally, this string of losses actually made Lucci a household name.)

Part of the WCPD major crimes unit, when the Paul Christos stabbing case came through, the life Carpentier led inside the DU usually meant at least one day or more a week of staying overnight and working twenty-four to thirty-six hours straight. Her husband knew that when Alison didn't show up for dinner, she was likely working a hot case that was going to take her away from the family for as long as she was needed.

"I kept a few changes of clothes at the department," Carpentier said. "If you caught a homicide, you did not go home until your leads ran out."

Carpentier prides herself on being a "nosy bitch."

"I'll start off busting a pickpocket," Carpentier explained, "and wind up taking down an entire credit card fraud ring."

So when they sat Sheila down, inside the Westchester County PD headquarters, and began asking her what was going on, Carpentier was immediately curious as to why there was no obvious motivation behind Sheila's mumbled responses. What had sparked this violent episode between a wife and her husband? Where was the reason, however stupid and licentious it might sound, for this woman to take a knife and stab her husband repeatedly?

They ended up bringing Sheila to the interview room several times. First, Carpentier was told by Sheila that Paul came home with wounds and she did not know how he got them.

"But I really am not learning much," Carpentier commented, looking back on the interview. "She tells us that Paul came home and he was stabbed . . . and she's not giving us much at all. She's not making any sense. The entire situation is not making *any* sense."

Looking at it, Carpentier considered that she had her case in the can. Paul had given a statement that Sheila had tried to kill him. They had the knife and other evidence from the condo.

Open and shut?

"I could have just packed it all up, went home, and called it a day," Carpentier remarked.

Yet, something told Carpentier to keep talking to Sheila. Find out why. What had driven this woman to nearly kill the man she supposedly loved?

"I had to know! Why did this woman stab her husband? There *had* to be an explanation."

Sheila was a wreck. It was 7:28 P.M. on that Sunday when the first interview started. Sheila wore a gray hoodie-type sweatshirt she had tossed on before helping Paul out the door. She had her arms on her lap as they began. Her dark black hair was wild and frizzy. Her shoulders were slumped; her head was leaning toward her right. Sheila stared at the table and a cup of hot chocolate in front of her at times; she looked at Carpentier at others. Sheila seemed to be on the back end of that mania phase, now coming down.

Carpentier sat to Sheila's left. Every question she asked seemed like a struggle for Sheila to answer. Even the time Paul got home, Sheila could not pin down the hour. She talked in complete circles, not making sense. But then, after thinking about it, she would come up with one of those aha moments that *still did not* yield much information.

Only a minute and a half into the interview, Sheila went from talking about how Paul went to New York that day— "He drove"—to a muttering, nearly incoherent few sentences, beginning with this lie: "He was on the ground . . . bleeding . . . and I . . . I get nauseous around blood. . . . He wanted me to look at it to make sure it was okay. And I looked at it, and it was not bleeding . . . but . . ."

Baffled by the comment, Carpentier asked: "You looked at his shirt. You pulled his shirt up. You *didn't* see anything?"

Granted, Sheila had bypassed explaining the entire game and how it had started.

"I didn't see anything . . . ," Sheila said, stumbling through her interview. She was obviously dancing around the question.

Carpentier sat quietly, knowing that Paul had been stabbed three times. Viciously. Violently. With a tremendous amount of thrust. Yet, here was the suspect in that crime telling her she hadn't really seen any of the wounds.

"I mean, it's your husband," Carpentier pointed out. "Did you lift up his shirt?"

"Sure," Sheila said. Then she finally admitted: "I saw the wounds on his chest."

"How many were there?"

Sheila pointed to her chest, where she believed Paul's wounds were, and seemed to count them off to herself. "I saw two. . . . I think there were two."

It was easy for Carpentier to tell that Sheila was lying and knew exactly what she was talking about. At times, Sheila came across as calm. She would play up the *"poor me, poor me, have some sympathy here for me and what happened"* role. It was laughable. She carried on and on, making little sense, trying to cloud each answer with several different explanations of one enormous lie.

But this only made Carpentier more curious.

Sheila broke into an explanation about Paul asking her during that moment on the floor if the wounds were superficial or deep. She told Carpentier they were superficial. "Then . . . that's it . . . that's it. . . . I took him to the hospital."

So there it was. This was Sheila's story: from Paul coming home, walking in the door with stab wounds, to driving him to the hospital.

Carpentier pushed. What time? When? Where? What did

you do that day? Begin at the beginning. Let's go through it all, step-by-step, moment to moment.

Sheila reacted to Carpentier's slight pressure by grabbing at her own hair and pushing it up on top of her head in great frustration, almost as if she was going to lose it and explode in a rage. However, she quickly regained her composure and once again started to talk.

In circles.

Carpentier coached her through the day. Sheila was confused about times. She did not want to commit to any specific time and tie it to any specific event.

Carpentier couldn't understand it. The incident had occurred just hours before, but Sheila could not recall what exactly she had done at a specific time.

Why can't she remember? Carpentier thought.

"Did anybody call you?" Carpentier asked.

Sheila shook her head. "No . . . no." She was contradicting what she later would claim when she said Nelson called and asked if he could come over. These were easily verifiable facts.

"Did you call anyone?"

"No . . . no."

Another lie.

"What were your plans for [Paul] on this evening?" Carpentier wondered.

Great question.

"He wanted to watch the Oscars," Sheila said, taking a sip of her hot chocolate.

They went back and forth about times. Sheila would not commit. She said at one point that shortly after Paul came home, she wanted to take him to the hospital, but he wanted to lie down. He was having trouble breathing, Sheila explained. She couldn't understand why.

Ten minutes into the interview, Carpentier focused on the

car ride to the hospital. The way Sheila played it off was that she had no idea how her husband had been injured. It was as if something had fallen from the sky and punctured him. But now, realizing he was hurt, she decided she needed to get him to the hospital quickly.

"I kept asking him, 'Are you all right? Are you all right?' as we drove. . . . 'How's your breathing? Do you want to lay down in the back?' . . ."

"Now, did he tell you how he got these wounds?"

Sheila shook her head, indicating no. Then she changed the subject, mentioning how Paul was saying at the time that it was becoming harder and harder to breathe as they drove to the hospital.

"And any reason why you didn't call 911 at the time this happened?"

Sheila shook her head again, then looked away. "I didn't think . . . I thought, 'I'm going to take him to the hospital.' It was right there. . . . My mom could come. . . . I . . . I . . . uh . . . I didn't think."

"So what happened on the way to the hospital? How come you didn't make it to the emergency room?"

Sheila waved her hand. "I thought of going to the emergency room. We went to school here. I thought the emergency room was there. . . ."

Really, how in the hell does she not know where the ER is located? Carpentier thought.

The detective wasn't biting. She asked a simple question of Sheila. When Sheila had gone to school at the same facility, didn't she take tours of the emergency room? For crying out loud, her mother worked at the hospital. Sheila had to know where the ER was located.

"I thought I remembered it was there," Sheila answered, totally blowing off the question. "So we got out and we walked up to the entranceway," she said, leaving out the entire bit about them having the knife fight on the edge of the parking lot. "I walked with him. And then . . . it wasn't the emergency room. . . ."

There was still that little problem of why Sheila never called 911. Carpentier kept asking the question. Why not even then, while they were outside the hospital? If Sheila couldn't find the ER, why not call and ask where the heck it was?

Sheila said by that point she had lost her phone.

How convenient.

Which was why, she continued, she took off in the car: to go find an ambulance.

"But there were two men out front. . . . Did you ask anyone to call 911?" Carpentier pressed. "Did you scream out for anyone to call 911?"

"After I saw them, I said, 'Call the ambulance. . . .'"

Lie.

"Because the guy was spending time on the phone, and I said, 'Call the ambulance. . . .'"

Lie.

"I did find the emergency room, when I left. . . ."

Lie.

"It was right around the corner. So I came running back to take him there. . . ."

Lie.

"To see if an ambulance could come there. . . ."

Lie.

"[Paul] said, 'Don't leave me! Don't leave me alone. . . .'"

Lie.

Lie. Lie. Lie.

For more than two hours, Sheila Davalloo lied her way through telling the tale of this day. Sheila's subterfuge only made Alison Carpentier, already suspicious, that much more interested in figuring out how the hell Paul wound up with all those stab wounds, close to death; and his wife was doing nothing more than backpedaling, telling stories that did not make any sense.

Moreover, not once, during this part of the interview, did Sheila ever ask how Paul was doing.

"I mean, Sheila, I find it odd," Carpenter said, well into the interview, "you're an educated person—"

"Well, it is odd," Sheila interrupted. "Yes . . . the whole thing is odd."

Carpenter went through Sheila's story, breaking it down: Paul comes home. He's bleeding. Sheila doesn't dial 911. Doesn't ask the neighbor for help. And so on.

"The fact that you're a medical person, and he's a medical person, I find it odd—" (Carpenter kept using the word "odd.")

"I don't know," Sheila interrupted, dropping her head into her hands. "I don't know."

"Sheila, you are going to have to start being honest with me, because I don't think you're being honest with me."

"I am," Sheila pleaded, now beginning to cry, picking up her cup of hot chocolate, staring blankly into the bottom of it. Sheila said she had no idea how Paul got hurt.

"Where's the knife?"

This got Sheila's undivided attention. She said: "I don't know about a knife."

"What if I told you, I *have* a knife."

"I . . . I . . . I . . . Well, I don't know. . . ."

"Are your prints going to be on it?"

"I . . . I . . ." Sheila shook her head, seemingly confused. "If it . . . I mean, if it came from our house, maybe. . . ."

"How would a knife get there at that scene?"

"I don't know. . . ."

A while later, Carpenter summarized her thoughts a bit for Sheila, explaining, "What I find here is an educated person being *very* dishonest. I want to know *what* happened today in your apartment."

"I'm in shock. . . . I don't know what—"

Carpentier cut her off. "No, you're not in that much shock, where you don't know the difference between a lie and the truth. And I believe you *know* the difference. . . ."

The tone of Carpentier's questions became a bit more commanding as she told Sheila straight-out that Sheila was lying, and that it was going to be a long night if she continued the charade. At one point, Carpentier said she had not come to work that day to play games with a liar.

Sheila, however, kept denying that she knew anything.

Then Carpentier dropped: "You know what Paul said . . ."

This got Sheila's attention again. She looked up quickly. *Paul.*

"Huh?" Sheila reacted.

"Paul said *you* stabbed him!"

Sheila shook her head. "No."

"Not once, but *twice*."

Sheila tried talking her way out of it.

"Right now," Carpentier said, "you're looking at attempted murder *if* your husband *doesn't* die. . . ."

"He's not gonna die . . . ," Sheila said, calling up those tears again, looking up a bit, trying to gauge Carpentier's reaction. "He's not going to die."

Then, as the interview carried on, investigators working the case discovered a phone number on Sheila's cell of a man she had called right in the middle of everything.

All they knew then was his first name: Nelson.

CHAPTER 64

AT ONE POINT late into the interview, Detective Alison Carpentier said, "Tell me about the blindfold?"

Sheila shook her head as if she didn't know what Carpentier was talking about.

"Tell. Me. About. The. Blindfold?" Carpentier demanded, saying the words slowly and deliberately, letting Sheila know the WCPD had done its homework.

Sheila shook her head again and mumbled.

"There was *no* blindfold?" Carpentier queried.

Sheila looked down. Played stupid. Shook her head no.

"You sure?"

"Uh-huh," Sheila said.

The problem with all of Sheila's lies was that she came across as the cat with the canary in its mouth, caught in the act, sitting on the kitchen floor, feathers sticking out of its mouth.

Carpentier said, "Tell me about the sock?" She meant the stocking.

"The sock?" Sheila asked. "It was part of the game."

Finally Sheila had admitted there was a game.

"Tell me about the game."

Sheila shrugged her shoulders. "It was just a game."

This sort of back-and-forth exchange—Sheila acting as though she had no idea what Carpentier was talking about; Carpentier laying out the facts, one by one—went on and on and on. Two hours' worth. Then three. Four. Carpentier asked at one point if the game had gotten out of hand.

Sheila said no. She had no idea what the detective meant.

"Sheila, do you think I'm making this all up and I didn't talk to Paul?"

"No, I'm just . . . ," Sheila responded right away, "I'm sure you did . . . but I'm . . . I don't know why you're saying all this."

Sheila placed the tips of her fingers on her temples and dropped her head as Carpentier explained how she couldn't help her if Sheila didn't start telling the truth.

"Sheila, just be honest."

"I would never hurt him. . . . I would never. . . ."

Sheila began crying and playing with a string on her sweater, looking down the entire time, shaking her head no. Another cop in the room handed Carpentier a piece of paper; the detective stopped interviewing so she could read it.

Sheila looked up, wondering what was going on. "Is he okay?" she asked, indicating that maybe that piece of paper was a note telling Carpentier that Paul had died.

"He's in surgery," Carpentier said.

"I would never hurt him," Sheila said, once more, through sniffles and tears.

"Sheila, you are going to have to explain what happened then."

"I'm afraid. . . . I'm afraid. . . ."

They continued the back-and-forth interaction. Sheila still would not admit to anything. It was only when Carpentier brought something up that Sheila would say, *"Oh, that? Yeah, maybe that did happen."*

"Go by what Paul says," she told Carpentier.

"No, I can't go by that. I need to hear it from you."

"Paul . . ."

"Tell me about the game."

"Paul's not covering up anything," Sheila said. She was hugging herself, as if the room had gotten suddenly cold. "I love him so much. . . ." Then she broke down and started bawling dramatically. "I'm embarrassed. . . ."

"Sheila," Carpentier said sincerely, leaning in close to her suspect, "I don't want you to be embarrassed."

"I don't want to talk about this . . . ," Sheila said through tears.

Carpentier became a little heated and told Sheila pointedly that she needed to explain herself. This was not going to go away just because Sheila didn't want to talk about it.

Sheila cried and put her head in her hands.

"We're normal people," Sheila said at one point as she lost control of her emotions.

After a brief period of them talking over each other, Carpentier said, "Sheila, did you stab him? Was it a game?"

Sheila wouldn't give it up. She kept saying, "Go by what Paul says."

Carpentier's instincts were spot-on. "Look," the detective explained, "you know what it looks like. . . . It looks that, you know, you might not have loved your husband. . . . You were trying to hurt him—"

"No! No."

"But how would I know that, unless you explain it to me?"

By 2:24 A.M., the next day, Sheila was talking about the game and how she held the knife and how Paul must have stumbled into it somehow and gotten hurt. She played it all off as some sort of touchy-feely game between a husband and a wife. They had rubbed objects on each other, and one of those objects—a knife—had somehow wound up in Paul's chest a few times—but, of course, she had no idea how.

The problem with Sheila's explanation, as Carpentier encouraged her to talk through it, was that as Carpentier reenacted certain parts of it for Sheila, asking her if that was what she meant, the stab wounds Paul had received would not have been to his chest.

"The first time, you told me it was an accident," Carpentier said as Sheila shook her head no and shifted uncomfortably in her seat, "and you held the knife, and he saw the blood, and he jumped up right away—"

Sheila interrupted Carpentier. "And I thought that's what made the center wound," she said, pointing to her midsection. "I don't know about a chair. . . . I don't know how the chair . . . I know the chair hit me at one point . . . and there was such a knee-jerk reaction. . . . He went straight into the knife."

Where was the dark figure? That elusive dark figure, whom Sheila would lean on later, wasn't anywhere near this explanation she gave to police. As she talked her way through what was a bevy of lies made up on the spot, Sheila was calm and lucid. She knew what she was saying.

Carpentier left her alone for a moment and walked out of the room, while a uniformed officer stayed in the room. Sheila stared at the table as she leaned on one hand, her elbow on the arm of her chair.

Returning, Carpentier explained that the interview wasn't really working for her anymore. If Sheila didn't want to start being honest, there was nothing else for them to discuss.

"I know. . . . I know," Sheila said. "This is all I can remember. I can't—"

Carpentier interrupted Sheila by outspokenly observing, "What it looks like . . . is almost a bad joke. . . ."

One stab wound, Carpentier said, Sheila might be able to explain away, but two and three? Well, there was an issue there, with this not being some sort of accident, but rather a deliberate attempt on the man's life.

Carpentier lit a cigarette at one point, sat back, and, blowing smoke toward the ceiling, told Sheila that none of this was adding up. There were the 911 calls she had never made. Why not? Who the hell did she call then?

"His mother and my mother. . . ."

Carpentier knew this was nonsense.

They discussed the NyQuil Paul had said Sheila tried giving him. "Wouldn't this make him drowsy and fall out?" Carpentier asked.

"No, no," Sheila said. "He wasn't in a lot of pain. It was more his breathing. . . ."

Carpentier flicked her ashes in an empty coffee cup on the table, crossed her legs, and listened as Sheila continued burying herself.

"No, I didn't think NyQuil would be that bad for him. . . ."

"He remembers clearly your conversations about the ambulance. . . ."

Sheila looked away, defeated. She shook her head. "I don't know. I mean, he probably wanted me to call an ambulance . . . but we never had a conversation about it."

When Carpentier questioned Sheila about Paul claiming she had attacked him inside the car in the parking lot, and he finally saw the knife and realized what was going on, Sheila responded, "That makes no sense. I would have done that *inside* the house! I would have *never* done it in the car in broad daylight, you know, at the hospital. That doesn't make sense."

"Well, now," Carpentier said smartly, "ten hours later, it *doesn't* make sense. . . ."

Regarding why she drove to the back of the parking lot and

not to the front of the hospital, Sheila said she tried finding the first parking spot that was open.

"That's weird," Carpentier said. "That you would try to find a parking spot and not pull up to the front of the door. . . . You parked far on the end, up a hill, instead of cutting across to go to the front entrance."

Sheila didn't have much of a response for that.

Carpentier said they found one of Paul's shoes there.

"His shoes weren't put on properly."

"Sheila, I have witnesses that heard him say, 'Get away from me!'"

"Well, he wanted me to leave. I mean . . . well . . . he wanted me to leave. . . . He wanted me to go home."

Carpentier pulled out a map of the hospital and parking lot and shoved it in front of Sheila. Another officer, a man in uniform, helped Carpentier as both began to pepper Sheila with questions about what happened, where, and why: Paul's sock was found here—why so far away from where you parked? Your cell phone was located over there—why so far away from the sock? You were parked here—why were you seen pulling at Paul, from the ground up here, on a bike path? Why did you take the path to the entrance and not cut across the parking lot—a straight line being the shortest—to get to the entrance quickly? Why didn't you flag down the man in scrubs, who was there in the parking lot and saw the two of you, if you wanted to help Paul?

"I can't explain any of it, because I—"

"Why did we find the knife over here?" the male officer asked, pointing with a pen to a location on the map.

"Paul had the knife—"

"He told me he took it out of *your* hand," Carpentier said.

"No, I didn't have the knife."

"He realized . . . at that point . . . this was no longer a game," Carpentier said somberly.

Sheila shook her head no again. "I wasn't out to hurt him—"

"Well, you did! You almost *killed* him," Carpentier quipped.

"But I wasn't out to do that."

Near three in the morning, Carpentier said, "Look, tomorrow you're going to court, and once that happens, I cannot help you. . . . My job is to find out the truth."

"The truth is," Sheila said, "I did not set out to hurt him. . . ."

The word "snapped" came up. Paul thought maybe Sheila had a momentary lapse of reason, Carpentier explained, and perhaps Sheila snapped and tried hurting him. Then when she came out of it, Sheila tried helping.

Contrary to what Sheila would later argue, she kept saying she didn't snap. She knew what was going on the entire time.

"If I wanted to kill him, if I wanted to harm him in any way," Sheila explained, "I would have done it in the [condo]—"

"It *was* done in the [condo]," Carpentier said.

The Westchester County PD was ultimately going to believe Paul, Carpentier explained. As Carpentier put it, the evidence pointed to "all of Paul's ducks in a row." She told Sheila pointblank: "The evidence makes it appear to be calculated."

Near the end of this second, and last, interview, Sheila said, "I know I can't live without him. . . ." This statement was made after Carpentier told Sheila that, without a doubt, the detective believed that Sheila had tried to kill her husband and that the Westchester County law enforcement knew of "problems" in the marriage because Paul's mother had already told Carpentier that Paul slept at her house for an estimated twenty days throughout the past year.

"He takes care . . . I mean, he . . . he takes care of everything emotionally for me. I cannot survive without him."

Carpentier wasn't buying it, and made a good point by saying: "With truth, it's easy to be consistent, because it just flows." She explained how Paul had told the same story of what happened—both before he went into surgery and after he came out of surgery.

The other point Carpentier caught Sheila on was how, as Sheila had learned that Paul was going to survive, she began to tell different versions of what had happened, all based on Paul's version—which made Carpentier think that when Sheila first sat down, she honestly thought Paul was not going to make it, so she told this tale of him coming home bleeding and being stabbed. But now, since Paul was alive and talking, Sheila found herself having to talk her way out of it all.

Sheila declined to write a statement.

"Look," Carpentier concluded, "do what you have to do and get bailed out and check yourself into [somewhere] to get some help, a psychiatric center."

"No, no . . . I'm sure I have problems, but I don't want to say that I tried hurting him because I—"

"I'm not saying that, but I do think you need a de-stressing. . . ."

Then, after a few additional formalities, they locked up Sheila Davalloo.

CHAPTER 65

PART OF WHAT worried Carpentier was the idea that someone else could have been involved in attempting to kill Paul. When the WCPD found Nelson's name on Sheila's cell phone, the theory arose that perhaps he was somehow involved with Sheila in attacking Paul. Sheila's cell phone had dialed Nelson's number right in the middle of the incident with Paul. Why was Sheila calling a man during a supposed "game" with her husband wherein he had been stabbed? As the WCPD looked at it, at the time Sheila had made the call to this Nelson person, Paul was literally dying and in need of medical attention.

"I had to make sure there was no one else involved," Carpentier explained. "And then, I needed to find out *why* this crime was committed."

Carpentier was proudly living up to her "nosy bitch" reputation.

From the time the call of the incident had come in and Carpentier was busy interviewing Sheila that night, well into the next morning—and on top of the search warrants served on Sheila and Paul's condo, and Sheila being arraigned the following morning, March 24, 2003—the detective never let go of the idea that she had to speak with this Nelson person.

And then another issue came up: Nelson lived in Stamford.

"So we couldn't just go trampling on their jurisdiction," Carpentier clarified.

Carpentier had Nelson's phone number, but she didn't want to call him. If he was involved, she did not want to give him a heads-up that law enforcement was sniffing around. What Carpentier wanted to do was go to Nelson's apartment and knock on his door.

Surprise the guy.

All they had at this point, however, was Nelson's first name. That was all that Sheila had labeled on her cell phone under his number.

"Look," Carpentier said to her partner, James Clarke, a former NYPD officer who had transferred to the WCPD some time ago, "every affair happens at work. Let's give Sheila's work a call and ask for a Nelson . . . See what happens."

"Sounds good to me," Clarke said.

At some time during the day on Monday, March 24, 2003, Carpentier called Purdue Pharma. "Listen, I just got off the phone with a gentleman who helped me a lot . . . a Nelson Something. I forgot his last name. Do you know who I'm talking about?"

The receptionist said, "Sure. Nelson Sessler."

"Oh yeah, that's it. Thanks!"

Great police work.

"We were hoping there was only one Nelson in the building," Carpentier recalled. "And there was."

Carpentier took the name and ran a quick background check. Nothing but Nelson's address and a few tickets came up.

She then called the SPD and asked if they could run a quick background check to see if Nelson had any history of felonious behavior.

She waited.

"And they never called me back," Carpentier said.

So she called and asked again.

No one returned her call.

"So I said to myself, 'Frick them!' But to be fair, there was a kidnapping going on in Stamford that day. . . . The FBI was around . . . and they were terribly strapped. It had been a crazy night for all of them."

Still, Carpentier did not want to sit on this lead. She smelled something foul. Her gut feeling was too strong. This Nelson Sessler character, she knew, was connected to the stabbing somehow.

"Let's just hop into a vehicle right now"—it was early evening—"and head over to his apartment in Stamford," Carpentier's partner suggested.

"You know what, let's do that."

And off they went.

CHAPTER 66

NEW YORK POST headline writers had a ball with the story on that Monday. PSYCHO KNIFE WIFE screamed one headline. *Westchester woman accused of cuffing her husband, blind-folding him and repeatedly plunging a paring knife into his chest—piercing his heart—has been charged with attempted murder, and is being treated at a mental hospital,* the accompanying article said. Another newspaper, the *Norwich Bulletin* in Connecticut, ran with: KINKY-STAB SUSPECT CALLED PSYCHOTIC.

Coming out of the fog he'd been in from surgery and the entire incident, Paul felt bad for Sheila. Feeling stronger, he saw her as sick, mentally unstable, and pledged his support.

At work that day (and those that would follow for quite some time), Nelson Sessler received several voice mail messages from Sheila, who had made bail and checked herself into a hospital, per Carpentier's suggestion. In the first voice mail, Sheila said, "I have a family emergency . . . so I won't be around today." As time went on, and she didn't show up for work, Nelson recounted, "It changed to she [had] the flu . . . and then it changed, I think one time, [to] 'I'm taking care of my brother.' You know, there were many, many calls that she had left."

Sheila Davalloo, the consummate liar, continued to hold on to Nelson Sessler as she waited on the courts to proceed with prosecuting her for the crime of aggravated assault and attempted murder.

CHAPTER 67

THE DRIVE TO Stamford from the WCPD did not take Carpentier and her partner more than an hour. And so, on March 24, 2003, as darkness settled on Stamford, Connecticut, Carpentier and Clarke found Nelson's apartment and walked up to the door.

Carpentier "banged and banged," but there was no answer.

"Neighbor?" Clarke suggested.

Carpentier knocked on Nelson's neighbor's door.

A woman answered.

"Does Nelson Sessler live there?" Carpentier asked after identifying herself and Clarke as police officers.

"You're here about that murder, aren't you?" the neighbor asked.

"Um . . . no . . . we're here about an attempted murder, actually," Carpentier corrected.

There seemed to be some confusion between them. Carpentier was referring to an attempted homicide; the neighbor was certain they were there about a homicide.

"His fiancée who was killed," the neighbor said. "Right?"

Carpentier and Clarke looked at each other. *What*?

Sometimes, in police work, all it takes is asking the right

question and then a case that has gone somewhat cold is thawed rather quickly.

"'Fiancée who was killed'?" Carpentier asked, puzzled by this remark.

"Yeah . . . his fiancée was murdered about four months ago. You should talk with the Stamford PD."

What the frick? Carpentier thought. She looked at Clarke. She could tell he was thinking the same thing.

The question on their minds as they drove away from Nelson Sessler's apartment complex toward the Stamford PD was: How could an attempted homicide *and* a homicide (if what the neighbor said was true) not be connected in some manner of speaking? It was nearly impossible. There are no coincidences in murder.

Greg Holt wasn't around when Carpentier and Clarke arrived at the SPD and began talking about what they had found out. Listening to what Carpentier was saying, an on-duty officer took off to his desk and called Greg Holt.

"Anna Lisa's breaking wide open, Greg. Get in here!"

Holt had heard this before. He sighed. He had just gotten home for the day. Nonetheless, he showered, dressed, and hopped back into his car.

With Greg Holt there, and Tom McGinty out working on a case, Carpentier explained again what they had uncovered.

Carpentier sized Holt up after meeting him, calling Greg the "old-school type" of detective. "I was thinking he didn't want to hear from us about a case they had been investigating for a while. At first, he wasn't hearing anything I had to say."

"Alison Carpentier is a great detective," Holt later said. "Just the best. Right on top of things."

After they sorted it all out, Carpentier asked, "Do you have any evidence we could look at?" Carpentier believed they were onto something much bigger than what they had started out to investigate.

Greg Holt said, "Follow me."

They went into the evidence room and Holt pulled out the 911 tape. He popped it into a cassette recorder and hit PLAY.

Carpentier stood and listened. Just a few words in, she said, "That's Sheila Davalloo."

It wasn't hard for a detective who had just spent the better part of an entire night interviewing Sheila to recognize her voice.

"That's who?" Holt wondered, surprised by the revelation. "No. No. . . ."

Carpentier and Clarke took a look at the crime scene photos. They studied them for a few moments.

In what Carpentier described as a flip from his earlier assessment, Holt said, "No female did this homicide."

"Look at the photos," Carpentier explained. "They're pulling hair, kicking. . . . If this was some two-hundred-pound guy, he would have taken her out with a punch. It appears to me like it's equal weight here."

"No, no," Carpentier said Holt told her.

"This was a catfight!" Carpentier said, referring back to the crime scene photos, adding, "I'm going to convince you."

"No, you're not going to convince me," Greg Holt said, according to Carpentier.

After the disagreement was settled, Carpentier said she wanted to interview Nelson Sessler. "I believe he was having an affair with Sheila Davalloo."

"No way," one investigator told her. "We've spoken to him over and over and he never mentioned that name. We've looked at all his phone records. We feel he was very devoted to Anna Lisa."

"Well, that's fine," Carpentier said, "but I'd like to find out for myself."

A fresh detective sitting in front of Nelson might be just what it took for him to come clean.

The SPD agreed to allow Carpentier to sit down with Nelson Sessler inside the SPD. "So," she explained later, "they could control the interview." Carpentier was fine with that. It was their case, their witness. She didn't want to interfere, but only clear up what were questions she had about her case back in Pleasantville.

"Once we heard that Nelson Sessler was in between a homicide and an attempted homicide," Greg Holt later said, "there was no way it was a coincidence. There had to be a connection."

CHAPTER 68

THERE CAN BE only one explanation why, on Tuesday, March 25, 2003, at 9:35 A.M., Nelson Sessler called the SPD and notified them about Sheila: His neighbor must have said something to him the previous night. According to a report by Tom McGinty, Nelson, however, claimed that he was calling because a few colleagues at work that day told him about the stabbing at Sheila's condo and showed him a newspaper article. Nelson testified later, though, that this happened on that Monday, not Tuesday.

(Maybe he just mixed up the days, who knows?)

Tom McGinty was working "extra duty" on Atlantic Avenue when he looked down and saw his cell phone buzzing.

Sessler sounded excited and upset, McGinty wrote in his report of the call, *as he told [me] about a co-worker at Purdue.*

This was four months and two weeks *after* Anna Lisa's murder.

"I just learned that Sheila Davalloo was arrested for stabbing her husband in New York," Nelson told McGinty. "Do you think she could have killed Anna Lisa?"

"How did you find out about the stabbing? Where, exactly, did the stabbing take place?"

"A coworker came up to me at work. . . . I'm really upset and leaving work for the day."

Still, at no time during that phone call or other contact Nelson had with the SPD that day and the days before, did he admit that he had an affair with Sheila.

Meanwhile, Detective Carpentier sat down with Nelson inside the SPD on Thursday, March 27, and spoke to him, first asking about Sheila.

Nelson referred to Sheila as his "coworker" and "friend." She was someone he knew from work. He walked her dogs once in a while.

Not a word about the recent trips they'd been on together, alone. Or the dinners. Or the sex. Or the phone calls.

Carpentier listened. When Nelson finished, she said: "So how long have you been sleeping with her?"

McGinty was in the room. He stared at Nelson. He knew the answer. The SPD had asked Nelson repeatedly about affairs and ex-girlfriends. Not once did Sheila's name ever come up.

"I wasn't sleeping with her," Nelson said. "We were good friends! I walked her dogs and helped her out. That's it."

Carpentier rolled her eyes. "Come on, Nelson. . . . You're not driving from Stamford to Westchester, New York, *without* getting laid."

There was a beat. A period of silence. "All right . . . all right . . . we're having an affair!" Nelson admitted.

Tom McGinty, Carpentier recalled, "went ballistic at that point."

McGinty screamed, "Are you *kidding* me? We've been talking to you for *how* long? And now you come up with this?"

"He was really, really pissed," Carpentier said.

McGinty had every right to be.

By withholding information, Nelson had, in effect, lied about the affair every time he chose not to talk about it to the SPD.

Carpentier made a point later, saying, "I don't know that they would have looked at Sheila closely. She had had a good job. Made a lot of money. Married. She seemed normal. Men are pretty narrow-minded when it comes to female homicides," Carpentier added, with all the respect in the world for the SPD and McGinty and Holt. "Women are capable of real terror. Most men are inclined to think that females are not involved in these types of very bad and violent crimes."

After Sheila's name was brought into the case, everything fit together. They checked her entry/exit log at Purdue right away. Sure enough, on the day of Anna's homicide, Sheila came in at 8:09 A.M., left the building at 10:53 A.M., and reentered the building at 1:53 P.M., before leaving for the day at 4:34 P.M.

Back in New York, Paul Christos, whose stabbing had initiated this entire new thread of the investigation, was feeling markedly better. In fact, he was discharged on that same day.

Armed with this new information about Sheila, Carpentier decided that she'd have to go over to Paul's and interview him one more time. Now that they had Sheila and Nelson as lovers, and Nelson's girlfriend dead, the WCPD had a motive in its case.

Sheila needed to get rid of Paul.

It all fit.

CHAPTER 69

PAUL FELT A LOT better than he looked. The guy had been stabbed three times, nearly left for dead, underwent emergency open-heart surgery, and was home just four days after it had all occurred.

All considered, Paul Christos was lucky to be alive.

Carpentier went to see Paul and laid out the facts for him with as smooth a brushstroke as she could: No 911 calls were ever made from the home or Sheila's cell phone (records obtained by the WCPD had proved as much); Sheila was having an affair with a guy named Nelson, who had even shown up at the condo on the night Paul was stabbed; and Sheila had called Nelson at 4:59 P.M., right around the time of the stabbing.

Paul sat with his jaw on the floor.

Stunned.

"He's been coming over to your condo for over a year," Carpentier explained, knowing how painful this was going to be for a guy who was still, arguably, in love with his wife. She told Paul how she had gotten the info straight from Nelson.

The brother story . . . I'm an idiot, Paul thought.

Paul considered the news and then laid out the Jack and Melissa story for Carpentier—which brought an important name into their dialogue: Anna Lisa.

After that, it all came together.

Paul gave the WCPD and SPD his consent for them to search the condo. The SPD and WCPD found the empty stun gun box, an empty box for a Taser (and the purchase receipt), the bugging device, the night vision goggles, the pills, a photo of Nelson holding his guitar, ticket stubs to a U2 concert at the Meadowlands in New Jersey, and plenty of other incriminating pieces of evidence tying Sheila to what looked like a premeditated, well-thought-out plan not only to kill Anna Lisa, but to murder Paul as well. All so Sheila could have Nelson Sessler to herself.

Paul was devastated, of course, but not all that surprised.

"Within . . . seconds it all clicked for me," Paul said later.

With Nelson and Paul, the SPD realized, it now had two substantial assets in its quest to indict Sheila on murder charges, and, hopefully, with any luck, shove the evidence in her face and break her. If Sheila admitted to it all, the end result would be so much less emotionally exhausting on the family.

CHAPTER 70

THE SPD WAS interested now in Nelson Sessler and what else he had to hide. On April 1, 2003, Greg Holt went to Purdue Pharma and found Nelson working.

"Not here," Nelson said. He didn't want to talk at work.

They agreed to meet back at the SPD sometime later that day. Holt had set up an interview with Sessler the previous day, March 31, but Sessler blew it off. He never showed and never called, at least as far as Holt knew. This was a red flag to Greg Holt. Why wasn't the guy now beating the SPD's door down to fess up to everything? After all, Nelson Sessler could be charged.

Nelson and Holt continued the meeting outside Nelson's work.

"I called at eleven last night," Nelson said nervously. "Look, I let it ring four times and got scared and hung up."

"I was at my desk, Nelson," Holt said. "The phone never rang."

Nelson didn't respond.

As they talked, Nelson explained how he had spoken to several high-profile attorneys in town and they had advised him not to talk to the police. He claimed he didn't "like that advice," but he was following it, nonetheless.

"Why isn't Tom calling on me?" Nelson asked.

"Detective McGinty is busy with something else."

"I've dealt with him all along and I do not want to change now," Nelson said.

Holt knew that Tom McGinty had built a rapport with Nelson, and Nelson trusted Tom. But here was a detective from the SPD calling on a witness and asking about a murder case.

Serious stuff.

"Are you refusing to cooperate with police, Nelson? Are you saying you do not want to talk to us? Why the sudden change in your behavior?"

"I do not like the advice I'm getting from lawyers," Nelson repeated, "but I am going to take it."

From there, Nelson continued to mention Tom McGinty's name and asked repeatedly why McGinty couldn't interview him.

Holt finally said, "If Tom was present, would you talk to us?"

"Yes," Nelson said.

"Okay."

"Actually," Nelson then added, thinking about it, "no, I won't talk to him, either."

Nelson had a notebook with him. As Holt talked, Nelson was jotting down things. Holt tried ending the conversation several times, but Nelson kept it going by asking additional questions.

"If you are going to talk to us and cooperate and help, I will continue speaking with you," Greg Holt explained, his patience running short, "and if you say you no longer want an attorney. If you cannot say that, I need to leave."

Nelson closed his notebook. He walked away.

It would be the last time Greg Holt ever spoke to Nelson. As Holt watched Nelson walk away, the detective thought back on something that had bothered him throughout the entire investigation. The SPD had hired the NYPD's technical assistance response unit (TARU) to film Anna Lisa's New York wake back in November 2002. TARU sent undercover officers to the wake and surreptitiously filmed the entire thing. No one knew or was aware. Holt had been studying those tapes for a lead or two—some sketchy character roaming around, or maybe a conversation between two people who didn't know anyone was listening.

He found none of that. However, while Holt watched the tapes, there was something that Nelson did at the wake that made Greg Holt suspicious of him.

"You could see him walking around, greeting people, like he was running the thing, and every once in a while, he would retreat to, like, this corner and you could actually hear him wailing, sobbing loudly. It was bizarre. But then when he turned around, there were no tears. In my opinion, the whole thing was fake!"

Holt stood there as Nelson left: *What else are you hiding?*

CHAPTER 71

THE FOLLOWING DAY, April 2, 2003, Greg Holt, Yan Vanderven, James Clarke, and Alison Carpentier took a ride out to the county correctional center in Valhalla, New York, where Sheila, who had been arrested on attempted murder charges and jailed, was once again waiting on an opportunity to make bail. Holt brought along EJ Rondano, the SPD's forensic evidence collector. They had a search warrant for Sheila's body signed and ready to execute.

"Mrs. Davalloo," Greg Holt said, introducing himself and those with him, "we're here to collect your DNA."

Sheila said fine. Holt remarked later that she was "more than willing to help us any way we needed."

Part of what Holt was thinking—once they heard from Paul that Sheila had a mentally unstable brother—was that perhaps that red truck spotted at Anna Lisa's on the morning she was murdered (which they could never nail down and find) was Sheila's brother's. Possibly, he had knocked on Anna's door for Sheila. It might have been a way to get Sheila inside. The brother might not have even known he was being played.

"Not everyone believed the 'red truck story' that Gary Riley gave me and Tom," Holt explained. "No one believed anything Riley said, actually. Me too. But that one thing, I believed him on. Why would he lie about a red truck parked in front of Anna's, a guy knocking on her door, and a woman with black hair standing under her porch?"

The obvious theory here for Holt was: If Riley lied about that, he would have come up with a much larger lie. The report was vague. Riley had no idea who it was that they were looking for.

There was that, and a thousand other questions that the SPD had for Sheila.

Looking at her, Holt could not believe "how unattractive Sheila was, as compared to Anna Lisa."

Why would Sessler ever pick her over Anna Lisa? Holt thought as Rondano took swabs of Sheila's mouth and samples from her hair.

They stood in the middle of what Holt described as a "huge, *huge* squad bay (inside the prison, where Sheila was being held), prisoners and guards all roaming about, shuffling around."

As they were finishing up, Sheila called Holt aside. "Could I speak to you?" she said. It was clear Sheila wanted to talk. She seemed comfortable with Holt.

"Yes, yes, of course." Sheila was full of emotion as they chatted, but she was also "very stoic." She seemed to be playing dumb, almost in a patronizing way.

Looking around, Holt said, "I do not want to talk here in front of all these inmates and guards. . . . I don't want your business being out in the open. You know what I'm saying?"

"Yeah," Sheila said, nodding her head in agreement, looking around. "Thanks for recognizing that."

"You're expected to make bail anytime now, right?" The thought was that Sheila was going to be released that day or later that night.

"Yes," Sheila responded.

"Maybe later today we can chat, when you're out of here."

"Okay. Yeah. That sounds good. When I'm out of here."

"Makes sense, right?"

"Yes. Can I have your business card?"

Holt handed Sheila his card. "I'll return [as soon as you make bail] and we'll talk."

Detective Holt called that moment a "fatal mistake—I'll never forgive myself" for not talking to Sheila right then and there. "Cops don't like correctional institutions when talking to suspects. A lot of stuff goes on in jail."

Still, as Holt viewed it later, an opportunity had been lost.

Sheila looked down at Holt's card. She waved it. "Yes, yes. Okay. I *want* to talk to you."

When Holt got back to Stamford, he called Sheila's parents, anticipating that they were heading over to the jail to bail Sheila out. He spoke to Sheila's mother. She sounded sincere and cordial.

"Very nice," Holt recalled about her mother.

Sheila had been arraigned again that day and her passport was confiscated by the court and handed over to the WCPD. Holt explained this to Mrs. Davalloo.

"Oh, okay," Sheila's mother said, surprised by this. "We'll be heading down to bail her out later tonight."

Holt left out that he and the SPD had served Sheila with a search warrant that day. Within this time period, the Davalloos and Nelson Sessler believed there was no way Sheila could have murdered Anna Lisa. They believed it to be some sort of misunderstanding, which would be cleared up as soon as Sheila was sprung on bail and had a chance to explain herself. The only one on board with the SPD, besides the WCPD, was Paul Christos, and only halfheartedly. There was still something within Paul that would not allow him to believe entirely that Sheila had murdered Anna Lisa.

Denial.

Holt called Mrs. Davalloo back later that night, around ten-thirty. Mrs. Davalloo said she was going to bail Sheila out.

Holt and the gang were at the jail, waiting to talk to Sheila, simply because she had not yet been bailed out. Sheila had seemed so eager to talk earlier that day. They wanted to get it done. They figured they'd wait at the jail; and as soon as Sheila was sprung, Holt could make his move.

They waited and waited. After a time, Holt put in a call to the guards to round up Sheila so they could speak with her. It was time to talk, no matter where they had to do it.

But Sheila never came.

Something was up, Holt knew.

Where her parents had been "very cordial" during the first phone call, Holt now had two "extremely confrontational" people on his hands. Mr. and Mrs. Davalloo were on the phone—both of whom he had spoken to at various times when he had called back after Sheila refused to meet with them. Now they were angry and outspoken.

"Her hair and saliva was illegally taken without her lawyer present," Mrs. Davalloo told Holt. She was livid.

"I was there, and there was a court order, I can assure you," Holt explained.

"Go to hell," Holt claimed Mrs. Davalloo said to him. "We're not going to help you."

"Will you be bailing her out?" Holt asked. "She really wants to talk to me. She told me earlier. I'm here waiting on her, but she hasn't come."

"No, we are not bailing her out! And we do not wish to speak with you any longer."

Dial tone.

Holt kicked himself. Why hadn't he found a darn closet earlier and allowed Sheila to talk?

After midnight, Holt went back to the jail and asked one of the guards to wake up Sheila and have her come down and speak with him.

This time, she came.

Holt read Sheila her rights.

"You ready now to chat?" Holt asked. Sheila was "sobbing and crying" hysterically, Holt recalled.

"I want to," she said, "but I've been told not to talk to you without my attorney here."

"Let's go," Holt told his colleagues. They began walking out.

Sheila started crying. "I want to . . . but I'm being told not to."

Holt stopped.

Sheila continued to cry as she walked away with a corrections officer.

Holt wanted to scream. From the way she was crying, how she was acting, the sobs and the drooped shoulders, Holt believed Sheila wanted to give it up.

"She was ready."

CHAPTER 72

IN MAY, NELSON Sessler went to the SPD, alongside his lawyer, to offer a suggestion. It seemed Nelson was willing to work with the SPD now and had jumped off the *"I cannot believe she did this"* ship and onto a barge that was moving in the direction of Sheila Davalloo being a cold-blooded sociopath and murderer. To SPD investigators, Nelson was beginning to sound worried that he might be charged with a crime.

"I'd like to tape conversations with Sheila for you," Nelson told the SPD. He outlined how he was willing to contact Sheila and wear a wire or record phone calls—whichever way the SPD wanted to handle it.

Between May and September 2003, Nelson contacted Sheila twice and recorded each conversation, in every instance calling her with the sole intention of getting Sheila to talk about Anna Lisa, hoping that maybe she'd slip up.

The two conversations Nelson recorded and handed to the SPD began with Nelson bringing up Anna Lisa and asking Sheila about her. All it took was for Nelson to mention the name and Sheila went off on a tangent, emphasizing and stressing, in a long-winded way, that she'd had nothing to do with Anna's murder. It was clear right away that Sheila was not stupid enough to fall for Nelson calling her and asking about Anna. She realized he was fishing.

Thus, Sheila was very careful. Nelson asked, for example, "Do you remember the last time you saw [Anna Lisa]?"

Sheila talked in circles, as she generally did when lying, stating, "Actually, we started talking and I said I'd really like to know you more." Sheila was referring to a time when she and Anna worked in the same building and Sheila had just purchased her condo and was thinking of inviting Anna over to check it out (which sounded contrived and unbelievable on its merit alone). "And she wanted to show her place to me. I said, 'Great!'"

And then, almost as if she took the question as an opportunity to plant herself in a position where she was inside Anna's condo (just in case the SPD found DNA), Sheila gave Nelson this line of nonsense: "You know, and that one time I went over to her place, and I think another time with a bunch of other people she had invited. She was very sociable. I guess the last time I saw her was . . . I said hello to her and then I was like—I want to say it was like before Christmas— or maybe not. . . ."

As their conversation continued, Sheila talked and talked and talked. At times, Nelson had trouble getting a word in.

"Is there anything else you want to tell me?" Nelson asked, squeezing his way into another rant by Sheila.

"The bad news is that I cannot tell you much."

"And the *good* news?"

"That I *can* tell that . . . I had nothing to do with it—I'm sorry, Nelson. I'm sorry."

"So there's *no* news? The same news! Soon we'll know the *real* news?" Nelson said, sounding frustrated and impatient.

Nelson also asked about Paul and what actually happened that early evening in March. There seemed to be so many mixed stories. Nelson wanted Sheila's version.

"The fact that you're so adamant about knowing what happened to Paul that day really scares me," Sheila responded. "Like you'll make me trip . . . because all you want is to find out what happened."

"Sheila, I never knew that you were living with Paul."

"I wasn't *living* with him."

"You were married and living with him!"

"I was *not* living with him," Sheila said adamantly. She was firm in her lies, as though she believed them herself. "This is all [what] the police think. They retracted that from the paper. [I was] not living with him." She paused. Then she tried to make her point a bit more emphatically with a sarcastic, rhetorical set of questions: "Where was he? You came over so many times. Where. Was. He?"

Sheila then broke into a colorful bombastic monologue about the police and how they often lie to witnesses to try and gather information about them in order to screw them royally. She insisted she had not been living with Paul when Nelson began coming over in 2003.

An absolute, unequivocal untruth.

"Paul and I," Sheila explained, stretching this lie for as much as she could get out of it, "in fact, when we *were* married, [but] we did *not* live in the condo together. I was—I mean, I wanted to move in with *you*. I wanted us to move in together—"

"Sorry," Nelson said. "Choking on my coffee! All right."

"Anyway, listen, I can only do so much, you know. I cannot—my hands are tied. I cannot—"

"I'm just saying," Nelson interrupted, "it would help me a lot if you just tell me what happened to Paul so that I can just go off and say, 'This is what happened.'"

"Yeah, but that won't—"

"It's black-and-white," Nelson said forcefully. "It's not gray. So it's—"

"But that wouldn't help *me,* Nelson."

And there it was: *me, me, me.* Sheila was protecting herself once again.

"Just to say . . . ," Nelson tried asking.

"That would make my life more difficult."

"How does it make your life difficult?"

"It does. It does!" she responded.

"What happened, regardless of your life?" Nelson pressed.

"No. . . ."

Nelson was losing his footing with Sheila. He had gotten caught up in the moment. Talking to Sheila could have that effect. At one point, Nelson said he was going "back to England" and wanted—deserved—to know the truth before he left. He said he realized Sheila was someone who made up stories, but he was okay with that now. Still, why couldn't she just come clean? Forget everyone else.

"Well, why . . . why . . . When I tell you over and over again . . . several times, I said that somebody else did it! Why is it important to know—why, when, how?"

"Because it's still all a mystery," Nelson countered.

It's important to note here that there was no conversation about the dark figure anywhere. It would have been easy for Sheila to say she was having hallucinations. She could have explained to Nelson that she was battling this dark and evil force she could not control. Heck, the amount of time they spent together, if the dark figure was an absolute, Nelson would have probably experienced her mentioning it at some point. But Sheila never referenced it.

If Sheila was referring to that mythical dark figure when she said "someone else" did all the things she was being accused of, she failed to work it in. This would have been the perfect opportunity to plead with Nelson and let him know that she was sick, psychotically ill.

And yet, when this exchange is studied, there are carefully

thought-out explanations on Sheila's part. One might argue that an insane or temporarily insane human being could not make up such elaborate lies designed to counter truth.

Near the end of this call, Sheila admitted she did not trust Nelson anymore. She talked about how she feared that any information she gave him would end up coming back to bite her at a later point. She was certain Nelson was talking to other people and hunting for information.

In the end, Nelson was about as helpful with these calls as he had been the entire time. He gave nothing to the SPD that it could use against Sheila.

"Nelson did what was asked of him, but nothing further," said one law enforcement source. "He really did not want to be involved, as I think he thought more of his . . . 'lies by omission' might come out. He just wanted this whole thing to be over with as soon as possible."

CHAPTER 73

SHEILA'S LAWYER MADE it known by the end of the summer that his strategy in her upcoming trial, now set for 2004, was going to be a "psychiatric defense." Sheila was going to claim that the dark figure had made her do it—and that she didn't recall much of what had happened.

Whatever she wanted to argue was up to Sheila Davalloo, of course. Westchester County prosecutors were ready for anything Sheila dished out. They had all they needed to put her away for a long time. It was going to be a matter of due process.

Sheila had been arraigned the day after she stabbed Paul. Her bail was set then at $25,000, with an initial charge of assault in the first degree being the only felonious problem in her life. After posting bail several days later, however, Sheila left the Westchester County Jail and voluntarily admitted herself into the Behavioral Health Center of Westchester Medical Center (on the campus of the Westchester County Jail) as an inpatient. She had been admitted on April 4, 2003, and went there directly from jail. She was discharged from the Behavioral Health Center in July 2003; but as that discharge neared and the investigation into what happened with Paul intensified, the court raised her bail to $50,000. Sheila, however, was allowed to live with her parents, who had posted the bail. (This sort of treatment doesn't happen to poor people, incidentally.) She had been indicted during this time by a grand jury—which had increased the charges to attempted murder and another count of assault.

Those were major crimes. Sheila was facing serious time.

Truthfully, there was no way that Sheila could talk herself out of this one. And if Sheila thought the judge in her case (ultimately she would choose a bench trial, facing only a judge and no jury) was not going to find out about her being a suspect in Anna's death, she was kidding herself. The idea that judges and juries don't know about prior cases and don't pay attention to the media is an ignorant opinion.

In today's world of instant news coming all day long, there is no way to block it out, save for retiring to a mountain retreat with no power source.

Meanwhile, addressing him as "sweetheart," Sheila wrote a few letters to Nelson. These letters, at face value, might have seemed like an attempt on Sheila's part to try and win her old flame back and get him to come around to her side. But when looked at objectively, they were a well-thought-out plan to mount a defense and plant certain bits of information into the public. With every perfectly written missive Sheila sent, infused with that extreme hubris of hers that she could not hide, Sheila also used the page as a pulpit to address herself to the police. It was so obvious what she was doing with these letters, it was embarrassing to read them.

She told Nelson in one letter that she was "now glad" he had told the police about them. In light of that, she insisted, she was "not the least bit worried or upset" that he had done so.

As if Nelson actually gave two shakes about what she thought at this point.

Sheila went on to say how, if she had known about Nelson and Anna Lisa planning on making house together or even dating, she would have "stopped seeing" Nelson in an instant, and she "felt sorry" for Anna.

Really?

Sheila had not only stalked Anna and Nelson, and spoken to countless coworkers about them, but she had listened to Nelson's voice mails.

If that wasn't enough, Sheila had the nerve to say she would have contacted Anna Lisa and "maybe warned her" about Nelson.

She ended the paragraph by claiming she would have "felt sympathetic" toward Anna Lisa, "not murderous," finally concluding this senseless collage of lies with one of her stupid, adolescent poems, which she had likely plagiarized a large part of.

"Pathetic" and "cowardice."

Those are the two words that ring in one's ears as the letters are read. And to think how Sheila could have chosen not to say anything only brings another layer of disgust to her character. The fact that she actually had the nerve to say she felt sorry for Anna showed how cold and uncaring and unremorseful she truly was.

"Like I have always said," Detective Alison Carpentier later commented after reading this letter, "it's all about Sheila. When I interviewed her, the only time she cried was for herself—*never* for Paul. She wants to always say, 'Why is this happening to *me*?' and play the role of the perpetual victim. 'Poor Sheila.' She will never confess. She used to tell Paul . . . that she couldn't have done the murder because she can't stand blood. I guess it didn't bother her when she was plunging that knife into Paul's heart. If you talk to her now, she would say she understands why Nelson doesn't bother with her. In reality, she is very angry at him for leaving her. She is mad he doesn't believe her and feels he has picked Anna Lisa over her by not standing by her during this ordeal. . . . The letters do not surprise me—classic Sheila Davalloo."

CHAPTER 74

THE SPD HAD sent out the tape of the 911 call to a well-respected voice-analysis expert for comparison. If they could get an expert on record saying he believed the voice on the 911 call was Sheila's, it would add to the amount of circumstantial evidence investigators were collecting, now including countless witness statements detailing how Sheila had talked to them about this "Jack, Melissa, and Anna Lisa" narrative. In the SPD's eyes, a solid case for murder could be brought against Sheila. But as February 2004 approached, with Sheila's attempted-murder trial set to begin, Sheila was only a suspect in Anna Lisa Raymundo's murder.

In his review of that crucial 911 call, voice-analysis expert Thomas Owen concluded that the caller exhibited "psychological stress, voice quiver, and somewhat constricted speech." Owen claimed in his detailed report to the SPD that his company, Owl Investigations, was certain, however, that the 911 caller's stress was undoubtedly caused by "fear and anxiety," which was "reflected vocally." Owen then listed all the characteristics that were similar to the person he believed had made the call. A forensic voice analyst, Owen used computers to match Sheila's voice up to that of the 911 caller.

When he looked at it all as a graphic and charted the two calls side by side, there was no doubt in his mind.

It is the opinion of this examiner, based on my education, training, certification, and experience, that the voice on the 911 call I examined is that of Sheila Davalloo. I make this opinion to a reasonable degree of scientific certainty, Owen concluded in his report.

Sheila couldn't hide from herself. She could deny—and she would—that it was her voice, but the science proved different.

Contrary to Owen's opinion, though, several people whom the SPD had interviewed and played the tape for claimed they could not recognize Sheila as the caller.

CHAPTER 75

THE ENTIRE ARGUMENT from Sheila's camp during her February 2004 bench trial on attempted-murder charges was that she "didn't mean to hurt her spouse." Sheila's hired medical gun walked into the courtroom and explained Sheila was "psychotic" and did not intend to cause Paul harm.

She couldn't help herself, in other words.

A dark figure took over.

Westchester County assistant district attorney (ADA) Dan Schorr put up his own doctor countering Sheila's, a man who had interviewed Sheila at length and claimed after a detailed evaluation that Sheila knew exactly what she was doing. Sheila had problems, no doubt about it—but they did not involve her mind being taken over by an evil, dark figure.

The most compelling evidence, of course, came from Paul's dramatic personal story of having been attacked by the woman he knew as his wife. Paul was charming and came across as genuine and blameless. There was no reason Paul had to lie under oath. He had not seen or spoken to Sheila since the incident. He harbored no resentment. He was more confused than anything. And with his soft, academic voice, Paul told the judge how it happened, step-by-step.

It was hard to discount this evidence. The guy was obviously torn and upset having to testify about such a terrible moment in his life—this, mind you, when many of the papers were calling what happened a "kinky" sex game gone wrong.

With Paul's testimony setting the stage, Alison Carpentier and other law enforcement came in to wrap it all up with a bow. Then an expert psychologist described for the judge a woman not psychotically ill in the manner she was arguing.

Thus, there was no getting out of testifying *if* Sheila saw herself walking out of that courtroom and into a mental hospital.

So, on February 9, 2004, that's exactly what Sheila did.

Sheila Davalloo looked well-rested and rather calm walking toward the stand, raising her hand, and pledging an oath to God.

Tom McGinty sat in the gallery, watching the trial, eagerly anticipating what Sheila had to say. McGinty was hoping to find something in her testimony to bury her on in the Stamford case. The Stamford district attorney (DA) was giving the SPD a hard time where it pertained to bringing charges against Sheila. He kept telling them to go back to the well—there just wasn't enough. SPD investigators were getting frustrated and impatient with the DA.

Opening her direct testimony, Sheila was asked by her lawyer, Theodore "Ted" Brundage, to digress. She should go back to those weeks prior to March 23, 2003. She should talk to the judge about who she was then, her marriage, how things were in her life.

Of course, Sheila couched her answer around what Paul had testified to previously: that their lives were "pretty erratic."

Then she began her campaign to bring in that dark figure, explaining how she was "not functioning one hundred percent." During this period of her life, Sheila claimed, she was supposedly losing a sense of her mind. This became the mantra that Sheila expounded upon in the courtroom, as though it was all part of her DNA. The drum of her being bipolar and acting strangely would now beat nonstop. Effectively, it was the only chance she had.

From the theme of her not being able to do even the simplest tasks at home to becoming a chronic painkiller addict, Sheila painted a portrait of herself as a broken woman, a woman in need of desperate help, a woman hanging on by an emotional thread and leaning on everyone around her.

In reality, however, Paul had said he checked the medicine cabinets in the house after hearing about this supposed drug addiction his wife had and found nothing but half-full and nearly full bottles of painkiller prescriptions (in Sheila's name), adding, "If she was a drug addict, wouldn't those bottles be empty?"

Bet your ass, they would have been!

Ted Brundage moved on to the interview Alison Carpentier conducted with Sheila right after she stabbed Paul with the intent of murdering him. Brundage needed his client to explain away her lack of honesty during that interview. He needed an excuse for Sheila's canned lies and aha moments of revelation.

"You didn't speak openly and honestly [to Detective Carpentier]," Brundage pointed out. "You told an hour-long lie—why?"

It was several hours, actually—but who's counting?

"Just out of ignorance and being scared . . . ," Sheila said, perhaps forgetting that the judge would view the videotape and see for himself that she didn't come across as someone frightened, but rather as someone falling over her own lies. The interview, after all, spoke for itself. Every time Carpentier approached Sheila with a new revelation that the WCPD had dug up, or something Paul had told them, Sheila tried swatting it away by saying something like, *"Oh yeah . . . that. Let me explain."*

So in trying to defend her, Brundage questioned Sheila about her memory coming back in pieces. Why was that?

"I was, I don't know, I'm not sure who I was protecting. I mean, in the beginning, maybe Paul was very embarrassed about the thing. . . . And then when the detective started coming out with [different parts of the story], I thought, 'Great, she knows and I can talk to her now.'"

Sheila said she had no recollection of stabbing Paul.

Not then.

Not now.

The direct questioning by Sheila's defense attorney was predictably brief. Less is always more when a pathological liar is put on the stand.

After a few more inconsequential questions, Brundage asked, "Did you intend to kill your husband on March 23, 2003?"

"Absolutely not!" Sheila uttered indignantly. "I mean, as far as my recollection serves me, I, you know, the world's a better place with Paul in it, and I know that, and have always known that. I have known that for ten years. I would never harm him."

One has to wonder why Sheila hadn't hired a violinist to come in at this point and play a little melancholy ditty from Mozart.

ADA Dan Schorr obviously had some questions for Sheila Davalloo. He began with what had become the theme of Sheila's life—the one emotion that drove this woman more than anything else.

"Prior to March twenty-third, you were *obsessed* with Nelson Sessler, right?"

"No!" she declared.

"No?"

"We had a sexual relationship, and that's about it."

Schorr reminded Sheila that she had told the DA's psychologist that she was obsessed with Nelson, as well as telling it to several other mental-health professionals she had seen at various times. Her *obsession* was on the record.

Sheila changed her tune and, from then on, she began referring to her relationship with Nelson as a "sexual obsession."

Schorr asked if she was disagreeing with having said she was obsessed with Nelson.

"I just never thought of myself as being obsessed with him because I kept getting tired of him," Sheila said.

Sheila would not agree with much of what the prosecutor had to say. It was as though everything the ADA brought up was grounds for Sheila to pick apart and deny. It became, honestly, nauseating to many in the courtroom. She came across as arrogant and unwilling to admit to anything.

They went back and forth for a long while, trading barbs. Sheila would often come around when she found herself backed into a corner with no way to lie her way out of it. And yet, even during those moments when she seemed to agree, she always managed to expand and expound upon whatever it was the prosecutor asked.

Schorr became a bit frustrated by this tactic at one point. He asked: "Well, in between the time you were stabbing your husband and driving to the hospital, *then* you were thinking of Nelson, right?"

"I don't think I was thinking," Sheila answered.

Schorr asked Sheila about the phone call she placed to

Nelson "while your husband was stabbed and bleeding in your home."

"It's possible," Sheila said, "because Nelson was going to come over that night or he said—"

Smartly, Schorr interrupted, saying, "That's *not* my question. My question is, did you place a call to Nelson Sessler while your husband was stabbed and bleeding in your home?"

"I don't specifically remember, but if the records say I did, I must have."

Schorr said he wasn't interested in what the records said, but if Sheila remembered calling Nelson.

"I do not remember," she said.

Asking the judge if he could "refresh" Sheila's memory, Schorr produced People's Exhibit Number 196, a photo of Sheila's cell phone.

Sheila agreed it was her cell phone.

Schorr explained that inside the memory of that cell phone was evidence that proved Sheila (or someone using her cell phone) called Nelson that evening at four fifty-nine—in other words, as Paul was bleeding to death on the couch. It was so obvious that when Sheila had made that call, she believed Paul was going to die, which would open up the opportunity for Nelson to come over for dinner.

That is, after she cleaned up the blood and got rid of Paul's body.

Sheila backed off and admitted that, yes, perhaps she *had* called Nelson, after all.

Schorr asked if she could recall what time she stabbed Paul.

Sheila said she hadn't a clue.

Then it was back to: "But you were thinking of Nelson Sessler [while calling him]?"

"I wasn't. I was thinking of Paul at the time."

"You were thinking of *Paul* when you called Nelson, or when you stabbed him?" Schorr asked.

"No, I was thinking of—"

But Brundage objected before she could finish.

After some discussion, they moved on.

As the testimony continued, Sheila was caught in repeated lies—although, true to her nature, she never admitted to it. It was like Carpentier was there once again questioning her. Whenever Schorr produced a document or piece of evidence indicating that perhaps Sheila wasn't being totally honest, there was that *"Oh yeah"* moment again from Sheila.

"You're talking about that. . . . Oh, sure, I remember now."

An interesting, if not laughable, moment came after ADA Schorr brought up the love triangle this way: "Now, isn't it true that when you were having an affair with Nelson Sessler, you actually told Paul about the affair, but you used fake names to say that other people were engaged in this affair?"

"I may have alluded to it, yes."

Imagine: *"I may have alluded to it, yes."*

"'Alluded to it'?" Schorr exploded, not allowing Sheila a pass on this one. "You actually talked about it *every* day a lot of times, didn't you?"

"Well, I mean, I alluded to it in the sense that I was talking very discreetly about it in terms of fake names, like you say."

"Didn't you tell Paul about a love triangle at work?"

Sheila: "I may have, yes."

"I may have, yes."

Sheila's testimony became ridiculous. And yet it proved how callous and shallow and heartless she was to sit there and give these answers with a straight face.

CHAPTER 76

ADA DAN SCHORR, using every bit of the arsenal of evidence he had at his disposal, submitted a copy of Fran Lourie's report from her conversations with Sheila back in late 2002. It was from that time when Sheila had sought Lourie's help in dealing with what she described then as a fantasy and obsession with a coworker, not mentioning to Lourie that she was, of course, married. In that report, Fran Lourie talked about how Sheila said many of her friends were sick and tired of hearing about the affair between her and Nelson (when she actually was prattling on at work about fictional Melissa and Jack).

"No friends of mine knew about Nelson," Sheila said after Schorr asked.

It was odd how when confronted with objective, seemingly incontrovertible evidence, Sheila would never admit to it entirely. Instead, quite abrasively, she'd come up with an excuse or some other way of explaining away what was an impartial opinion from a therapist or a doctor. And what became incredibly transparent as her testimony went on, beleaguered and contrived as it sounded, was that Sheila Davalloo was never going to admit to anything. Her truth was the only truth, and there was nobody who could tell her any different.

Schorr then focused his questioning on the game and the actual stabbing. But again, Sheila kept repeating herself with "I don't recall" and "I have no memory of that." Anytime ADA Schorr posed what seemed to be a quite easy, noncombative question to answer—such as, "You were blindfolded, right?"—Sheila could not just say "yes" or "no." Instead, she had to come up with some sort of long-winded explanation as to why she was saying "yes" or "no." Schorr asked if a chair was involved, for example, and Sheila responded: "Generally, the chair was involved, because all the pictures show the chair was broken."

Generally?

Always, from Sheila's perspective, the onus was on what the photos and/or reports or Paul had to say, not her. She would not take ownership of anything.

Her testimony was confusing.

Felonious.

Shameless.

Embarrassing.

Disrespectful.

Alarming.

Irresponsible.

Idiotic.

Sheila Davalloo was digging a hole for herself, lie by lie. A woman full of sin, jumping into the water, hoping for baptismal redemption, but knowing damn well she did not know how to swim, to begin with. This was Sheila Davalloo.

No judge was going to buy into this nonsense.

Schorr asked next about Sheila's supposed dark figure.

Contradicting just about all she had ever said about it, Sheila claimed she wasn't present for most of the game, adding, "The only time I saw a dark figure, which I'm not really sure what it was, was, you know, when I was scrounging around looking for another object and I saw a dark figure . . . in the vicinity of the kitchen area. . . ."

Regarding the 911 fiasco, Schorr said: "You never called 911, right?"

"I'm not sure if I did or didn't. If the records show I didn't, I didn't, but I may have. I should have called 911."

Three different answers.

"Okay," Schorr responded patronizingly, "*instead* of calling Nelson?"

"I definitely should have called 911."

"You told Paul you were calling 911, right?"

"No!" She was certain of this.

"You *never* told Paul you were calling 911?"

"No. If I did, I don't recall, and it would be, I don't know . . ."

Schorr tried to get Sheila to admit she had feigned a call to 911, but she was not going there, making the claim she would never do something so deliberate like that, especially to Paul.

Then it was back to the knife.

The dark figure again.

Traveling to the hospital.

The 911 call (again).

Sheila not knowing where to find the ER.

Sheila's mother had worked in the hospital for eighteen years, Schorr pointed out. How could Sheila not have any clue where that hospital was located? It didn't make much sense to a rational person with common sense. But if that's what Sheila wanted to put on record, Schorr maintained, so be it.

Near the end of his cross-examination, ADA Dan Schorr brought it back to Sheila's conversation with the county's psychologist and something she had said during that interview. It was a brilliant note to strike, leaving the judge with a solid taste resonating on his taste buds of who Sheila Davalloo was: "You told [our psychologist] these exact words, 'I know I lied to everybody.'" Dan Schorr paused. Then he asked, "Right?"

"If the report says I said that," Sheila proclaimed once again in her true narcissistic evasiveness, "I must have said that."

Schorr simply shook his head in disgust.

They exchanged a few additional words, and Sheila tried to talk her way out of being caught in yet another tight position.

Dan Schorr then followed up with repeating how Sheila had told the state's psychologist that she lied to everybody about everything.

"I don't recall saying that," Sheila repeated—and then perhaps slipped, adding, "But I have lied a lot, yes."

Schorr saw an opening and took it: "Thank you. Nothing further."

On redirect, Ted Brundage asked Sheila about Nelson. "Did you know him to be an honest person in his dealings with other people?"

"No! Nelson tells more lies than truths!" Sheila spewed the answer like venom.

Schorr objected. Nelson wasn't on trial here.

Brundage rephrased the question: "To your knowledge, was Nelson having affairs with more than two people at Purdue?"

"Yes."

Sheila then painted Nelson as a serial cheater, telling the court that all their coworkers at Purdue knew it.

After a few more questions, that was it.

Both lawyers indicated they had nothing further.

CHAPTER 77

AS TRIALS GO, this one turned out to be as close to a slam dunk as a prosecutor wanted to see come across his desk. Trouble was, in the reality of a courtroom, with a bench trial—same as if a jury had been chosen—anything was possible. Sometimes the judge (or jury) saw and heard things different from what was expected.

For ADA Dan Schorr, however, that would not be the case.

As Sheila was brought back into the courtroom to hear the verdict on February 19, 2004, Tom McGinty sat in the empty jury box watching her closely. McGinty was there to gauge Sheila's reaction, to see how she was going to take being found guilty of a crime. McGinty was beginning to believe that the stabbing was actually the final part of a premeditated plot to take out any obstacle in the way of Sheila and her obsession with Nelson.

Sheila stood with her hands folded. She moved her thumb over her other fingers while looking back and forth, side to side, around the courtroom. She gave the appearance of a professional—the researcher and highly paid pharmaceutical worker she once was. She certainly did not look like a woman who had viciously murdered one female and violently stabbed her husband repeatedly, with the hope of putting him in an early grave.

Then again, what does a heartless murderer and cold-blooded sociopath look like?

Here was a thirty-four-year-old woman standing before state supreme court justice Thomas Dickerson. She was twiddling her thumbs; and her mind, obviously, was moving a mile a minute. She showed no emotion. She didn't seem one bit sorry for putting the court or Paul through all that she had. Instead, Sheila Davalloo stood upright, as if waiting in line at the DMV. She seemed to want to get this over with so she could move on to whatever she had planned next for that day.

Dickerson read some legal mumbo-jumbo and then pronounced Sheila Davalloo guilty of assault and criminal possession of a weapon, as well as the major charge of attempted murder.

Sheila was going to be spending some serious time behind bars.

She never winced or reacted—besides, that is, displaying a slight smile as guards handcuffed her and put an arm on her shoulder to lead her away.

Being taken from the courtroom, Sheila needed to say something. So she stopped. She turned to one of the court officers and asked that they would "please give" her car keys to a family member. Here was a woman who had just been found guilty of attempted murder—not to mention being investigated for a brutal murder—and she was worried about her car.

Months later, Sheila was given the maximum penalty for her crimes. Twenty-five years in the pen. That would keep her warm and cozy while the SPD continued building its case against her for first-degree murder.

What no one realized then—as the Stamford case seemed to be coming together and looked rather good, now that

Sheila had shown a precedent for violence—was that it would take nearly a decade before Sheila found herself in a court-room again. It would be almost a decade before she would stand once more and face a judge or a jury—and, boy, there would be many revelations along the way as this new case moved toward potential prosecution.

ACT FIVE

THE DÉNOUEMENT

CHAPTER 78

PAUL CHRISTOS HAD filed for divorce back in May 2003. He was granted that freedom from Sheila by October 2004. Expediting the dissolution of the marriage did not stop Paul from caring about Sheila, however. To the credit of Paul's tremendous spirit and overall good-hearted nature, what worried Paul was that if Sheila had a psychotic brother, then she, too, could be mentally ill. If she was, Paul wanted nothing to do with judging her behavior and pledged to give her his unconditional support, regardless of what had occurred throughout their lives together.

Still, this did not mean Paul wanted to see Sheila on a regular basis or develop a new friendship with her. Between the stabbing event in April 2003 and Sheila's court case in 2004, Paul had no contact with Sheila. And yet there was one question plaguing him as he began going through the past few years of his life and that love triangle of Jack, Melissa, and Anna Lisa, which Sheila had brought into the marriage.

Paul finally spoke to Sheila one afternoon in the prison she now called home after her sentencing. He asked a question that had been on his mind for some time.

"Why didn't you tell me Anna Lisa had been killed?"

If Sheila had had nothing to do with the murder, why

wouldn't she include that information as part of the soap opera narrative—that Anna had been murdered? Why leave that important piece of the story out?

"If I told you that Anna Lisa had died," Sheila responded, "you would have stumbled onto the whole affair."

In a strange way, it kind of made sense. For Paul, he considered that if she had told him, "I would have learned that Anna Lisa was not dating a man named Jack—and that it was, in fact, Nelson."

As they talked further over a period of weeks, Sheila kept going back to that "dark figure" persona, giving Paul a description of what happened that evening inside the condo. "I saw this dark figure picking up a knife and hitting you with it," she told him. "But I do not have any recollection of doing it myself. It was the dark figure."

This statement was in total contrast to what she had testified.

Then Sheila admitted to Paul how, at one time, she "wanted to break into Anna's condo and hide under her bed."

The lock pick set . . .

Paul was taken aback by this, obviously. It was beginning to seem as though Sheila was not only obsessed with Nelson, but with Anna, too.

"Why did you want to break in, Sheila?" Paul asked.

"I wanted to get under the bed and then hear what their conversations were," Sheila explained.

Paul asked if this was why she had purchased the stun gun.

"Yes," Sheila told him. "Because if I had gotten caught underneath the bed, I would have had something to protect myself."

This was certainly behavior that could lead to bad things happening to good people. But what Sheila next said was so off the mark—yet in total symmetry with her hubristic, narcissistic character—that Paul had to think she had not only stabbed him willingly and with malice, but she had murdered Anna, too.

"I'm thinking of writing a fictional account of Anna's murder," Sheila explained to Paul. "What do you think?"

He was speechless.

CHAPTER 79

GREG HOLT AND Tom McGinty kept their minds open where it pertained to who had murdered Anna Lisa Raymundo. They had a good feeling about Sheila as the culprit. The evidence was building toward her role in the crime.

"But we just weren't sure," Holt recalled.

And there was nothing worse for a case than a cop putting blinders on and heading down a path—especially at this stage in the game.

So the SPD submitted to the state crime lab the DNA search warrant evidence that they had collected from Sheila at the jail.

The problem was, Holt explained, that "nothing moves in a DNA lab for months. . . . You wait and wait."

It's the nature of police work. Things take time. Particularly science.

Tom McGinty was curious about the injury Sheila had sustained to her hand. If it looked as bad as it had two weeks after the murder (when Paul and others had reported seeing it), if Sheila had cut herself while killing Anna Lisa, then there must be a record somewhere of her going for treatment. She couldn't have cut herself that severely and not gotten someone to look at it.

On a hunch, Tom McGinty took off one day. Here was a cop, as tenacious and patient as a spider, following his instincts. He was not some fly-off-the-handle rookie looking to muscle up some answers, but rather he was an old-school detective doing what any investigator should do when faced with brick walls. McGinty knew that if Sheila Davalloo had used a local—or even not-so-local—medical center or walk-in strip mall medical stop-and-go that she wasn't smart enough to use a fake name or even drive one hundred miles out of the area. What Sheila had done in trying to murder Paul was proof to McGinty and Holt that Sheila Davalloo, as much education as she'd had, was not at all intelligent.

McGinty drove around Westchester County, spending an entire day, going to every "doc-in-the-box" he could find, asking about Sheila and her cut finger. He'd started out going to hospitals. However, hospitals were a bit harder to get immediate medical info from without a warrant. And a hospital, the detective surmised, was probably not going to be Sheila's first choice.

Driving away from one hospital, McGinty came upon a medical center, a small one in a strip of other buildings.

McGinty parked and walked in. "Let me ask you this," he said to the woman at the counter, "can you tell me whether Mrs. Davalloo was treated or not? . . ." The woman looked at him and thought about it. Then she took off into a back room.

When she returned, the woman said, "Yeah, looks like she was treated here . . . back last year."

That was enough for McGinty to complete a search warrant and obtain those records, which proved that Sheila Davalloo was indeed treated for a "significant laceration" the day *after* Anna Lisa was murdered.

What were the chances of that being a coincidence?

With that information, on top of everything else they had developed, McGinty and Holt felt a strong case was building against Sheila. So as 2004 wound down and the spring of 2005 came, heading toward three full years since Anna's murder, the SPD took what they had to the prosecutor's office and met with state's attorney (SA) James Bernardi.

"Not enough," Bernardi quipped. Bernardi was one of those prosecutors who liked to have his cases wrapped up tightly, no fray or doubt. He wanted evidence he could easily explain to a jury.

Clean-cut, with clay gray hair and a runner's body, Bernardi had that gaze of a prosecutor, cutting and deliberate. He respected juries. He knew that it was a rough job for an average American to put aside his or her everyday concerns, show up, and pay full attention while sitting in that jury box—and if the prosecutor didn't have the proverbial aha moment to break out during the trial, Bernardi knew it was a crapshoot, no matter how certain the investigators were of their case.

In fact, as they developed more evidence and felt their case was growing stronger by the month, all the SPD heard from Bernardi was "Still, not enough. . . ."

Bernardi told the SPD over and over that he wasn't taking on Sheila Davalloo until he had "something that will win the case."

"They wanted to offer her twenty years," one law enforcement source said. "Bernardi was hopeless. He kept telling us, 'We'll *never* win this case.'"

"And every time we'd go over there with a new morsel," said that same investigator, "it was like, 'Not enough.'"

Frustrating doesn't even begin to explain what these cops went through with James Bernardi and the state's attorney's office (SAO).

Apparently, the Stamford-based prosecutor was scared that even with all of the evidence they had, a circumstantial case against Sheila Davalloo would not transform into a guilty verdict. Some voice expert wasn't going to cut it. A laceration to the hand of the suspect treated the day after the homicide was not enough. One of the biggest blows became that the state medical examiner's office could not say Anna's body had any stun gun marks on it. They had photos of the marks. But as Dr. Henry Lee later pointed out, "There was no ruler next to the marks. . . ." So there was no way to judge the size or scope of the two burn dots on Anna's body. Effectively, the dots could be anything. There was nothing backing up the notion that Sheila used a stun gun on Anna.

Near the end of the year 2006, after a fairly quiet year (2005), McGinty and Holt developed a piece of information about Anna Lisa they believed could help significantly. So McGinty got Nelson Sessler on the horn and asked him about it.

"Look, have you ever told Sheila that Anna Lisa was raped twice?"

Nelson became "upset and puzzled," McGinty later reported.

"Never . . . never," Nelson said.

"Are you *sure* that you've never heard of such an allegation?"

Nelson thought about it. He explained the only time he "thought Anna might have been raped" was when he spoke to someone she knew very well after her murder and this person told Sessler that some guy "might have done bad [things] to Anna while she was at Harvard." But that was the extent of it. Nothing else.

"But I'm absolutely positive that I never told Sheila about this."

"Did you have sex with Sheila in North Carolina at any time while you were with her in those weeks before Anna Lisa's murder?"

Sessler said no. He then insisted to McGinty that he had

"stopped having sex with Sheila months prior to Anna being murdered."

And yet after the murder, beginning in early 2003, Sessler picked up the relationship again and started sleeping with Sheila.

Hope, once again, turned into dust.

CHAPTER 80

HOLT AND MCGINTY had developed a tight, personal connection to Anna Lisa's family, her sister, Bernadette, and her father and mother, Renato and Susan. As they chatted about the case throughout the years, Holt could hear the pain in their voices and sense the edginess and anxiety that the case against Sheila was going on and on with seemingly no arrest in sight.

"They would listen and they were patient," Holt remembered. "All the time that went by, there was never any pressure from them. They never went over our head and called the chief to ask, 'Why isn't this case being solved?'"

The Raymundos, to their absolute resolve and understanding and faith, always believed time would eventually catch up to Anna's murderer.

The vibe Holt got from them always was "We trust you two guys," Holt and McGinty.

"It breaks your heart," Holt recalled. "Because nothing was happening."

The state's attorney, as the summer of 2007 passed, still wanted nothing to do with prosecuting Sheila Davalloo.

It seemed as if Sheila was going to get away with murder.

CHAPTER 81

THERE WAS ONE day while Greg Holt was at home recuperating from back surgery (that car accident injury he had sustained years earlier during the Florida trip had never healed properly) and his phone rang.

Holt put the television remote down and answered.

"It's Tom. You going to be around today?"

"Yeah, yeah. What's up?"

"I'm in court right now, but can I stop by afterward?"

"Tommy, come on, you don't need an invitation to come over here."

They hung up. Holt walked back to the couch, stopped, and stared at the telephone: *This is odd. . . . That's not Tommy.*

Something was up.

Tom McGinty walked in some hours later and stood before Holt.

Holt knew his partner. "He's got something," Holt recalled. "I could tell by the look on his face."

"What is it?" Holt asked.

"We got her!" McGinty said, cracking a stolid smile.

"What . . . what are you talking about?"

McGinty explained that he was in court that day when a colleague sought him out to tell him the DNA they had submitted so long ago had come back. After processing the DNA from Anna's condo, a small speck of blood on the faucet handle in Anna's bathroom matched with the sample Sheila had given freely that day in jail. In fact, on that faucet handle was a mixture of Anna's and Sheila's blood.

Science had confirmed it.

"Son of a bitch . . . ," Holt said. "That's it! We got her, Tommy."

And suddenly, just like that, a completely circumstantial, evidentiary case had gone from lukewarm to steaming hot as it turned into a forensic case. Sheila's DNA—her blood—had been found inside Anna's condo.

There was no reason for Sheila Davalloo's blood to be there.

So Tom McGinty then went back to Nelson Sessler and asked about any Christmas parties at the condo, get-togethers, or any other social situations where Sheila could stake the claim that she was inside Anna's condo.

Nelson said no way. There was not a chance he would have ever had Sheila over to the condo. Anyway, Sheila and Anna did not know each other. They might have bumped elbows at a company event when Anna worked at Purdue, or passed each other in the hallway, but they were not even acquaintances.

Besides, why would Sheila's blood be inside the condo even if she had visited Anna Lisa herself under a social situation? And taking it further, why would that blood be found mixed with Anna's and still be there days, weeks, or months after a supposed visit?

"We tried to close every door and were able to prove that she had never been over to Anna Lisa's condo," Holt explained.

As they sat and studied the case from Sheila's point of view, an alarming reality became clear to Holt and McGinty. As Greg Holt explained it, Sheila Davalloo must have "meticulously" planned and carried out Anna Lisa's murder. Based on the evidence they had, there could be no credence given to the notion that Sheila had flown off the handle into a fit of anger and then effectively snapped.

"Think about it," Holt theorized, "this was not a spur-of-the moment or jealous-rage type of crime. But she was concocting this love triangle and she had to know—and this is very important—that Anna Lisa was taking that day off and working from home, and had to know that Sessler was not going to leave the [Purdue] building at all, that he wasn't taking a half a day or going on a road trip. She had to *know,* moreover, what unit Anna lived in . . . the *exact* door to knock on. . . ."

Indeed, the meticulous preparation and plotting this murder took was evident in the case they built against Sheila. As the picture came into focus, the reality of how desperately Sheila Davalloo needed to kill Anna disgusted Holt and the SPD: Sheila had freely chosen a target and carried out this violent, brutal crime.

Equally disturbing, Greg Holt thought (same as many other cops involved in the case), was that Sheila must have also prepared herself and her body forensically for the murder because of the lack of forensic trace evidence found—i.e., wearing a hat or a hairnet, gloves, certain type of clothing, etc.

Calculated premeditation, indeed.

For Sheila to claim later—if she was going down this road—that a dark figure took over and murdered Anna Lisa (the same as it had attacked Paul) would not work in this situation. Sheila carefully executed this crime of murder with absolute precision and passion. Even the fact that months prior to the crime she had purchased a stun gun proved, without a doubt, she was thinking about harming Anna before she had done the job.

And yet, Sheila Davalloo, within that careful planning, never banked on the common factor that no murder is perfect.

There are always anomalies.

Contingencies.

Mistakes.

In this case, her blood mixing with Anna's on a faucet handle inside the downstairs bathroom in Anna's condo.

That small speck of DNA alone was going to bury Sheila Davalloo.

CHAPTER 82

A LEVEL OF frustration had been building between the SPD and SA James Bernardi. The SPD was wondering what it had to do in order to get the guy to sign off on an arrest warrant.

"We have what we have," said one source within the department, "and we're [asking] the court to sign off on a murder warrant and they *just* won't do it."

Months turned into years.

For some, frustration turned into resentment.

What it amounted to from the perspective of the prosecutor's office was that the pressure wasn't on the SAO to investigate or begin preparing a case *until* the arrest warrant was issued. So the SAO could keep telling the SPD or any other investigating agency in the region under its jurisdiction: "There isn't enough—keep digging. We want a little more."

The difficulty in asking for more, any seasoned investigator knew, was that sometimes a case just didn't get a little more and the prosecutors had to take a chance and move on with what they had.

Bernardi, many agreed, had a "great legal mind." The guy was vicious and thorough in a courtroom. Yet, he also came across as a prosecutor who was being distracted by surrounding circumstances. There were cases on top of cases, not enough help, budget cuts, and interfering politics.

This was the last thing a cop with a strong case against a murder suspect wanted to hear.

It got to the point where McGinty and Bernardi stopped talking.

"We had to put someone else in the room with them when they got together," one source said. "There were many arguments."

The SPD felt they were being held hostage by the state's attorney's office. There was no other prosecutorial agency where they could take the case.

CHAPTER 83

JAMES BERNARDI WAS finally convinced (if still quite reluctantly) by November 2007 that the SPD had enough on Sheila to at least make an arrest. Taking Sheila to trial was going to be a whole new fight for the SPD and the state's attorney.

In McGinty's extremely detailed arrest warrant, the gold nugget was included within item #55, in where McGinty wrote about *numerous items collected as evidence from the Raymundo residence. . . .* Add that to Sheila's DNA submission from prison and there was the smoking gun. Bottom line, according to McGinty's meticulous and expertly written warrant, that mixture of Sheila and Anna's blood on the faucet handle found by forensics included *a frequency of individuals who could be contributor[s] . . . [to the tune of] 1 in 28 million to the African American population . . . 1 in 8.5 million in the Caucasian population . . . 1 in 25 million in the Hispanic population.*

Even more important, one investigator pointed out, "That blood speck on the faucet that turned out to be Davalloo's could not have been there too long when we found it because of the humid environment bathrooms are susceptible to."

In other words, it wasn't as if Sheila had visited the condo a month before and haphazardly left behind her DNA.

CHAPTER 84

ON DECEMBER 29, 2008, over one year later, Tom McGinty and several colleagues drove from Stamford, Connecticut, northwest up to the Bedford Hills Correctional Facility, in Bedford Hills, New York, to serve Sheila with an arrest warrant on a single charge of murder. The reason for the long pause between issuing the arrest warrant and serving it became a matter of buying extra time for the SAO.

"There was a specific time limit that once she was arrested, Bernardi had to bring her to trial in Stamford because she was an out-of-state prisoner," a law enforcement source explained. "So she was not arrested until Bernardi felt he was ready, which he never did. He offered her twenty years to plead (five years *less* than she got in New York for attempted murder) and told us this case was not a winner, 'circumstantial only.' She obviously did not take the plea and forced his hand to go to trial."

Typical Sheila Davalloo.

McGinty transported Sheila to the SPD for booking at nine fifty-six that morning.

The trip . . . and the booking, McGinty later wrote, *went without incident.*

Thirty-nine-year-old Sheila Davalloo was charged with the

murder of Anna Lisa Raymundo six years after Anna's violent death.

Sheila's bond was set at $1 million. Fairly standard for this type of situation—however, it didn't really matter, seeing that she was serving twenty-five years for attempting to murder Paul.

Sheila was then brought back to Bedford Hills, where she would begin the process of preparing for the fight of her life.

CHAPTER 85

IT WOULD BE nearly three years from Sheila's arrest on murder charges until the case went to court. Sheila pleaded not guilty, obviously. There was no way she was going to admit to murder, much less the brutal murder of her love triangle rival, when she couldn't—and wouldn't—confess to stabbing her own husband amid a cavalcade of evidence.

By the time court proceedings began and Sheila's trial got on track, nearly ten years had elapsed since Anna Lisa's murder.

It was almost nine years, nearly a full decade.

Justice sometimes requires patience.

In a major blow to the defense that Sheila was mounting, in September 2011, Stamford Superior Court judge Richard Comerford ruled that during the murder trial James Bernardi and his prosecuting team could use Sheila's past conviction of attempting to murder Paul. Sheila, of course, was hoping to get it tossed.

Judge Comerford explained to the court on Thursday, September 1, 2011, how he had based his decision on the legal argument that the 2003 attempted murder charge and later conviction established "motive" and particularly displayed a clear link to the murder of Anna Lisa. As detrimental as it would be to Sheila's record, that case did not fall under the state of Connecticut's Code of Evidence prohibiting "past crimes or acts to be used as evidence to demonstrate a defendant's bad character or criminal tendencies."

In effect, it was the polar opposite, the judge said with his ruling.

Sheila hadn't hired a high-profile attorney to represent her; she had opted instead to use public defender Barry Butler, an entirely competent, recognized, respected, and seasoned trial attorney. In his oral argument against allowing what was a precedent for violence, Sheila had displayed, Butler explained how the earlier conviction in New York would greatly "influence the jury" in Stamford to believe Sheila was a violent person.

Uh, well, could she deny she was not?

Comerford was adamant. Sheila's past was pertinent. It was coming in.

Jury selection was set to begin in October.

CHAPTER 86

DAVE MICHEL HAD lived in the United States for twenty-five years, and now he sat inside the jury box taking questions from both James Bernardi and Sheila Davalloo. Still, with all those years behind him as an American citizen, Dave could not shake his conspicuous, thick French cadence. His English was good, but Dave's French inflection was very noticeable.

As jury selection was delayed, and it was now heading into January 2012, Sheila Davalloo had decided between her last motion filing and the court hearing regarding evidence that she would represent herself. Sheila was going to take control of this train and steer it into a not guilty verdict. She was certain of it. Sheila entirely disregarded the old saying: *"A defendant representing his- or herself has a fool for a client."* She chose, instead, to act as her own attorney and face a jury on charges that could result in a lifetime behind bars.

This decision exemplified Sheila's hubris and narcissistic personality. The woman could not allow for the least bit of handing over control. She had to think that she was in charge of everything.

As jury selection continued on January 4, 2012, what miffed Dave Michel right off the bat was when Sheila—parading around the courtroom in a dark blazer, a button-up, collared shirt, and dress pants, with her thick black hair pulled back and tied in a tight ponytail—decided to address Dave in French after hearing his thick accent.

"Bonjour," Sheila said.

"Hello," Dave said back, adding later, "It was a dirty trick. I was there to be a juror, to be neutral. She heard my accent and immediately tried to get to my French side. And because I ignored that, I guess, it is part of the reason why they both picked me."

Quite interesting, Dave Michel had moved to Stamford in 2006. Before that, he had lived in Westchester County, but, according to what he told the court, he had never heard of the stabbing case. What's more, Dave had purchased a house just two blocks from where Anna Lisa was murdered.

Regarding Sheila deciding to represent herself, Dave Michel believed that most of the jurors probably believed it was a major mistake on her part.

"I just didn't understand the point of it," Dave recalled. "But I made no judgment on her decision. She seemed to be a very smart woman. She obviously had issues as well."

What Dave noticed about Sheila as the trial got under way was how she would enter the courtroom in a businesslike manner. "Not showing any emotions." The word that came to mind, Dave said, was "prosaic."

One of Sheila's favorite questions for prospective jurors: "Do you believe I am presumed innocent despite being on trial for murder?"

Another showstopper, quite easily giving away part of Sheila's hand: "Do you think police officers always tell the truth?"

Judge Comerford explained to the packed courtroom that the trial was expected to last between three and four weeks.

* * *

After a jury was chosen, Sheila argued against having cameras in the courtroom.

Her reason?

"Stage fright!"

Sheila claimed she wouldn't be able to do her best if she was on display. She would suffer from "performance anxiety" if cameras were recording her every move.

"I cannot speak in front of a camera," Sheila argued before Judge Comerford. "I really don't think I will be doing very well with a video camera pointed in my direction."

In the end, the judge ruled against Sheila, and allowed cameras in the courtroom.

Producers from NBC's *Dateline,* among others, rubbed their hands together after hearing the decision.

CHAPTER 87

TESTIMONY GOT UNDER WAY on January 24, 2012. Patrolman David Sileo talked about how after the 911 call, he arrived, with a colleague, at Anna's condo to find Anna dead on arrival.

In the courtroom, front and center, where they would sit and listen to every day of testimony, Susan and Renato Raymundo shifted in their seats as Sileo described what he saw. It was heavy on their hearts to listen as an officer of the law defined the crime scene as "brutal and bloody," and the victim was their child.

Setting the scene was the necessary thing, and the prosecutors were obligated to do it; bringing in the players who would tell the story of who murdered Anna was quite another.

In that regard, first up was Paul Christos. Was there another man alive who could explain the manipulative, calculating, and pathological nature of Sheila Davalloo's lies? Could James Bernardi bring in anyone else to enlighten the jury on just how prolific and disturbing Sheila's love triangle creation had been? But more than any of that, here was a witness who had survived an attack by the one person the prosecutor claimed had planned and carried out Anna Lisa's murder. This was as close to an eyewitness as this trial would see.

As if projecting how she felt, Sheila wore all black on this first day—before beginning with his work life, Paul was asked to point his ex-wife out to jurors.

Paul then discussed how they met.

Where they went to school.

Their friends.

Then, of course, the love triangle.

To which, Sheila objected. She wanted the court to excuse the jury so she could argue whether or not it "was a love triangle or if it was love."

Readers are most likely shaking their heads right now.

Love triangle came out the winner.

Paul described the love triangle in exhausting detail as jurors listened curiously, trying to wrap their minds around what sounded like a story someone had made up. For the person who had not heard about this convoluted fantasy and lie created by a woman who had decided to represent herself, it must have come across as a joke. Sheila was no doubt an intelligent woman. Paul was equally, if not more, intelligent. Yet this love triangle story sounded as though it was ripped from the pages of a trashy drugstore romance novel.

As Paul told this story of Jack and Melissa and Anna Lisa, Sheila wrote things down and kept herself busy. She smiled at times and winced at others. There was no way out of this for Sheila Davalloo. She had created the scenario so she could cheat on Paul inside the man's own home. And by the time Paul was finished with the love triangle story, it was clear to anyone paying even the slightest bit of attention that Anna Lisa was the third wheel in the narrative. She was keeping Jack and Melissa from being together.

Bernardi put up a matrix of the love triangle. A computer-generated, blocked presentation of this enormous lie, simplified in writing, so jurors could refer to it in the context of Paul and Sheila's lives.

The stories Paul told jurors began to paint a picture of a woman obsessed with a man—a woman willing to do anything to keep him.

Bernardi had Paul describe the night vision goggles, the recording devices Sheila hooked up at work to Nelson's phone, and the relentless tenacity that Sheila displayed every single day she was involved in the love triangle.

How repetitious it all became.

Redundant.

Ridiculous.

And then, all of a sudden, shortly after Anna's murder, it stopped, Paul told jurors.

Just like that.

Sheila did not talk about it anymore.

Bernardi brought up the cut on Sheila's hand.

Paul spoke of how his then-wife said it happened while opening a can of dog food.

"All right, did it look like an old wound that was healing over?" Bernardi wondered.

"I wouldn't say that old," Paul responded, "but certainly not actively bleeding. I suppose the tissue hanging out looked a little dry. . . ."

When it seemed as if the noose could not get any tighter for Sheila, Bernardi, as though he was conducting an orchestra and working a crescendo, brought up Sheila's brother and the weekends he would come over to the house.

Bernardi asked Paul if he had seen anything around the house that indicated someone else had been staying there.

Paul described finding odd clothing and extra wineglasses. He told how Sheila would often wash the sheets.

Then Paul testified how the visits from her brother increased as the beginning of 2003 came.

"Yes, I was getting tired of it," Paul stated. "I said, 'Your brother has to be told that we're married.'"

And this was when Sheila—Bernardi was competently saying with his line of questioning—realized that she needed to make a decision and get rid of Paul. He was becoming a nuisance, an obstacle, in her rekindled love affair with Nelson.

As February led into March, Paul explained, taking jurors back to the year 2003, Paul kept up the pressure for Sheila to tell her brother they were married.

This gave Bernardi the opportunity to begin asking about what happened on March 23, 2003. For jurors, they had no idea what was coming. As Dave Michel later explained, he had never heard about Sheila's previous arrest and that attempt on Paul's life.

Indeed, to anyone following this story and not knowing the details, especially for a juror deciding Sheila's fate, that trapdoor holding Sheila up was about to pop open.

CHAPTER 88

PAUL CHRISTOS HAD an inherent genuineness that could not be disavowed. He spoke with an honest, well-refined astuteness. A listener could not help but believe Paul on virtue alone. The guy was not a man scorned; rather, he was a victim in this love triangle who had almost lost his life to the same maniac who had murdered her rival. Paul was lucky to be alive. However, he didn't come across in a needy, martyred way—especially after having endured the ordeal that he survived. His presence and composure as he began to tell jurors what happened on the day Sheila tried—not once, but twice—to kill him was enough to exhibit how fortunate this man felt to be there testifying.

Paul wore a dark blue blazer, white shirt, and striped tie. He spoke with authority and purpose, addressing his comments to the jury at times, and to Bernardi at others. If he was nervous, Paul did not show it.

The game came up. Paul held his own, explaining yet again that it was not sexual play in any way, despite how some folks desperately wanted to believe it.

"The blindfold was a pair of panty hose," Paul explained.

"Could you see through them?" Bernardi asked.

"No," Paul said, "not clearly. . . ."

Paul and Bernardi discussed the items that Paul and Sheila used in the game.

Then Paul described how at one point, not long after the game began, he felt as if a "heavy weight" had been dropped on his chest from high above. How deliberate and alarming this had been to Paul.

The chaos in the house, Paul explained, was obvious after this weight had been dropped on his chest. He could hear it going on around him. Sheila was all over the place.

"She sounded like she was in a panic" when she called 911, Paul told jurors, adding how Sheila was even "panting" much like a dog out of breath at one point. And he was certain: Sheila had called 911.

Not once, but twice.

This was riveting testimony and jurors were locked onto it.

Paul described how Sheila told him she loved him, and that he was very brave. These compliments, of course, happened after she stabbed him in the chest.

And as they sat in the living room, waiting on an ambulance that was not coming, Paul said he believed Sheila. He considered they might be able to work things out. It wasn't, in fact, until they got to that back parking lot of the medical center when Paul realized his wife was trying to kill him.

The tension in the courtroom was nearly audible as Paul told his story. The mere fact that he had placed his hand over the blade of the knife to try and wrestle it out of Sheila's hand was stunning testimony. There would be no way for Sheila to talk this fact away, like she had tried with so many other irrefutable incidents in their life together.

Paul's direct questioning by Bernardi carried on all afternoon. Bernardi even brought up that now ubiquitous dark figure, asking Paul if Sheila had told him about it "as far as your stabbing was concerned."

"Yes," Paul explained.

"What did she tell you?"

"She saw a dark figure was present. That she saw it picking up the knife and hitting me with the knife, but she didn't have any recollection of doing it herself. The dark figure did it. And then she could see the aftermath of that figure."

Ending his direct, Bernardi asked Paul to focus on Sheila wanting to break into Anna's condo and how she had purchased a stun gun for protection in case Anna caught her.

Sheila stood and objected, saying, "There's . . . I don't . . . I don't understand the relevance of this, Your Honor."

Judge Comerford encouraged Bernardi to refocus his questioning more on how the stun gun and breaking into Anna Lisa's condo was connected to the case.

With that, Paul told jurors how the stun gun was for Sheila's protection, should anyone discover her underneath Anna's bed.

After a few additional, inconsequential questions, Bernardi looked down at his notes, raised his head after a moment of reflection, and said, "You know what, on that note, I have no further questions."

CHAPTER 89

SHEILA STOOD. The dark blue suit coat she wore displayed the figure of a woman who had lost a bit of weight. Sheila's frizzy, curly black hair, now with streaks of gray, was pulled back tightly and tied behind her head. Sheila held a piece of paper in her hand.

"Good afternoon, Mr. Christos," Sheila addressed her ex-husband. There was no chance for Paul to respond, because Sheila broke directly into what was her first point of contention: The "fictional triangle that was, you know, some kind of relationship going on at work. . . . In my description of that, isn't it true that I *never* spoke to you about the word 'love'?"

"You said Melissa loved Jack, yes."

"I . . . I actually said she *loved* him?"

"Yes."

Sheila then spun her questioning, as bizarre as it sounded, on Jack, the love triangle, and if Paul believed everything she had told him about it. This tactic by Sheila was as obvious as her lack of experience as a lawyer: She was trying to tell the jury that this love triangle was a fantasy; and just because she had told Paul something about it, it didn't mean it was true, or that she had done it. Oddly, Sheila's questions were far longer than Paul's responses. She was pushing an agenda here, trying to plant seeds, using the questioning as a way to argue her case. Sheila wasn't about to give up or admit to anything without arguing it to the point of confusion. And when she felt she had lost an argument, or that Paul would not back down, Sheila moved on, changed subjects, and asked an entirely different question about an entirely different subject.

Regarding the lock pick set, for example, the idea that she was going to hide in Anna's condo, spy on Anna and Jack, stalk them, listen to Jack's phone calls at work, and so on, Sheila said, "So, could I have been telling you these stories to engage you?"

Objection.

Speculation.

The judge agreed.

Sheila withdrew the question.

The judge asked Sheila to stop editorializing her questions and previous answers. Stick to asking pertinent questions, Comerford explained. This was not some sort of opportunity for Sheila to present her opinions about certain facts and wrap a dispute around a question. And the way in which Sheila stood there, looking down at that piece of paper in her hand, reading from it, suggested she had written a manifest she wanted the jury to hear.

Sheila focused on Paul's memory next. How good was it after ten years?

Paul stuck to his answers, realizing, of course, what Sheila was trying to do.

Sheila was out of her league—not only in dealing with witnesses during a murder trial, but having to stand and question her ex-husband, who was not about to back down to any of her obvious bullying.

She even argued what kind of dog food they used to purchase.

Paul said mostly dry food, but sometimes canned.

"So you don't remember me saying that it was a can of pumpkin at Thanksgiving time?" she asked, referring to the day she had supposedly cut herself at home on a can of dog food.

"No."

Did it matter, really, whether she said the canned good was pumpkin or dog food? The fact Paul and the prosecutor discussed was that she had lied altogether about cutting her hand inside the home and had actually sustained the injury long before.

Sheila brought up the game, initiating a series of questions that were all over the place. She went from one topic to the next, not making too much sense.

During the incident inside the house, she said, "I did, basically, everything you had requested of me?"

Paul agreed. Then he added, "*Except* the 911 call."

"But, Mr. Christos, you don't know if I *didn't* call 911, correct?"

"I know that you did *not* call 911," Paul said, leaning into the microphone.

"How do you *know* that?"

"Because there was [no] record from our phone [of a call] ever placed to 911."

Sheila changed the subject.

As Barry Butler, Sheila's legal counsel sitting in to help her, asked the court if he could approach the bench with Sheila, the judge declared that the day was just about over, anyway, and now was as good a time as any to break.

All agreed.

CHAPTER 90

THE NEXT DAY started on a more dreadful note. Dr. Harold Wayne Carver, chief medical examiner for the state of Connecticut, took the stand. Carver listed his credentials before explaining to the jury that the ME who had performed the autopsy in Anna's case, Dr. Thomas Gilchrist, had died in 2009. Carver was picking up his colleague's duty. (Sadly, some months after testifying here, Carver would be handed the grave task of conducting the autopsies and addressing the families of those twenty children and six staff members savagely murdered in a Newtown, Connecticut, school, which would become known as the "Sandy Hook Massacre.")

After a series of questions regarding how many autopsies the ME's office performs each year and how the doctors go about their business of dissecting bodies, Bernardi asked Carver how Anna Lisa died.

"Miss Raymundo died as a result of multiple stab wounds," Carver stated. "And, also, a contributing factor was blunt traumatic injury to her head."

"And manner of death?"

"It was classified . . . as a homicide—and I thoroughly agree."

From there, they talked specifics and evidence photos. The

main point of Carver's testimony was to explain to the jury how brutal Anna's murder had been, how she died, and what type of weapon the ME's office believed had been used to kill her, which Carver noted as "a knifelike object that had one sharp edge and one dull edge."

They talked about the wounds Anna suffered, one by one. In the courtroom was a large computer screen, about the size of a car hood, standing next to the witness stand, on which photographs, some gruesome and shocking, were displayed for jurors. Witnesses and attorneys also referred to the screen at times. This stark reality of the crime scene brought the case to an entirely new level of disgust and clarity. The brutality and pure hatred Anna's attacker displayed was never more permanent and present than when photographs depicting the attack and its aftermath were put up on that screen for everyone to see.

On and on, Carver's vivid, clinical testimony continued. Every wound Anna suffered was talked about and referred to as a number.

Just before Bernardi concluded with his direct, an interesting discovery was presented. Examiners had come to find out, Anna had a bit of blockage in one of her major arteries. Carver quickly ruled out that the blockage had anything to do with her death (just in case), but, he added, "She was headed for a heart attack someday, but she hadn't had one yet."

If Sheila was as smart as the academic degrees she had earned suggested, she'd tread lightly here with her cross-examination of this man. Carver was a professional—a well-respected medical examiner who had forgotten more than Sheila knew. Carver understood his way around a courtroom and had met many a hostile defense attorney; he'd testified countless times, talking about dozens upon dozens of murders. Moreover, Carver was not some sort of hired gun to come in and say what the SA wanted him to say; he worked for the state. He was there to represent what the state of Connecticut had uncovered during the autopsy of a homicide victim. More than that, Carver was a hulking man, with what some described as "an ego," and he would not take lightly to a woman accused of murder, representing herself, trying to badger him on minuscule issues of insignificance.

If bitten, make no mistake: Dr. Harold Wayne Carver would certainly bite back.

As she began, there was no mistaking the fact that Sheila Davalloo did not care where she tread, only that her foolish points were made through her oftentimes bizarre soliloquies disguised as questions.

"The medical examiner at the time had characterized the victim, Miss Raymundo, as being well nourished, correct?" Sheila asked.

Carver hesitated a bit, then replied, "Yes."

"And I don't mean to be indelicate about this, but is it possible that you can elaborate on that?"

"Well—" Carver tried to say before being stopped by Sheila's interruption.

"Even though you didn't—"

Bernardi shook his head and stood. "Your Honor, I'm going to object about 'well nourished.' I mean—"

"It's in the report!" Sheila said.

"He *gave* the weight and height . . . ," Bernardi clarified.

This was one of those technical phrases medical examiners used: "well nourished," as opposed to "malnourished." Sheila was trying to capitalize on words that medical examiners all over the country used every day to describe dead people. It was ludicrous and insulting to the victim.

Not being prompted by anyone, Carver then explained

how the ME's office went about noting a person's weight and height and why they did it.

Sheila wouldn't give up. She was trying to make a point—however inconsiderate it came across. She said, "She was not—would not be considered fat, but would you consider her somewhat robust with being five—"

"She's . . . She's—" Carver tried to say.

Sheila interrupted again, adding, "five-two, one hundred fifty pounds."

"She's plump," Carver finally let go, perhaps falling for Sheila's mockery and victim bashing.

"Okay."

As this discussion about Anna's weight and size continued, Sheila focused on the second part of her argument by comparing her size and body mass to Anna's, finally letting everyone know where her argument was headed.

The judge had finally heard enough and encouraged Sheila to move on, saying, "Let's go."

"I'm—" Sheila started to say.

"You have any other—" the judge tried to say over an explanation that Carver wanted to get in.

All three were talking at once.

The judge then said, "Stop." He paused. "Do you have any *other* questions?"

"Yes, Your Honor," Sheila said.

"Let's go!"

Sheila moved on to two fingernails that had been broken off Anna's hand during the struggle for life and death. She wondered why the ME had removed the remaining portion of each nail from Anna's hand.

Bernardi objected.

The judge asked Carver if he wanted to elaborate on the fingernails and if it was relevant to Sheila's line of questioning.

"In this setting," Carver explained, "a broken nail is part

of a pattern of a fight. And as I said, Dr. Gilchrist recognized this and chose to remove the two broken nails that remained against the possibility of matching them up to the broken pieces if they were ever found. . . ."

Sheila moved on to the location of Anna's stab wounds; she seemed to be interested in the fact that most were to Anna's face and neck. Why she focused on this was never made clear.

Sheila's questions again became longer and more drawn out, giving the jury an indication that she was perhaps trying to push an agenda more than ask astute questions relating to the homicide.

Part of Sheila's latest diatribe—the only way to describe this sort of bullying type of questioning—consisted of a theory that there might have been two weapons used, one of which could be a pair of scissors.

It made little sense.

Sheila talked about the dumbbells next. She called them "free weights." Sheila's contention here was that if Anna's perpetrator has used a dumbbell to bash Anna in her head, there would have likely been more severe wounds made to Anna's skull.

Carver agreed that weights can create much more trauma on a human head than what was found.

Sheila should have stopped there. However, she pushed the bar by breaking into a talk about a person's height and how far the "assailant" would have to lift a dumbbell above his or her head to cause the wounds present on Anna.

Bernardi objected, saying it was conjecture.

"Hold it," the judge said, agreeing. "You're in an area of total speculation here, Miss Davalloo—"

"Your Honor," Sheila pleaded.

"You're in the area of *total* speculation," the judge repeated more sternly, sending a clear message.

"I understand," Sheila said, backing down.

A few questions later, Sheila looked over at the judge, came out from behind her table, and said, "If I can approach the witness, Your Honor, I would like the witness to look at a—a wound on my finger. A cut on my finger. Is that all right?"

"Sure, go ahead," the judge allowed. "I don't know where you're going with it, but go ahead."

Bernardi watched with curiosity.

Sheila walked over to Carver and extended her hand, showing the doctor her scar from the so-called canned-pet-food injury.

Carver studied it.

"Now, Doctor, in looking at that wound on my thumb, what kind of observations can you make about that?"

Rookie mistake: Never ask an open-ended question.

Sheila had just tossed the dice.

She waited.

"Well, first of all—" Carver began, but Sheila interrupted him yet again.

"And feeling and touching it," she said.

"It's healed, so it occurred significantly more than six weeks ago. Second of all, it is a straight linear scar on the pad of your finger. It is a healed cut, with something that was sharp and capable of producing a—a straight line as opposed to a piece of busted drinking glass in your . . . in your dishwasher, probably not."

If Carver had stopped there, maybe Sheila could have escaped the question without any serious damage. Not to mention, there's a second rookie mistake that good trial lawyers don't ever make: Never ask a question you don't know the answer to.

Thus, Carver went on to note that he, in fact, had "considerable experience" with these types of cuts and explained for the jury that Sheila's wound was in an "unusual place to cut yourself. . . ." Then the bombshell: "If your next question," Carver surmised, doing a bit of speculating himself, "is going to be, 'Is it within the range of wounds that could be seen in an altercation involving a knife?' . . . Yes, it is! . . ."

Snake eyes.

"Okay!" Sheila said sarcastically. "Thank you for obliging. I . . . It's just . . . all I really wanted to know is, it's more than a paper cut, correct?"

Bernardi smiled.

Carver agreed it was much deeper than any paper cut.

Sheila moved on to a question about Anna's stomach contents, which led to a long-winded discussion without the jury present regarding caffeine and its effects on the body. Sheila was wasting everyone's time with her repeated, meager attempts at poking holes in the state's hard evidence. Every time she tried to make a point, it backfired.

By the end, Sheila launched into a line of questioning surrounding a theory that the murder may have been sexually motivated based on the possibility of blood being found in Anna's anus.

Carver did not think this was possible.

After Sheila wrapped up her cross-examination, Bernardi focused his redirect on science and how pathologists draw the conclusions they come to regarding sexual assault and rape. Bernardi was clear, concise, and direct. It wasn't hard to understand that Sheila was trying to create something here that wasn't true.

On her recross (the second time), Sheila again asked about blood inside Anna's anus, not being able to let this subject go.

Carver finally cleared it up by saying the average human being suffers from hemorrhoids and this was most likely the reason for the minuscule amount of blood the ME had found.

But Sheila kept pushing.

They went back and forth, recross, redirect, several times.

Finally Bernardi gave up and told the doctor he had nothing further.

Sheila agreed.

Paul Christos stepped back into the courtroom to finish his cross-examination.

CHAPTER 91

ON THE AFTERNOON of January 25, 2012, Paul Christos sat down in the witness-box for a second time, hoping to conclude his testimony. With any luck, Paul would conclude his testimony by the end of the day. Harold Wayne Carver was finished. Although Bernardi did not have to prove it, the case was now focused back on the motivation aspect of the crime. Bernardi had positioned Paul to show a violent precedent and also to talk about that love triangle, the faked 911 calls, and Sheila's all-around character.

Sheila continued her cross-examination by asking Paul to recall the entire 911 incident. Talk the jury through what he remembered, step-by-step. Sheila was, one could argue, stuck on this. The idea that she might be able to raise doubt in Paul's story of her calling 911 seemed almost implausible. She was better off admitting to the lie and dealing with it. Yet, within her questioning of witnesses and choice of topics to focus on, Sheila Davalloo displayed her immense hubris and narcissistic personality: She felt that if she talked about a subject long enough and managed to put in her own thoughts—however awkward and silly they were—the jury would toss aside pure facts and would rely on her delusional, grandiose notion of telling a lie long enough until people believed it.

There were two facts here that Sheila fundamentally (even ignorantly) avoided: One, Paul said he heard Sheila make two 911 calls; and two, there were no records to back up those 911 calls.

Period.

Either this event occurred or it didn't.

As Sheila continued with her line of questioning about the 911 calls, there came a point when she sounded tired. Her voice went up and down. She paused for longer and longer periods.

Finally she gave up the fight.

Paul had a scar down the center of his chest—the remnants of open-heart surgery—that looked like a night crawler earthworm. This was on top of three additional scars Sheila had made by plunging that knife into him.

Sheila locked onto the scar next. She talked about how Paul, after divorcing her, still went to visit her in prison. She wanted Paul to talk about the concern she had shown for him, the scar, and his injuries during those (few) prison visits.

"Correct," Paul agreed. "Yes."

Sheila said she'd even asked Paul during one visit to see his largest scar, the open-heart surgery remembrance.

"Correct," Paul said.

"And I mentioned that poss—" Sheila started to say, but then she needed a moment, stopping to catch her voice. It sounded as though Sheila was cracking. "And I had mentioned that there could possibly . . . be a way . . . to reduce the scarring . . . correct?"

One courtroom bystander later said it was here when he saw Sheila glance over at the clock in the courtroom before this moment began, as if her emotional reaction was by design.

"Yes, that's true," Paul said.

"One moment, Your Honor . . . ," Sheila said.

"Sure," the judge responded.

James Bernardi said, "Your Honor, the state has no objection to a lunch break at this point."

"I can . . . continue, yes," Sheila said, with her tears beginning to flow.

She then took another long pause. And taking a sip from a cup of water, struggling, she tried again: "Regarding the guessing game, you said in a previous hearing"—it was apparently getting tougher as she continued—"that the guessing game was actually fun, correct?"

"Correct," Paul answered. He watched Sheila closely. Paul knew this woman better than most in the courtroom. Something was happening.

"That you seemed to be having a good time playing . . . I . . . I . . ."

Sheila couldn't do it.

Barry Butler, her legal adviser, spoke up, saying: "Take a minute."

"Do you need a break, ma'am?" the judge asked. "Would you prefer a break?"

"Yes . . . yes, Your Honor," Sheila indicated.

Judge Comerford broke for lunch.

While the courtroom cleared, Sheila dabbed at her eyes with a tissue. Then she began to nervously arrange her case files. Most said later it "appeared" Sheila was crying. With Sheila, it was hard to tell. She was perhaps crying; yet no one could be certain if she was feeling sorry for Paul and what she had done to him, or for herself and the lifetime behind bars she faced.

Paul came down off the stand.

Bernardi approached him. "Hey, Paul, do not fall for this tactic. She's just being manipulative and trying to get the sympathy of the jury. It's all an act."

Paul considered this to be a "very plausible" theory.

A corrections officer sat with Sheila during the break.

"Why are you crying?" the CO asked.

"I'm upset about how cold Paul was to me on the stand."

"Sheila, come on, why wouldn't he be cold, given that you tried to *kill* him?"

When Paul later heard about this conversation, he said what the officer didn't realize was that the last time Paul had seen Sheila during a prison visit in 2007, he was civil and friendly to her. Sheila had effectively thought she'd molded Paul into an ally. She considered she had won Paul back over to her side.

"For most of my visits, I was civil and friendly, because I was trying to continuously ask questions about Anna Lisa's homicide," Paul remembered later. "Of course, another reason I was civil/friendly was that, at the time, I still cared about Sheila's situation in prison. Yes, I'm embarrassed to say that, but, unfortunately, it's true. I still had some denial and found it difficult to stop caring about her situation altogether. So I kind of saw the visits as twofold—see how she's doing and keep asking about Anna Lisa. All of my visits (they were infrequent) ended when she was formally arrested in late 2007, since I knew I would be a prosecution witness and I could have no more contact with her. Also, she would obviously figure out that I was on the side of the prosecution after her arrest. Whenever she would say something incriminating, I would report back to Tom McGinty. But besides a few minor things about the stun gun, she never confessed to anything about Anna Lisa . . . so I'm not sure my questioning was very effective for trial purposes."

Still, Paul believed when Sheila saw him act coldly toward her on the stand, it upset her because she wasn't used to seeing him that way.

"In fact, she actually started to cry when she was referring to that prison visit where we had talked about my scar.

It's definitely self-serving, of course. I suspect she just felt that she was fully abandoned by me at that point. You would think she would have figured that out, already given that I was a main prosecution witness. But [for] Sheila, it's all about her. . . ."

CHAPTER 92

SAME AS HER 2004 trial, there had been no one in the Stamford courtroom during Sheila's murder trial in 2012 supporting her. Sheila's mother showed up for half of one day and part of another, but that was it. This fight for her freedom was apparently Sheila's alone.

After lunch, Sheila collected herself and made an announcement. "I apologize for earlier," she said. "I seem to have John Boehner's affliction." The Speaker of the House of Representatives, John Boehner, had been known by then to have strange weeping spells while on the House floor.

With that bizarre explanation out of the way, Sheila continued questioning her ex-husband—except she now focused on the "guessing game," as she referred to it. Sheila wondered if Paul, while blindfolded, believed she had been running around the house grabbing items and applying them sensuously to his skin so he could guess what they were.

Paul said yes, of course, that was the game.

"Okay," Sheila continued, again taking things a step further than she might have wanted to, had she been a lawyer, "and you thought at the time it was—you thought I had a seizure and I had fallen on you. That's the sensation that you could tell from your standpoint?"

Objection. "That wasn't his testimony," James Bernardi clarified.

"He could answer it," the judge replied. "She's asked him whether he *said* that."

Bernardi tried objecting again, but Sheila started to ask her question.

The judge interrupted and overruled the objection.

Finally Paul piped in and clarified things: "That was *one* speculation I had, correct."

Sheila talked about the pain Paul "didn't" feel at the time; in other words, he simply felt winded and generalized pressure on his chest.

Paul agreed, adding how he was sweating, too.

Sheila wondered whether Paul could recall for the jury her screaming at that point in the game.

"After that second thrust, yes," Paul answered.

Sheila mentioned how she had been in a state of panic as they realized together that Paul was bleeding.

"You said," Paul began, "'I think I hurt you. You're bleeding.' You were panicky. You put the dogs in the other bedroom. And then I heard you on the—when you picked up the phone, you . . . seemed to be in a state of panic, correct."

Sheila had Paul go through the breaking of the chair, the removal of the blindfold. Then their realizing something had happened, but they didn't know what.

Paul did not dispute any of this.

Yet, Sheila's true point came when she stated how she had, in fact, not left Paul immobilized and blindfolded, as if she had done the right thing in the moment.

Paul said he agreed.

From there, Sheila talked about pulling up to the hospital and how Paul never objected to where she parked the car.

"No," Paul disagreed. "I asked you . . . is this where the emergency room was. I'm not sure of your response. You might have said, 'I think so.' I *assumed* it was nearby and we could walk to it."

Paul had this plain, nice-guy-next-door way of articulating his answers. When he was certain of something, there was no doubt he was speaking from the heart. And when he was unsure of something, he had no trouble admitting it. Paul Christos made a very compelling witness.

They talked about struggling for the knife.

Sheila made a point to say Paul believed she was "out of it" while holding the knife.

"Yeah, you were rambling on about your brother at that point," Paul confirmed. "Things like that."

Then Sheila moved on to how strong a hold Paul believed she had on his jacket as they fought outside—Paul was struggling to get away and move toward the ER entrance.

Within all this senseless questioning, it became obvious Sheila was trying her best to downplay her role in stabbing Paul in the parking lot, while, at the same time, desperately trying to keep him from getting medical help. It did nothing to boost Sheila's credibility; more or less, all it did was show the jury how methodical and manipulative she had been in trying to keep Paul from getting help after stabbing him while he was blindfolded.

By the time Sheila finished asking Paul about the struggle on the lawn and how they wrestled in the parking lot, her second agenda became obvious: "Okay, and very last question, Mr. Christos, you, at some point, you had . . . had started speaking, well, the Stamford Police started asking you some questions. And one of those questions they asked you was about my physical strength, correct?"

"Correct."

"They had asked you about my upper-body strength specifically?"

"Yes."

"And what was your response to that?"

"I believe my response was, I didn't think you had much upper-body strength at that time."

And so it was clear now that Sheila was trying to tell the jury she wasn't strong enough to manhandle Anna Lisa, who was the more "well nourished" of the two. Perhaps a more powerful person had murdered Anna.

It was more than a stretch to suggest such nonsense at this juncture of the trial. After all, James Bernardi had established already that he believed Sheila Davalloo had used a stun gun to gain control over Anna Lisa.

CHAPTER 93

NELSON SESSLER WAS the one other witness besides Paul Christos who would prove to be the most damaging for Sheila Davalloo and her quest for acquittal. The Sessler/Davalloo relationship/obsession was, truly, at the center of all this violence. Through no fault of his own, Nelson was the reason why Sheila had flown off into this rage. Sheila had been obsessed with Nelson—and perhaps still was—and dreamt of the two of them one day being together. This was her ideal man—until, that is, she got sick of him and focused her obsession on someone else (there would always be someone else). Some trial watchers theorized that Sheila's sole reason for representing herself was built around questioning Nelson.

SA James Bernardi, however, had first crack at Nelson Sessler, who was encouraged right away to speak up if he wanted to be heard. Nelson had a habit of speaking softly, as though ashamed of what he had to tell the jury.

As he walked into the room, jurors judged Nelson. One juror later said Nelson came across as cocky and sarcastic. This particular juror instantly felt disconnected from Nelson, as though Nelson had spread some sort of negative pollen throughout the room.

"I didn't believe him at all," this juror said later.

Sessler had moved south in 2005, married three years later, and had a daughter with his new wife. It was almost as if everything Anna Lisa (or maybe Sheila) had dreamt of having with Nelson, he had gone on to do.

Nelson still worked for Purdue Pharma, a ten-year man at the company by now.

Bernardi asked Nelson to tell the jury about his highest level of education.

Nelson had a doctorate, he said.

After introducing Anna Lisa, Nelson talked about how they lived apart, but also together. He spoke of how they met, where they hung out, mutual friends, how they got along, and what they did together.

Smartly, Bernardi asked Nelson to talk about how clean Anna kept her condo, especially the bathrooms.

Nelson said she often kept the place spotless.

Bernardi then asked Nelson to tell the jury how he met Sheila and how she had lied about being married, and how he eventually found out the truth after she stabbed Paul.

"Sheila said that she had a handicapped brother, a mentally challenged or retarded brother that she took care of, and elderly parents, and volleyball," Nelson explained as Sheila sat, staring at him, more or less looking through him. "And that those three items took up most of her weekends. . . ."

According to Nelson, he broke it off with Sheila as he grew closer to Anna Lisa and things became serious between them. He said by the summer of 2002 (he never gave an exact month or date), he was no longer intimate with Sheila. As far as Nelson felt, Sheila had been a fling, an affair at the office. It was fun for a while, but it had run its course.

What he didn't know, of course, was that breaking it off

with Sheila was like putting a bullet in a chamber, locking it in place, and pointing the barrel directly at Anna. By Nelson brushing Sheila off, he had fed the flames of a madness already kindling inside her. How could he have known this fatal, deadly action would occur?

Nelson then discussed how he'd tried to fix Sheila up with a friend of his, but that friend wanted nothing to do with her.

Bernardi had Nelson explain the entire pathology behind his relationship with Sheila.

How Sheila followed him to North Carolina.

How she obsessed over him at work.

How she called and called.

How she fixed it so she could work in his group.

"All right," Bernardi said. "Now, with regard to the defendant, did you ever discuss marriage with [her]?"

"Never."

"Did you ever take her to meet your parents?"

"No."

"Did you ever buy her anything?"

"No."

"Did you ever write to her?"

"No."

"Did you ever tell each other that you were in love?"

"Never!"

"Did you ever discuss living together?"

"We never did."

"All right—and you never took her to Anna Lisa's condominium?"

To make himself perfectly clear, Nelson said: "I *never* took her to Anna Lisa's condominium."

Nelson said he had never even had Sheila over to his apartment.

The rest of the afternoon went pretty smoothly for Nelson. He talked about the night before Anna was murdered and what they did. Then he spoke about how she was knitting that morning, after they'd had sex and before he left for work. He mentioned how he went to Donut Delight and then clocked in at work with his swipe card/badge. He went to a lecture at lunchtime in the building and never left the facility all day, until it was time to go home around five.

After that, a bit of emotion crept into Nelson's voice as he described going home to Anna's condo and finding the place crawling with cops.

CHAPTER 94

NELSON SESSLER NEXT explained how he was ruled out as a suspect. He did a very good job of it, with Bernardi talking him through those hours inside the boathouse and then down at the station. Within one of his answers, however, Nelson said something that, according to one juror, began to rub them all the wrong way.

"And I actually gave [police on that same night] the names of two girls I had dated in the past who suffered from, you know, depression and some other illnesses. But I did not mention Sheila Davalloo."

This was a fact Nelson had to admit. There was no way around this absolute omission of the person he should have mentioned first.

"All right . . . and in the weeks that followed, you never gave up, as it were, Sheila Davalloo's name. Is that correct?"

"No, I did not."

One could almost sense the next question as it came out of Bernardi's mouth: "Why not?"

Nelson took a moment. "Yeah, so, the day after . . . Anna Lisa was killed, there was an article in the paper, in the *Stamford Advocate,* that a 911 call had come in. And that a man was seen leaving the [condo]."

"Forget about all that. Why didn't you give her—Why didn't you give them her name?"

"I didn't think she did it. I . . . I . . . was—you know . . . The interrogation itself was pretty traumatic for me."

"Okay, you got accused of killing [Anna] at one point. Is that correct?"

"That's right."

Bernardi knew he needed to explain this one fact: Nelson did not think Sheila did it. Sheila was probably going to latch onto it during her cross.

After a few more questions, Nelson gave this explanation: "I was frightened. I was scared. . . . I [was] depressed. I didn't think she did it. I didn't really want her to get involved in it if I didn't think she did it. There was . . . I had never seen any anger or anything from Sheila."

Nelson admitted next that he failed to tell police he had sexual relations with Sheila before November 8, 2002.

"And you denied that when you spoke to the police the following March 23, 2003?"

"That's right."

"And that was a lie, correct?"

"That's right," Nelson said. "It was a lie."

The fact was that Bernardi could prosecute Nelson for his failure to be honest with police during the investigation. However, Bernardi explained with a question that since Sessler had decided to testify against Sheila and, in effect, admit to his lies during that process, the SA's office promised not to prosecute him.

"That's right," Nelson said.

Nelson's testimony continued throughout the day on Wednesday, January 25, 2012. He talked about every aspect of his relationship with Sheila. He talked about the morning he left the house. He talked about that phone call Sheila made on March 23, 2003, inviting him over for dinner. He told how he arrived to find police at Sheila's door, and the fact that their "romance" had been rekindled after Anna was murdered. By January, fewer than two months after Anna had been murdered, he was having sex once again with Sheila, using her as a shoulder to cry on.

The ski trips.

The dinners at Paul and Sheila's condo.

Walking Paul and Sheila's dogs around their neighborhood.

Going to work the following day after Paul was stabbed and being told what had happened.

Calling the Stamford Police Department . . . "and the individual who I spoke with, before there, an officer. And I told him that he should look into Sheila Davalloo." (The police report detailing this incident, if it is the same one Nelson described here, claimed to be two days later, not the next day. And, honestly, it's not that Nelson Sessler was perjuring himself on the stand. He was likely mixing up the days, because things were happening so fast, and the entire scenario of this murder was coming into focus before him. Not only did he just figure out that Sheila was married and had a husband, but that she could have possibly murdered Anna as well.)

"I was frightened. I was scared out of my wits because I had just . . . It seemed like some kind of setup. I was being asked to come down for dinner at a time where it looked like [Sheila] had stabbed her husband. . . ."

From that point on, Nelson talked about going to the Stamford Police and volunteering to wear a wire and record conversations with Sheila, which proved to be, in the end, fruitless.

Ending the day, a long and tiring one for Nelson Sessler, James Bernardi had his witness focus on a trip to Las Vegas he had taken. And who ran into Nelson inside the Vegas airport? None other than Sheila.

"It must have been destiny," Bernardi mocked. "Did you make any kind of arrangements to see her before then, or is this a *complete* surprise to you?"

"It was a complete surprise to me. She had said she was visiting friends or something. . . . I thought [she was headed to] California."

"She just ended up in the seat right next to you on the flight home?"

"Yeah. . . ."

"Okay," Bernardi said, "that's it for today."

CHAPTER 95

IT WAS JUST ABOUT 50 degrees Fahrenheit on the following morning, January 26, 2012, as court commenced. That's quite warm for New England in the heart of winter. Yet, 2012 would prove to be one of the warmest winters on record for the region.

That winter warmth outside the building would not translate inside the courtroom for Sheila Davalloo as Nelson Sessler took the stand once more and continued telling his story. Nelson began this day by telling James Bernardi that it was after he started receiving letters from Sheila that he got nervous and contacted the SPD to begin working with them on recording her. This gave Bernardi a chance to admit the letters into evidence so jurors could see for themselves how slick and sly Sheila thought she was in trying to create a diversion by talking about how compassionate she was and how much she hated the sight of blood.

One better, a court clerk read the letters into the record—while Sheila looked as if she were fading into her chair.

After being prompted by Bernardi, Nelson admitted that he believed Sheila's letters were a disguised attempt by her to deny stabbing Paul and killing Anna Lisa.

The problem with all of this for Sheila was that she could

not hide from who she was—the letters displayed a person who believed the lies she told would somehow translate into a new truth.

As the morning progressed, and James Bernardi and Nelson Sessler discussed the taped conversation Nelson had made with Sheila, the most important point that Bernardi wanted out there—hanging in the air for the jury to take in slowly—was one particular question Nelson had asked Sheila regarding the last time she had seen or spoken to Anna Lisa.

"She said before Christmas . . . ," Nelson testified.

Sheila had told him, Nelson explained further, that she and Anna had run into each other in an elevator inside Purdue Pharma's corporate office.

This was significant. If Sheila was going to argue she had been inside Anna's condo—hence, her blood on Anna's faucet handle—she'd have to go back and explain why she said the last time she saw Anna was at work in 2001.

This is where a liar gets caught all the time: the simple things.

Sheila's poetry came up next. Those quirky poems—if they can even be called such, without insulting true poets— she had written and included at the end of her letters to Nelson. Bernardi keyed on a reference in one poem: Nelson running away from Sheila like a deer. Bernardi asked how that made Nelson feel.

"Yeah, I did," Nelson said, meaning he had run away. "Scared as . . . hell from this woman. I never received anything like this before."

By the end of his direct testimony, Nelson told a story of Sheila surprising him in September 2003 at his apartment and he was frightened of her. Sheila had a manic look in her eyes. She had waited for him to come home, jumped out of her car, and ran up to him. He told police about it, but they said not to worry.

"I had no idea that she was so obsessed," Nelson claimed. "I . . . We had never had that kind of relationship, where we shared love—[the] word love, or future, or anything like that. So it was completely left field to me, all of this."

Bernardi looked down at his notes. Paused.

"Nothing further," the prosecutor said.

As Sheila shifted in her seat, undoubtedly thinking of how she would soon mount her first attack on her old flame, Judge Comerford took a ten-minute recess.

CHAPTER 96

SHEILA DAVALLOO WASTED little time pointing a finger.

"Good afternoon, Mr. Sessler. You—on the day of Miss Raymundo's murder, Mr. Sessler—you had a swollen red knuckle, a red mark on the side of your face, wrapping around your ear, and scratches on your back, correct?"

Nelson was not going to be bullied, apparently: "Not to my knowledge," he said quite firmly. But according to several investigators that saw him on that day, he was injured.

Sheila got off the subject and focused on Nelson's character next, asking, "Mr. Sessler, you mentioned yesterday—with remorse, of course—that you had lied to the police?"

"Yes, I wasn't forthcoming to the police."

As Sheila continued questioning Nelson, always referring to him with her snarky tone ("Mr. Sessler!"), the judge had to pipe in because Sheila was becoming so heated that she wasn't allowing Nelson to finish his answers.

Sheila got hung up on the fact that Nelson had told police about two of his former girlfriends, but not about her. It sounded as though she was mad that he had not considered her important enough in his life to mention.

Then, after exhausting all she could in regard to Nelson's other girlfriends, Sheila went back to the idea that Nelson had something to hide, asking him why he had given police four different versions of what he did on the morning that Anna was murdered.

As he looked to Bernardi for guidance, all Nelson could say was "Um . . ."

Bernardi objected.

Sheila withdrew the question.

Question after question, it became awkwardly obvious that all Sheila was interested in was embarrassing Nelson Sessler. She asked him about falling asleep while in the boathouse that night.

He said he didn't recall nodding off.

Carrying on and on after the lunch break, it appeared Sheila might have taken on the role of attorney for this reason alone: to poke a stick at Nelson. She came across as scorned and bitter because he had slept with her and then left her. The tone of her voice was so incredibly vengeful at times, one had to wonder if she was going to leap from her spot in the room toward her ex-lover and lash out at him in a tirade. Her cross-examination accomplished nothing in the form of impeaching his prior testimony or even putting into question his behavior, other than catching him, perhaps, causing question that he didn't fall asleep or was not injured.

For example, Sheila talked about Anna's upper-body strength again and asked Nelson repeatedly how strong she was, and if he believed Anna was stronger than she was.

Then she moved on to the relationship Nelson had with Anna.

"Isn't it true that she would leave you messages [at work, on your cell], but you would not call her back?"

Nelson started to explain that when he was working, he didn't like to make personal calls, but Sheila cut him off, asking the same question, couched differently.

Then Sheila asked Nelson to qualify the "nature" of his and her relationship in 2002.

"We were friends—"

"I'm sorry?" Sheila snapped back.

"We were friends. . . ."

At one point, Nelson called the relationship a "fling," quoting what he believed Sheila had referred to it as at the time.

This made her mad.

"And during that time [of our fling], though, when you said after [we 'dated'], we would have sex, you . . . you also said that we would never spend the whole night together, correct?"

"That's right. I never stayed a night with you that I can recall."

"Okay—" Sheila started to say.

Nelson interrupted, adding, "Until *after* you stabbed . . . your husband."

Bernardi watched with warmth. It was actually entertaining.

"After?" Sheila pressed.

"I'm sorry," Nelson clarified, "*after* you stabbed Anna Lisa Raymundo. Or, after Anna Lisa Raymundo got stabbed!"

"Okay," Sheila added, not realizing what Nelson had just told the court. "So the way you—" she started to say.

The judge, however, spoke up, addressing the jury: "I want you to strike and disregard that last response."

"Sorry about that," Nelson said.

The testimony became confusing. Sheila bounced all over the place, never really finding a groove to get things moving in any direction that could help her. It was almost as if she had not prepared for the cross. It seemed she was simply barking questions off the top of her head.

For the remainder of the afternoon, Sheila focused her questioning on her relationship with Nelson: how he walked her dogs, how they went to concerts together. She stated she had always thought their relationship ended because they were not "sexually compatible." To this statement, Nelson replied, "No, I'm not sure what you mean by . . . sexually . . . *in*compatible."

Bernardi spoke up at one point and objected to a question Sheila uttered about Vegas and her chance meeting with Nelson. "I know Your Honor is going to tell this jury, anyway, but the facts in the question, all right, don't take the place of testimony. There's a lot in that question that sounds to me like someone testifying than—"

"I've tried to give the lady some—" Judge Comerford retorted to the prosecutor.

"I'll rephrase it," Sheila interrupted the judge.

"Latitude!" Judge Comerford finished. "That's why I stopped her and asked her to rephrase the question."

After that was settled, Sheila brought up the friend Nelson had tried to fix her up with.

It was another moment to roll eyes and shake heads: What the hell was her point?

Again and again, Judge Comerford reminded Sheila that she was "testifying here" and not asking questions.

Sheila then admitted a Xerox copy of a police crime scene photo as one of her exhibits. Bernardi quickly pointed out that it was a state police crime scene photo that she had photocopied—not an actual photo exhibit of her own.

Sheila was trying to show how messy Anna kept her apartment. The only problem was, the photo she was using had been taken after the fight and murder took place inside Anna's condo. It was not an accurate depiction of Anna's condo on a normal day.

She asked Nelson to take a look at the photo. Then she wanted to know if the dumbbells were in the same spot they were when he left for work that morning.

Nelson said he didn't recall.

Sheila finished her cross after asking if Anna wore blue contact lenses.

Nelson said he couldn't remember.

Bernardi had a few redirect questions, all of them centered on the 911 call. Concluding, Bernardi asked Nelson, "When you listened to that 911 call, did you have any difficulty at all recognizing whose voice that was?"

"No. That's Sheila Davalloo's voice," Nelson answered.

Pin drop.

Sheila declined to ask any more questions of Nelson Sessler, so another day in the *State of Connecticut* v. *Sheila Davalloo* was over.

CHAPTER 97

ON FRIDAY, JANUARY 27, 2012, James Bernardi's voice recognition expert, Thomas Owen, talked about how he had applied the proper science to the 911 call, but it took some time before he was able to match the voice to Sheila's. Owen explained that back in 2004 when he had first tried to test the call, he did not have the software to conduct the experiment he had wanted to do. In 2011, though, technology apparently caught up to Sheila Davalloo. With the latest computer software available, Owen was able to determine, beyond any doubt in his mind, that it was Sheila who had placed the 911 call on the day Anna Lisa was murdered.

"Yes . . . ," Owen said after being asked. "Sheila Davalloo is the person that made the 911 call."

Jurors then heard the call. And what's interesting about Sheila choosing to represent herself became the fact that throughout the entire trial, there was Sheila speaking out loud for jurors to gauge her voice and match it to the 911 call for themselves. They didn't need an expert to convince them.

Sheila had done it herself.

Several additional witnesses were called in next to make a case for Sheila leaving the Purdue Pharma building and

Nelson not leaving the same building during the time of Anna's murder.

In her grandest moment of the trial, Sheila objected to the idea that only one day of records was being examined by the prosecution and not a composite of the year to prove that it was a habit for her to come and go from the building because of her depression and to take her dogs for walks. Her leaving the building wasn't quite the anomaly the SA had made it out to be.

"If the state wants to show a narrow window and not the whole picture, that's prejudicial," Sheila explained to the judge, with the jury out of the courtroom.

Judge Comerford came back with a zinger: "I'm giving you a lot of leeway because you don't know what you're doing."

Sheila had made a valid point, however.

Comerford wound up allowing the records into evidence, which gave Sheila the opportunity to show, as she put it, "a pattern" of her coming and going from the Purdue Pharma building.

Needless to say, as part of that "pattern," as much as she wanted to renounce it, the evidence proved Sheila had left the building before Anna was murdered and returned shortly there afterward.

As testimony ended for the day, Bernardi brought up something that had been on his mind since the start of the trial four days earlier. He explained to the judge that he was growing increasingly concerned over how Sheila had been asking "inappropriate questions" of witnesses during her cross-examinations, which had mostly alluded to a theory she was trying to plant in the minds of jurors that someone else had murdered Anna Lisa. Bernardi talked about how she had, during a series of questions, tried pointing the jury in the direction of a murderer much bigger and stronger. "Without,"

Bernardi said, "having sufficient evidence" to support the theory.

In other words, Sheila couldn't make accusations that implicated some absent third party in Anna's murder, while asking witnesses questions without backing up those statements—exactly what they were—with evidence.

It was a solid legal argument. A lawyer cannot ring a bell for jurors without displaying proof that the bell actually exists.

"I understand she's not a lawyer, and she thinks she knows what she's doing," Bernardi told Judge Comerford, "but she doesn't. And the rules *have* to apply to her."

Comerford duly noted Bernardi's concerns and adjourned until the following Tuesday.

CHAPTER 98

THE STATE'S TRAIN hit overdrive on Tuesday, January 31, 2012, as Bernardi entered fifty pieces of crime scene evidence into the record, including the bloodstains found inside Anna's condo on the bathroom faucet handle. The newspapers referred to this move later as a "mountain of evidence."

And so here was the torpedo that would sink Sheila's ship—if there was any doubt in jurors' minds that Sheila had never been inside Anna's apartment. Things seemed to be lining up: 911 call (Sheila), obsessive, jealous, and rage-filled scorned lover (Sheila), forensic evidence left by the killer on a bathroom faucet (Sheila).

Sheila's blood on the faucet handle in Anna's bathroom mixed with Anna's blood was substantial. There was no explanation as to how that blood could have gotten there other than Sheila leaving it behind.

James Bernardi asked State Trooper Don Elmendorf if he could determine what happened in the bathroom on the day Anna Lisa was killed. Was there a reason why Sheila's blood might be inside the bathroom when, chances were, Anna was murdered in the living area near the kitchen?

"That someone was standing in front of the sink trying to clean themselves," Elmendorf testified, giving jurors a clear image of Sheila standing over Anna's sink, desperately trying to wash all the blood from her savage crime off her hands.

Further along, Elmendorf dismissed the notion that the murder could have been in direct relation to a botched robbery, saying that if that was the case, they'd expect to find items missing from Anna's condo. The SPD certainly had seen this scenario played out scores of times—someone breaks into a home, thinking no one is there, and begins committing the burglary; the homeowners surprise him (or her) and a fight ensues, sometimes ending in murder.

Nothing was missing, however, Elmendorf said.

Sergeant Richard Colwell was next up, and then State Trooper Matthew Riley, as the state hit its law enforcement stride: one cop after the next coming in and setting the scene of a brutal attack that pointed—after a lengthy investigation, taking several years—to one woman only.

Sheila.

As she sat and listened, Sheila didn't have much for any of these witnesses during her cross-examinations. Perhaps, as each officer talked about his expertise and how it applied to Anna's murder, the defendant/defense attorney realized that less was probably more. This was the time to keep her trap shut and to allow this extremely damning portion of the trial to get over as soon as possible.

The following day, February 1, brought more forensic testimony, this time from EJ Rondano, who had collected much of the forensics in the case, knew it all inside and out, and had escorted Anna's body to the ME's office for autopsy.

Rondano talked about lividity, that period when a body succumbs to death and blood stops pumping and gravity takes over, pulling the blood down to the lowest part of the body.

This type of testimony in any murder trial brings reality

back into what can sometimes become a procedural course of expert testimony. Here Rondano talked about a human being and how she had died and what happened to her body thereafter. Through the course of this testimony, Bernardi posted photos. So if anyone in the room had forgotten what Sheila's rage and violence had resulted in, there was Anna's battered and dead body, proving just how real her death was for her family and friends.

Rondano cleared up something Sheila had tried to say during one of her cross-exams. He told Bernardi that the ME's office had obtained oral, vaginal, and anal swabs to send to the lab for analysis—something he was supposed to do. One of his other jobs was to collect fingerprints from the scene and any potential POIs or suspects, which included James McBride, Gary Riley, Nelson Sessler, and several other possible suspects.

Bernardi wanted confirmation that Rondano had compared those prints to any prints found at the scene.

Rondano had.

There were no matches.

There was also some hair analysis Rondano had conducted. There had been "pulled hair" found at the scene.

Black hair, specifically.

Rondano said he checked the hairs against hairs he had pulled from POIs.

No match.

Then Bernardi asked about Rondano having extracted blood from Sheila. Rondano said he never drew blood from POIs or suspects; nurses did that sort of thing. Still, Rondano was there when Sheila's blood was taken, in order to make sure the chain of evidence was not broken.

All this did for Bernardi was show jurors how Sheila's blood was drawn, where it was sent, and how the lab came to its conclusion that, yes, Sheila was one of the donors connected to that smear on the faucet handle.

During her cross-examination, Sheila went after the blue contact lens that had come up previously. She asked Rondano if he was there when the ME found the lens.

He said he was.

"Where was it exactly, Officer?"

"I believe it was found in her hair," Rondano said.

"Tangled up in her hair?"

"Right."

Then Sheila got off the point.

Finishing shortly thereafter, Sheila asked Rondano about finding some blood in the boathouse.

He said he did.

And then Sheila, not following up, was done.

CHAPTER 99

SUSAN AND RENATO RAYMUNDO had been front and center for the entire trial, thus far. They were exempt from witness sequestration rules, since they were Anna's family, and they listened intently to the woman who, they believed, killed Anna have her day in court. After James Bernardi was finished with his direct questioning of Anna's parents, that same woman would be questioning them.

Renato was first. He talked about Anna's condo and how they had purchased it together with her.

Anna's father was a spiritual man, a devout Catholic, who appeared to be holding it together rather well, considering his . . . girl had been taken away from him far too early.

An intelligent and highly experienced trial attorney, Bernardi then had Renato focus on Anna's condo—in particular, how clean Anna kept the place, including the bathroom, and how often (four times per year) the Raymundos visited their daughter and actually cleaned the place themselves.

"All right, now, would you include the sink handle?" Bernardi asked, meaning in the scope of how spotless Anna kept the place. Was she that detailed a cleaner to make certain the bathroom faucet handles were washed?

"I cleaned the bathroom thoroughly," Renato said, "including the toilet bowl tank, the sink, the mirrors, the floor, the whole bathroom."

The last time they had visited Anna was on August 2, 2002, about three months prior to her murder.

The other point Renato made was that he and Susan had gone to Anna's condo after her murder in order to go through it. And during that torturous moment of walking around, looking things over, Renato said he and Susan did not notice anything missing.

Renato talked about their last communication with Anna—that phone message.

Bernardi said he was done.

Sheila stood and went right at Renato. She had no preamble to her questioning of the victim's father. She didn't say anything about being sorry that she found herself in a position to have to ask questions at such a horrifying time, under such dire circumstances.

There was no sign of her sympathizing with them in any way. She began, instead, with what amounted to a crass-sounding question out of left field.

"Isn't it true that you—or some . . . one of Anna Lisa's relatives—noticed that her house keys were missing?"

"Pardon me?" Renato replied.

"Her house! Her set of keys were missing—isn't that correct?"

"I can't recall."

"Okay, no questions, Your Honor."

Bernardi called Susan Renato next. Susan was beautiful, same as her daughter. She had a certain warmth and charm about her. Anyone watching Susan walk slowly to the stand could tell that this loss had been tremendous. It was a weight she'd been carrying since that moment Susan felt something had happened to Anna as she drove her own mother home from the hospital.

The obvious focus here was the phone call Susan had received from Anna on the morning Anna was murdered. Bernardi asked Susan to recall for the jury what she heard on her voice mail that morning.

Anna's sweet voice, so comforting for a mother to hear, delightful, elegant, saying those final words: "Hi, Mom and Dad. . . ."

As Susan recalled what Anna had said, she broke down.

They took a quick ten-minute recess so Susan could collect herself before Sheila began her cross.

Sheila again did not say sorry, nor did she feel the need to waste time—this, mind you, just after the witness had to take a pause because of an emotional breakdown.

"Good afternoon, Dr. Raymundo. Do you recall if . . . where your daughter kept her house keys?"

Susan said Anna placed her keys in a box close to the stairwell.

"Okay, do you recall if her house keys were missing?"

"No, I do not recall."

That was it. Sheila said "thank you" and sat back down.

At one point during the afternoon session, Bernardi again brought up the notion that Sheila was using witnesses in order to push a "third-party culpability" agenda she could not support with evidence.

Judge Comerford needed to rule on this ploy that Sheila was using.

Sheila took it a step further and argued that the state should make a video available to the jury that explained the "comings and goings" of Nelson Sessler from Purdue Pharma.

Bernardi had already established with certainty that Nelson's card was not swiped for him to leave the building on that day.

Sheila argued that he could have easily used someone else's card, same as someone else could have used hers, indicating a setup or a frame-job defense.

It went against logic, of course.

But Sheila reminded Judge Comerford how just last week the security director for Purdue had testified "that someone could have used another employee's swipe card to exit the building."

Judge Comerford then asked Sheila: "So you're point-blank telling me he's (Nelson) not a third-party culprit?"

"No, that's not what I'm telling you," Sheila replied.

Sheila wouldn't budge after Comerford kept asking. Instead, she attacked Nelson's character, saying she believed he had not been truthful while testifying, adding at one point, "Almost everything he said was a lie—and that raises questions!"

Bernardi was enjoying this as Comerford warned Sheila that she'd had her chance to challenge Nelson's credibility while he was on the stand. She couldn't now, as she questioned other witnesses, state metaphorically or otherwise within the body of a question that Nelson had lied. That was not how the legal system worked.

On objection, without the jury present, there was another issue Sheila brought up after two forensic investigators testified, regarding Bernardi retrying Sheila for the 2003 stabbing. Sheila said she wasn't going to have any of it. Bernardi couldn't do that.

Bernardi fought back aggressively, defending his witnesses, claiming their testimony helped to explain a window of opportunity where Sheila had actually called Nelson in between attacking Paul and feigning the call to 911. The stabbing, Bernardi argued, was part of a pattern of violence Sheila had shown with one goal in mind: getting Nelson back.

Concluding his thoughts, Bernardi ended on a rather powerful note, saying, "She may be the most peaceful person otherwise, but when it came to eliminating obstacles to Nelson Sessler, she was willing to commit murder!"

Sounded like a closing-argument line.

Comerford overruled Sheila's objection argument, but the judge cautioned Bernardi not to retry Sheila for stabbing Paul.

A lot of the discussion had centered on a witness who was yet to testify, a detective from Westchester County. As the day drew to a close, Bernardi promised that he'd have his witness ready by the following morning.

Comerford repeated his earlier warning to be very careful with the witness so as not to impugn Sheila's rights.

CHAPTER 100

THE NEXT MORNING, James Bernardi indicated that he'd changed his mind and would not be calling the Westchester County detective he had fought for the previous afternoon. Why take a chance now? As it was, the state was steamrolling Sheila. Allow due process to take place and this jury was going to convict Sheila on the evidence alone. The jury knew she had tried to kill Paul. They knew she had tried to keep him from getting medical attention. They knew she was serving twenty-five years for attempted murder. The details surrounding that crime, in the end, wouldn't matter. So Bernardi did not call Detective Alison Carpentier to the stand, after all.

He did, however, summon Pleasantville officer Anthony Prete, who had answered the call to head up to the hospital to find out what was happening in the parking lot.

Bernardi then called another witness on the morning of February 2, 2012, who sat and talked about cell phone records and how Anna used her cell phone to call her mother and father on the morning she was killed. What's more was that this particular witness also concurred that Sheila's cell phone had made a call at seven fifty-five on the morning Anna was murdered to her home in Pleasantville. All indications, according to the witness, were that the call from Sheila's cell phone was made in the Fairfield, Connecticut, region—which Stamford fell under. It was fairly obvious after this testimony that Sheila had, in fact, called Paul and was, quite possibly, sitting in front of Anna's condo, as Paul had recalled to police.

Tammy Mei had known Sheila since 1995 when they worked together at a Mount Pleasant, New York, company. Tammy was next up for the state.

A mother and wife, Tammy came across as a delightful stay-at-home-mom, who had believed in her friend at one time. Bernardi had Tammy on the stand to explain several key factors: one, to give some context to the "Melissa, Jack, and Anna Lisa" narrative; two, to speak about Sheila's obsession with the aforementioned narrative and how far Sheila went in listening to Nelson's phone calls and following him; three, how Sheila had asked Tammy if Melissa should confront Anna Lisa and let her know she was still seeing Jack; and four, that Sheila had asked Tammy and her husband about fingerprints and DNA.

All of it was powerful testimony. Unabashed. Entirely unimpeachable. Here was a friend of Sheila's coming in and telling the jury the truth of their lives, as she saw it.

During Tammy's cross-examination, Sheila referred to her friend as "Miss Mei." Sheila went after Tammy's memory and asked if Tammy believed her memory could have "faded in terms of time and information that you've provided in general to today and before this?"

What Sheila tried to suggest with this question was that Tammy had perhaps told the police one thing years ago and then had come into the courtroom and said something different. Yet, she provided no proof to back up her claim other than ridiculous, two-bit pieces of information that were meaningless in the scope of the case: such as how many days might have gone by between the times when they had not spoken.

Sheila also keyed in on the fact that Tammy recalled Sheila having told her that she'd met Nelson in a Texas airport. (In actuality, it was Las Vegas.)

Tammy responded by saying she wasn't sure of the town/state when she spoke to police five years before; and as she sat there, she still wasn't sure of the town and the state. What she was certain of, however, became the fact that Sheila just happened to "bump into" Nelson in the airport, as if it were destiny. Tammy thought that was strange and highly unlikely.

CHAPTER 101

BERNARDI HAD MENTIONED the previous day that he would be wrapping up his portion of the case on Friday, February 3, 2012. He never said how much a thunderous boom he was going to make with the witness he had chosen to rest his case on, however.

Dr. Michael Bourke had worked in the state forensic laboratory for nearly twenty years, several of those as the supervisor of the lab. The guy's résumé was too big for him to sit and recite orally, so Bernardi offered it up as an exhibit for the jury to look at themselves as they deliberated—an expert move by James Bernardi.

For the first part of his testimony, Bourke explained how DNA worked, along with the basic process of collecting and examining it as compared to examples from one's mother and father.

He then talked about how he received Anna's and Sheila's DNA and how the lab went about "purifying" it and then prepping it for testing.

"We generated a complete full profile from each known submitted," Bourke explained.

Now the lab had a DNA profile of Sheila and Anna.

Bourke talked next about how the lab also received a

separate sample from a faucet handle inside Anna's condo, which became known as "Item 8Z1."

Item 8Z1, Bourke said, "was represented to me as a blood-like stain from the handle of a sink."

The stain had a sufficient quantity of blood in order to make a good comparison, along with it being of the necessary quality the lab liked to see. This was textbook DNA testing. When law enforcement has a bloodstain and they have some donors, they test all three to see if there is or isn't a match.

Standard DNA profiling.

"All right," Bernardi said, "now, what was the result of your test?"

"I generated a DNA profile from 8Z1, which is a blood-stain from the handle of the sink that was a mixture."

Important word there: "mixture."

"And did the mixture—how did it relate to the known profiles [that] were submitted?"

"When I compared the mixture profile—and the definition, a mixture is that we see genetic elements that have to come from more than one individual. When I compared the mixture profile from 8Z1, the known DNA profile of Ms. Raymundo and the known DNA profile from Miss Davalloo were included as contributors to that mixture DNA profile from 8Z1."

Bernardi asked the doctor about other people he included in testing against the mixture found on the sink handle: Gary Riley, Nelson Sessler, James McBride, and several others.

"What was their relationship to that contribution to the . . . bloodstain?"

"They were eliminated. . . ."

Bourke went on to explain that in the mixture profile, there were only two different contributors.

Two.

Bernardi and Bourke then entered into a rather long,

detailed discussion about "touch DNA"—those everyday occurrences when people enter and exit buildings, wash their hands, open doors, and leave traces of their DNA everywhere they go. This DNA that Bourke had looked at—just in case Sheila wanted to claim she was over at Anna's and had washed her hands and touched the sink handle—was not that type of DNA. This was bloodstain DNA that had been left behind. The presence of blood was the root source of the DNA on the sink handle.

Bernardi asked Bourke to explain.

"We . . . detected genetic elements . . . that are consistent with the known profiles of Miss Raymundo and Miss Davalloo."

The only criticism that could be lodged at Bernardi for the course of the entire trial, really, was that he likely kept Bourke on the stand too long. Because after Bourke delivered that devastating line, implicating Sheila Davalloo in Anna's murder, telling jurors he believed the person who left that blood behind on Anna's faucet handle could have been no other person on this planet other than Sheila, Bernardi had Bourke talk about DNA and its scientific origins, beyond other things. What became clear, however, within all of this long-winded testimony was that Anna's DNA/blood had been found all over the condo. And Sheila's had not. What this proved, anecdotally, was that Sheila likely had worn gloves and protected herself.

In the end, Bourke was certain the contributors on the sink handle were Sheila and Anna in the neighborhood of one in every 8.5 million people.

Sheila started off her cross-examination by bringing in Nelson Sessler's name, once again raising the eyebrows of Bernardi and the ears of Judge Comerford. Here she was once again suggesting by osmosis—ringing that damn bell—that Nelson could have killed Anna.

In a series of questions to Bourke, Sheila made the assumption that Nelson's blood could have been inside Anna's condo as part of the scene; yet the SPD or the CSP did not collect it and submit it for testing. According to Sheila's logic, they had, in effect, missed it.

For the next half hour, Sheila asked silly questions, trying to poke holes in science. She was ineffective at getting anywhere.

Bernardi kept objecting on the nonfactual basis of the questioning, and the jury was asked to leave at one point.

The thing to do here was for Sheila to have her own expert, a hired DNA gun, come in and refute the state's findings. It was the only way to cause doubt—if even possible—in what was rock-solid science.

As a juror, a person either bought into the science or he didn't. There was no gray area.

Sheila questioned the doctor about several dumbbells found inside the condo with blood on them.

Concluding his testimony, Dr. Bourke explained the bloodstains "on three of the dumbbells contained" Anna Lisa's genetic profile, in addition to another "unknown contributor." The doctor said that "out of the thirty-nine samples" investigators had sent to the crime lab for testing, it was only the faucet handle in the bathroom that produced a match to Sheila.

"We're about ready to rest," Bernardi said.

Sheila stood after a lengthy discussion among the judge, Bernardi, and the jury, and she called her first witness, John Thompson, an information technology (IT) person from Purdue Pharma.

CHAPTER 102

SHEILA WORE A GRAY suit coat, a striped turtleneck sweater, and black slacks on February 7, 2012, a Tuesday. Her first witness, John Thompson, had admitted the previous day to being friends with Sheila outside work. In his brief testimony, Sheila put Thompson on the stand to say, essentially, he had heard the 911 call, but he did not believe it was her voice. It was strange she had focused on the 911 call right after a highly respected and decorated DNA specialist had placed Sheila at the scene of the murder by the fact she had left her blood on the sink handle.

This first full day of presenting a defense was slated to be Sheila's magic moment. She called Gary Riley, her one and only chance to gain any type of momentum. Although no matter what Riley said (save for begging for mercy and admitting to a murder he did not commit), ultimately it was not going to make any difference in what was an inevitable outcome.

What came across immediately as the morning session began was how much fun it seemed Sheila was having. As a narcissist, she was in her ultimate glory here. She controlled every aspect of this case right now, and the entire spotlight was on her.

Riley, however, would make things slightly interesting. He wore a black North Face jacket, and his glasses, as Riley sat down, were still tinted amber from the sun shining brightly outside the courtroom as he walked in. Riley looked as though he had lived a hard life. After being encouraged by Sheila, Riley said he had been down in back of Anna's condo on that morning, fishing off the pier. At first, he did not mention he was also burglarizing boats.

"In the parking lot," Sheila asked her star witness, "what happened after you finished fishing?"

Riley said, "I heard a scream. I came through the parking lot. I seen a man and a lady arguing." As he continued, Riley spoke of how, as he walked toward his car through the parking lot, he saw "another lady . . . on a staircase. . . . It was like a laundry area down there or whatever, and there was another woman walking a dog and she asked me what I was doing there. I just . . . left."

Confusing, to say the least.

Riley said he went down to the Duchess Restaurant after that to get something to eat, which was when he ran into some police officers, who asked him to go into the station for questioning.

As much as she didn't want to, Sheila had to bring in the burglaries Riley had been pinched for. He had served five years in prison on those charges.

After several more inconsequential questions, Sheila indicated she had nothing further for Riley. Apparently, he was there to say he had seen a few women in the laundry area of the condo unit Anna lived in, and also a man and woman arguing. Yet, as Sheila presented a photo of Anna to Riley, asking if that was the woman he had witnessed arguing with the man, Riley could not say it was Anna.

* * *

James Bernardi simply picked Riley apart, piece by piece, getting him to admit that he had lied to police repeatedly, had broken into boats down at the pier, served time in prison for it, was "heavily into alcohol and drugs in the fall of 2002," not to mention several additional character defects.

For some, it felt uncomfortable to sit and listen to Riley at one point as Bernardi hammered him on everything from the type of drugs he smoked to the amount of alcohol he consumed, to the criminal ways in which he made his money.

The hard questions went on and on. Riley never caved. He seemed to be telling the truth the best he could.

Finally Riley explained how he couldn't remember several statements he had given to police back in 2002, adding, "I didn't recall half of what I said back then."

"Because it's difficult to remember lies, right?" Bernardi suggested, not really looking for an explanation.

Sheila had several Purdue employees come in and, one way or another, say they didn't believe it was Sheila on the 911 call. Not quite science or expert opinion, but her point was clearly made. The DNA did not matter. What was important was that she did not make that 911 call.

Heading toward the end of the day, Sheila offered several pieces of evidence to the court without the jury present: a recorded conversation between her and Nelson Sessler back in 2003, information regarding cell phone towers and where they're located and how they ping calls back and forth, and a DNA test (mitochondrial in nature) on a hair sample supposedly found at the crime scene. In addition to that, Sheila asked the court if she could talk to the jurors about a "bloody sock found in the condo complex parking lot more than a month after" Anna's murder.

The problem with all this evidence was that Sheila could

not produce one witness to corroborate any of it. She simply wanted to toss it all into the pot and allow jurors to have a look at it.

Judge Comerford listened, but he denied each piece of evidence based on "relevancy concerns and the lack of expert witnesses to testify."

With that, Sheila indicated she had finished her case.

Judge Comerford said that closing arguments—which, unlike opening arguments, were allowed in Connecticut— would take place on the following day at two o'clock in the afternoon.

Sheila spoke up, however, after this announcement. She had something to say.

Bernardi looked up at the judge.

The judge nodded for Sheila to speak.

"This is a circumstantial case," Sheila argued. "I understand it's in the hands of the jurors, the triers of fact. There are no eyewitnesses or murder weapon. No one knows what the intent of the perpetrator was."

Sheila then motioned for an acquittal.

Judge Comerford did not hesitate to deny the motion. "The court has heard enough evidence to let a jury decide. . . ."

Gavel.

CHAPTER 103

CASES ARE NOT won on closing arguments; it is simply a way for the attorneys to wrap up a trial that has, many times, gone on far too much longer than it should have. A bow needs to be put on certain pieces of evidence so the jury understands why a particular witness sat in the chair and testified, or why a particular item had been entered. For prosecutors, it's also a way to remind jurors of witnesses who testified earlier in the trial.

Judge Comerford explained to jurors that in Connecticut the prosecution "has an opening and closing [at the end of the trial]. Miss Davalloo has a right to make an argument in the middle."

Each side would get an hour, Comerford warned. No more.

Beginning, James Bernardi did what most prosecutors do: He thanked the jury for its service; he talked about the single charge in front of them ("murder"); he broke into a brief discussion surrounding the law and reasonable doubt.

In a smart change of pace, Bernardi then focused on what he described as the key factor in reaching a reasonable-doubt verdict. He encouraged jurors to keep "the emphasis . . . on the word 'reasonable.'"

Further along, Bernardi added, "there is no special formula. You use your common sense to see what is accurate and what is honest testimony. And then you . . . determine from that testimony, are you firmly convinced of the defendant's guilt?"

The next order of business for Bernardi was Harold Wayne Carver's testimony and how several of the wounds Anna sustained were defensive. Then he talked about the fact that Anna had been bludgeoned on the top of her head and stabbed "deliberately" (good choice of words there) with one particular blow to the chest "intended to kill—there's no doubt about that."

Bernardi moved on to intent. Sheila went there that day with the *intent* to murder Anna in order to get her out of the way so she could have Nelson all to herself. She did not go there to talk. Or to confront Anna. Or to warn her. Or to give her an ultimatum. Sheila Davalloo, this prosecutor made clear, had a premeditated plan to murder Anna Lisa.

The problematic situation Paul Christos found himself in, Bernardi argued, was that he knew about the love triangle and also wound up in Sheila's way.

So Sheila decided that he had to go, too.

In case jurors had forgotten, Bernardi went through each piece of evidence he had presented that "proved" Sheila's obsession.

The stalking.

The night vision goggles.

The lock pick set.

The plane ticket purchase and the "destiny deception climax" (another set of choice words) with Nelson Sessler on the airplane.

The fake names of "Melissa" and "Jack" and the love triangle.

As far as corroborating evidence, Bernardi pointed to the

911 call and the expert with an "exemplary résumé" he provided to explain it.

"He said that's her!"

If jurors wanted to toss this out, however, Bernardi pointed out, and rely solely on one piece of objective evidence: "There is DNA," he said calmly.

Taking it one step further, even if a juror wanted to toss reasonable doubt into that one in 8.5 million chance that the faucet handle contributor could have been someone *other* than Sheila, Bernardi expertly explained in layman terms, ask this one question: "Could that *other* person be randomly chosen and also have the *same* connection to this case as Sheila Davalloo?"

Of course not. It was impossible.

Bernardi spoke of how his forensic witness had explained how the faucet handle had just been cleaned, save for the bloodstain. That Sheila's and Anna's blood mixed together was no "stray secondary transfer."

Bernardi reminded jurors how Nelson Sessler testified he had "never" taken Sheila over to Anna's apartment.

If one took all of those facts together and looked at each separately, impartially, there would have to be only "one compelling conclusion, and one compelling conclusion alone that you came to. And it is consistent with her guilt!" Bernardi took a pause. Then the hammer: "Her DNA in the bloodstain was put there by her as she cleaned up after the murder."

Bernardi kept it short, about fifteen minutes. As closings go, this one was a skillful concluding argument hitting all the right notes.

Sheila came out and immediately touched upon the reason why she had decided to represent herself—or, rather, one of the reasons: So the jury had "ample opportunity to listen to" her voice, she said. In the scope of the case, she "felt it was important." If they heard her speak throughout the trial, they would be able to tell themselves without a doubt she had not made that 911 call.

Sheila hammered the state for not mentioning "burden of proof" and presumed to go on and explain it herself. It sounded forced and tired. She was not a lawyer. Why would she try to be one?

A few minutes in and Sheila broke into a rant about a hypothetical situation of her being accused of stealing papers and the prosecution's burden of proof to prove she stole them. It was ridiculous. This went on and on. A wasted metaphor on a piece of evidence the state had not produced. It had no lasting effect.

Five or six minutes later, Sheila asked this question: "Did the state prove to you that I was there on that day of November 8, 2002? Did they prove I was physically there? Well, they can't do that. But they are bringing in my entry/exit logs for Purdue Pharma, where I used to work, for that day. And they're saying that *that* gives me the opportunity to be there."

She failed to mention here that her DNA placed her at the scene of the homicide. Instead, she labored on about how many times she had left the building in the days before the murder.

Then, after this long-winded explanation of the times and days she entered and exited the building was finished, she launched into her own DNA argument.

"They want you to believe that from the DNA evidence on the sink handle," she began, but she never finished this statement. "The sink handle, for some reason, was a resubmission to the laboratory. I can't get to the bottom of what [or why] this was resubmitted. . . ."

DNA evidence is routinely resubmitted because it can take forever to process.

As quick as she broached the subject of DNA, Sheila got off it and focused on the state's argument regarding intent.

Then she hammered Nelson, calling him a liar.

She returned to the DNA, arguing that it was not found in the "immediate crime scene," but rather in an "adjacent bathroom on the sink handle."

Further, "And then they want you to ignore Mr. Riley. . . . He told them in 2003, on two occasions, that he saw an altercation between a man and a woman—and he pointed to the building in the case."

Bernardi stood. He'd heard enough nonsense. "Your Honor, I don't believe that that's evidence in the case."

True, Riley never said that.

Sheila continued. She touched on everything from the 911 call and how many witnesses said they couldn't be certain it was her, to how "they want to convict me on some poetry" she sent to Nelson.

From there, Sheila had an easel brought out and she said, "I'm going to give you fifteen reasons what, all together, adds up to reasonable doubt."

She noted the "blue contact lens" found in Anna's hair and how neither of them wore blue contact lenses. The "bloody sock"—which sent Bernardi up on his feet to object, saying that none of this was in evidence and that Sheila could only argue the facts in evidence. And, furthermore, this was a closing argument, not testimony.

Judge Comerford asked the jury to leave so they could hash it out.

When they continued some time later, Sheila went back to describing her fifteen reasonable doubts. No witness saw her there at Anna's condo was number three. No murder weapon was number four. "Inconsistent testimony" on the 911 call was number five. No hair evidence, number six. No fingerprints, seven. Eight was that a search of her car had yielded nothing (though, she never said that search took place four months after the murder). Nine was her relationship—"the [state's] so-called motive"—with Nelson. Ten was "unknown DNA mixed" with Anna's. (Unknown? The state had proven it was hers!) Eleven was the idea that "items were missing from the condo" (something that had never been proven). Twelve consisted of a twenty-five-pound dumbbell being moved fifteen to twenty feet inside Anna's condo, which Sheila claimed she would seriously struggle to do. She didn't mention thirteen, but she skipped right to fourteen, calling for jurors to look at the scissors found inside Anna's condo. Finally she got to fifteen: Gary Riley's testimony.

"Thank you, and God bless," Sheila concluded.

She did not bow.

Bernardi had sat and allowed the nonsense of Sheila and her fifteen reasonable doubts because, in the end, he had the final word of the trial.

CHAPTER 104

JAMES BERNARDI HAD somewhat of a suave demeanor. This guy said something and you believed him. It wasn't that he had that solemn burden of truth hanging over his head, but Bernardi had stood in front of enough juries to know when the end was near. He never wanted to prolong it. If he did that, then he'd come out looking like the bad guy. Still, even with that being the case here, Bernardi had a lot of trash to clean up from the mess Sheila had made of the justice system.

He explained that jurors, in general, are "not parents. I mean, if you've been a parent . . . it's tough being a parent. It really is."

This statement was based on a sympathy argument Sheila had launched into near the end of her closing. She was, in effect, asking jurors for their sympathy and thus placing a burden on their shoulders for making a decision that would send her away for a lifetime. It was a sneaky, dirty move on Sheila's part to try and appeal to a juror's moral underpinning. In his rebuttal, Bernardi needed to convince jurors that in seeking justice, they were doing the right thing—the legal thing. No one needed to feel guilty about sending a woman who murdered another woman to prison. It was justice—plain and simple.

He encouraged jurors to take any sympathy they had and place it on the victim's family—where it belonged.

"Just focus on the facts," Bernardi encouraged. "And those facts in this case show, beyond a reasonable doubt, that she did this crime."

Bernardi didn't need to go through every single opinion that Sheila had presented as fact. Instead, he beckoned jurors, as the judge would soon instruct, to reach down and "if your recollection differs about the facts, of either anything that I've told you or anything that she said . . . you disregard it. And you go with your recollection of the facts, because that's your job—your job as fact finders."

After thinking about it for a moment, Bernardi decided to go through and attack several of those fifteen "reasonable doubts" and dismantle them.

It wasn't hard. He pointed out that Gary Riley was an admitted liar.

Disregard.

That the talk about the dumbbell being moved was in reference to a photograph, not testimony.

Disregard.

The fact that Sheila herself pointed to there being no forced entry into Anna's condo.

Regard: and also focus on the fact that Sheila had a lock pick set.

No weapon being recovered.

Disregard: "It's easy to flee with a murder weapon—as we saw with the stabbing of Paul Christos."

Lack of fingerprints?

Disregard: "All somebody had to do was wear gloves."

And on and on, Bernardi went, admonishing each of the fifteen points Sheila had made.

About ten minutes later, Bernardi wrapped it up, concluding, "I wish you Godspeed in your deliberations. Once again, I'm confident that your verdict will be guilty, because beyond a reasonable doubt, the evidence here is *overwhelming*. . . ."

CHAPTER 105

JUROR DAVE MICHEL was one of the more outspoken jurors among the bunch.

"I had mixed feelings about the case at the beginning as we began to go through the trial," Michel said later. "Of course, here we are and we're going to pass judgment. I wanted to be able to take the most step back, as possible, and get the whole picture."

At first, as he sat and listened to the testimony, Dave Michel thought there had to be two people involved in the murder.

"As they presented evidence, it was like a roller coaster for me."

The question that Michel and other jurors routinely asked themselves while listening to testimony or looking at evidence became: Is this proof?

"You want to make sure, as a juror, that you pass judgment on something that you're really, really convinced of," Michel said.

Dave Michel had no regrets about how he voted and what the jury ultimately decided. He did have serious concerns about some of the evidence, however.

For example, the "sound graphics" on the 911 call tape

that were analyzed by Bernardi's expert: "That was really sketchy," Michel said, and other jurors concurred. For Michel, he had studied science. The tests that the prosecutor's expert did, Michel noted, were not scientific in any way. "To make just one comparison of just two voices"—Sheila's and the 911 caller's—"is not scientific, experimental proof. You'd have to do the same with other voices."

The prosecution's expert did not do that.

As the jury deliberated, they asked for several tape-recorded sections of the trial to compare to the 911 call. They wanted to hear Sheila's voice on tape up against the 911 call.

"And to me," Michel said, "that was over-proof. I mean, that's her! That is her voice on the 911 tape."

So, in the end, Sheila was right to keep trying to drum home the point that it wasn't her on the 911 tape. It was the 911 tape, after all, that convinced the jurors of her guilt. She somehow knew that, suspected it would be the case, and tried to persuade them she wasn't the phone caller. Her instincts were right. Her desire to kill wrong.

"The recording of her voice in court totally matched the voice on the 911 tape."

Michel and several other jurors had no doubt about it.

In effect, the jury had done its own experiment very similar to what Bernardi's expert had done. And that alone was the "complication" of reasonable doubt for Dave Michel and other jurors.

As soon as they sat down and voted for the first time, Sheila was found guilty.

The DNA was "indicative" of her guilt, Michel explained; and the numbers that the statistics presented—one in 8 million—were a good bet, he added.

"To have a piece of her DNA there [at the scene], to me," Michel concluded, "that was proof, that was evidence."

There was no separation in the jury room, Michel explained.

"There were some jurors convinced sooner than others, because we all think differently, and we're all individuals."

The jury mostly believed Sheila's decision to represent herself was a "big, big mistake."

"Why do you think it was a mistake?" Michel asked the roundtable gathering of jurors at one point in the deliberation room.

"Well, for one," said a juror, "she was just awful defending herself."

"I didn't think she was that awful," Michel said. "But I have nothing to compare her to."

What was "most astounding" to the jury as a whole, Michel said, was Paul Christos's testimony. No one on the jury had known about Paul before he sat down and told his story.

"I don't think any of us were expecting to hear what Paul Christos had to say," Michel explained.

The story Paul told verified for the jury that Sheila was devious and violent and had motive to kill Anna. It seemed to all come together when they put it into the context of Paul's stabbing.

"When he was describing this to us, it was shocking. . . . After that, there was no question that she was trying to get rid of him."

The jury, according to Michel, "all hated Nelson Sessler. I thought he was a scumbag and a dirty liar. In the jury room, we all decided not to go by any of his testimony. We all knew he was a liar and [we] did not want to pay too much attention to his testimony."

It was the way he talked, Michel said.

"At one point, I even considered that maybe this guy, Nelson Sessler, was an accomplice. And then as the trial went on, it didn't make sense that he was an accomplice."

And so, on Friday afternoon, February 10, 2012, the

Raymundo family finally got justice for Anna Lisa when the jury found Sheila guilty of murder.

Susan Raymundo, sitting in court and intently listening, dropped her head in her hands and wept openly as the jury foreman announced the verdict.

Sheila sat down, crossed herself in a religious gesture, and then dropped her head into her lap.

In total, the jury started deliberations on Thursday in the late morning and took the entire day and most of Friday before coming back with its decision.

It was two-thirty in the afternoon when a marshal handcuffed Sheila and took her out of the room. She faced twenty-five to sixty years when sentenced. If she received the lighter end of that sentence, Sheila would still be an old, decrepit woman when she was released, seeing that first she had to serve twenty-five years in New York for attempting to murder Paul.

Outside the courtroom after the verdict, reporters asked Renato Raymundo how he felt. Anna's seventy-year-old father, who had not missed one beat of the trial, bowed his head a moment, thought about it, and told reporters: "We got what we were asking for after all these years of suffering. It does not replace our beloved daughter Anna Lisa. . . . She was the perfect daughter . . . an excellent human being."

CHAPTER 106

FOR HER SENTENCING on April 27, 2012, Sheila wore a purple blouse, black pants, and large, black-framed glasses. Her hair was tightly wound in a braided ponytail. She looked tired and frequently rubbed her eyes. This was not the outcome Sheila had expected; anyone who had known her before she became a murderer could never have predicted her life would end up like this. Sheila was a smart, intelligent human being. She was a gifted pharmaceutical researcher, who truly could have done the world some good with her work.

Renato Raymundo took the stand and talked about Anna and the immense loss his family has experienced since Sheila had taken Anna's life. It was the years waiting for justice—ten in total—that had caused Renato and his family, he said, "mental anguish and uncertainty." He'd had trouble getting the images of Anna's final moments of life out of his head, he explained, as tears ran down his cheeks. It had been devastating.

The local victims' advocate read a letter from Anna's sister, who could not be there because she had children to take care of back home.

The message in the letter was that Anna's death deprived the world of a caring, loving human being—a woman who would have gone on to share her gifts with the world and make it a better place.

In the letter, Anna's sister referred to Sheila as a *heinously ugly creature, both inside and out . . . a cold blooded killer, who plotted, calculated, planned and executed the murder of my sister.*

Susan Raymundo came next. She talked of a firstborn daughter who inspired her family and the world. The lasting image Susan was going to carry to her grave, she said, was her daughter at her funeral, looking different "from the beautiful daughter I remembered."

Susan blamed herself for "not being able to protect" Anna Lisa.

James Bernardi went next, telling the court exactly what a prosecutor who won the case would say.

Barry Butler, Sheila's court-appointed attorney, representing her for the sentencing, talked about how long a sentence it would be for Sheila and gave the court some numbers to consider. The judge, Butler argued, did not have to sentence Sheila to the maximum. She would serve plenty of time even if the court went lenient on her.

When Butler was done, Judge Richard Comerford said, "I just want to remind you that Anna Lisa Raymundo's sentence is final!"

Then Sheila spoke.

Not much of a religious person while growing up or when she was married to Paul, Sheila began by thanking God for giving her the "courage and the strength to stand" in the courtroom and face her accusers and punishers. She talked about how "difficult" it had been to hear the "bitterness, anger, and just a lot of agony" that had been directed at her during the proceeding.

From there, she went down a list, as though giving an Oscar speech, thanking everyone from her parents to judge to the Department of Corrections to friends and the jury, Barry Butler, the state police, the prosecutor's office, the Stamford Police. In there, somewhere, had to be the kitchen sink, but then that was something that had sunk her—the DNA she left on a bathroom sink handle, rather.

Finally, in her own self-aggrandizing way, Sheila said something to Anna's family, noting how she was praying for them.

"I was shaken by the fact that they lost their faith, when my faith has increased insurmountably in the past ten years."

Sheila promised that if she could, she would take away the Raymundos' suffering. She was taken aback by the resentment and fury of Anna's sister in the letter read to the court and said she would pray for her, too.

Concluding, Sheila never admitted guilt, but she said she hoped the sentence would bring the family some solace and closure.

Now it was Judge Comerford's turn.

He evoked Shakespeare first, calling "murder" a "most foul" crime. But the sentence he was about to hand down, Comerford added in what would become a rather strange way to begin a sentencing speech, it "'is the sentence imposed by a mere mortal. I fear for her that someday, as Dante once told us, she will pass by the gates of the city of Dis. She will move to the seventh circle, the deep valley, the pit of the river of blood. That's well beyond my pay grade.'" He took a moment to reflect. Then: "'She better make peace with the Ultimate Judge—I hope she does.'"

After he gave the court a little lesson in faith, Comerford asked Sheila to stand up.

"'On the charge of murder, the court will commit the defendant to the Commissioner of Corrections for a period of fifty years to serve. That sentence will be served consecutively to the sentence that has been imposed by the people of the state of New York.'"

Sheila was forty-two on the day of her sentencing, just about to turn forty-three on May 11, 2012. It would be 2079 before Sheila ever had a chance for release (2075 if she managed early release from Bedford Hills Correctional Facility for Women in Bedford Hills, New York). If she happened to live that long, Sheila Davalloo would be between 106 and 110 years old on the day she walked out of prison.

"After the verdict was announced, we all felt a collective sigh of relief," Paul Christos said as a concluding thought. "I was so happy for the Raymundo family that they finally received justice for Anna Lisa. It was a very painful ordeal for them, and the verdict and sentence were long overdue. Sheila had every opportunity to take responsibility for her actions over the years. Instead, she chose to deny it, remove her public defender, represent herself, cross-examine the Raymundos and myself, and actually *enjoyed* putting on a show with complete arrogance. [She is] a true psychopath that ultimately got what she deserved. Anna Lisa was a wonderful person, and I hope she can finally rest in peace now."

EPILOGUE

SHEILA DAVALLOO FILED an appeal, obviously. They all do. It's the due process of America's justice system. That appeal is still outstanding. No decision has been made as of this writing.

I wrote to Sheila, not expecting a response. In my letter, I offered basically the same things I offer most incarcerated killers I want to write about:

I'd like to know if you'd be interested in being interviewed for [my book] project. It would be up to you how you wanted to participate; totally on your terms. I could interview you through the mail and we could talk about everything, or you could begin to call me. I believe there is a story here beyond the media hype; and, in all of my books, I like to give everyone involved the opportunity to tell his or her side of the story. Please let me know if you would be interested. Be happy to answer any questions you might have. . . .

Sheila answered almost immediately, thanking me for showing some "interest in [her] case." She explained how she had "viewed" my Web page and found it to be "impressive."

First the charm.

Then the terms.

Sheila proceeded from there to tell me how she was being approached by all sorts of media, but she had "kept everyone at bay" in lieu of her search for an appellate attorney. She said she was hoping to "raise funds" for legal counsel on her road toward appeal by "licensing pictures or other similar avenues." This (coming up with the cash) had been, she added, her "number one priority" since her conviction. Interestingly enough, she closed this paragraph by explaining that while the "public's perception" of her and her "point of view" were equally important, her reputation and how people felt about her were the lesser of her two top priorities at this juncture: selling her story and finding counsel.

The letter was written in that perfect script of Sheila's. I'm incredibly fascinated by her penmanship. I have never seen anything like it.

Further along, Sheila asked me to help her find legal representation, and, in turn, she would be more than "willing to give" me her "full and even exclusive cooperation."

I recall reading this brief letter while standing over my desk—and cracking a smile.

I wrote back. I mean, look, why the hell not!

Thank you for writing back in such a timely fashion. . . .
I would gladly pay a small, nominal fee for photos
that interest me, providing you have the right to
release them. I have so many photos already from the
court file, I'm not sure I'll need many more.
As an objective journalist who has never paid a

*source, I cannot help financially with your search for
representation. . . .*

*I'd love to hear from you, either by phone or mail.
I'm here if you'd like to present your story to my
readers. . . .*

I never heard from Sheila again.
Surprised?
I didn't think so.
Knowing she'll read this book, however, I'd like to say this:

*Good luck and good riddance. You murdered a won-
derful human being for no other reason than your
own selfish needs, not to mention for a man who did
not even want you—and you did not even have the
nerve or the guts to admit it when the evidence against
you proved overwhelming. You tried to kill a man who
loved you and put up with you—and never said sorry
to this man or apologized to him for making his life a
living hell for the time he knew you. You're a killer and
a narcissist. You claim to have found God. You better
hope He has found you.*

One final note: There is a detailed conversation in this
book between Sheila Davalloo and Fran Lourie, a therapist
Sheila went to see in 2002. Some might wonder how I was
able to put this conversation together with that all-important
patient confidentiality relationship in place between a client
and his/her therapist. Lourie's notes from these sessions with
Sheila detailed what they discussed. I put those notes into a
conversational narrative.

These "progress notes" became part of the court file
under subpoena after Sheila was arrested and charged with

the brutal murder of Anna Lisa and the attempted murder of her husband, Paul Christos. These notes prove Sheila had lied repeatedly to everyone around her—including her therapist. Finally, and this is essential, Sheila signed a disclaimer for Fran Lourie before treatment. In that disclaimer Lourie clearly outlined this patient/therapist confidentiality agreement, along with the caveat: *It is my intention to keep our relationship confidential within the limits of the law.*

ACKNOWLEDGMENTS

I WOULD LIKE to thank Jupiter Entertainment for thinking of me throughout the years when it comes to great true-crime stories. Jupiter stayed with the Davalloo case for ten-plus years and always kept me informed. When it came time for me to write this book, everyone on staff was extremely helpful with encouragement and material.

It gets kind of redundant writing the same list of people at the end of every book. So I will just say here that my family and friends, colleagues, and those working for me, are the foundation of what I do, and I could not continue my work without any one of them. To thank some and not others seems unfair to me. So I will use the old cliché to say, *"You know who you are!"*

When it comes to my readers, I am always at a loss for words when trying to say "thank you," because nothing I can say is, in my opinion, enough. You are the most important part of my work. I am grateful to each one of you for tuning into my series, *Dark Minds,* on Investigation Discovery, and reading each book I have written. I am honored and humbled by your dedication and willingness to spend this time with me. Thank you for coming back, book after book. You are the best—I mean that sincerely.

SPD officer Theresa Vitti was instrumental in making sure I had all the photos (some of which I published and others I used for research purposes only), reports, and other documents and materials I needed in order to complete this book. I am very grateful for Mrs. Vitti's help (and greatly appreciated and enjoyed the extensive tour she gave me of the SPD), along with Greg Holt, Captain Richard Conklin, and the entire SPD staff, including the chief, who displayed to me his confidence and gratitude that a writer such as myself was taking on this case. I am continually humbled by and grateful for the respect law enforcement shows me.

Likewise, I am indebted to Paul Christos for his honesty, integrity, and trust. Paul revealed details about his and Sheila's life together that he had never told anyone. I appreciate his candidness and the fact that he never got sick of answering my dozens upon dozens of e-mails.

My publisher, Laurie Parkin, and the entire team at Kensington Publishing Corp. are the best publishing people I have worked with. I want to extend a continued thanks to all of you. In addition, I need to thank my longtime editor, Michaela Hamilton, who has been an instrumental part of my career for well over a decade now, and also a great friend. We've done nearly twenty books together and Michaela's passion for what I do continues to grow with each book. I am indebted and grateful, not to mention amazed, by Michaela's drive to see me succeed. There is a ton of work that goes on behind the scenes of each book, and I want to point out to the team at Kensington that I realize how hard you all work on my behalf—and I'm very grateful for it. Once again, Stephanie Finnegan—thank you!

I would like to extend my sincere appreciation to everyone at Investigation Discovery and Beyond Productions involved in making *Dark Minds* the best (nonfiction) crime show on television: Andrew "Fazz" Farrell, Alex Barry, Colette "Coco" Sandstedt, John Mavety, Peter Heap, Mark Middis, Toby Prior, Peter Coleman, Derek Ichilcik, Jared "Jars"

Transfield, Jo Telfer, Claire Westerman, Milena Gozzo, Cameron Power, Katie Ryerson, Inneke Smit, Pele Hehea, Jeremy Peek, Jeremy Adair, Geri Berman, Nadine Terens, Samantha Hertz, Lale Teoman, Hayden Anderson, Savino (from Onyx Sound Lab in Manchester, CT.), David O'Brien, Ra-ey Saleh, Nathan Brand, Rebecca Clare, Anthony Toy, Mark Wheeler, Mandy Chapman, Jenny O'Shea, Jen Longhurst, Anita Bezjak, Geoff Fitzpatrick, John Luscombe, Debbie Gottschalk, Eugenie Vink, Sucheta Sachdev, Sara Kozak, Kevin Bennett, Jane Latman, and Henry Schleiff.

As you can see, it takes an army to make a television show.

I also need to extend my deepest gratitude to the families of my *Dark Minds* road crew, as well as my own, for allowing us to take the time we need on the road to shoot the episodes. It's a lot of time away from home and I realize the sacrifice all of you make on my behalf, especially the children: India, Ivo, and April—and, of course, spouses Bates and Regina.

Where would I be without Mr. John Kelly, criminal profiler extraordinaire, mentor, friend, sometimes therapist, and business partner? Thank you, JK, for your hard work. Your dedication to catching bad guys is admirable and an inspiration.

Enjoy this exclusive look at M. William Phelps's
next real-life thriller coming in hardcover
from Kensington Publishing in 2014. . . .

The Killing Kind

*With a ticking clock and victims' families demanding
justice, law enforcement enters into a race
to catch a Southern serial killer.*

CHAPTER 1

ON OCTOBER 29, 2009, somewhere near one forty-five in the afternoon, York County Sheriff's Office (YCSO) detective Alex Wallace, a seasoned, dedicated cop with a dozen years behind the badge, took a call to head out to the 1200 block of Robinson Yelton Road in York County, South Carolina.

When later asked, Wallace referred to this area of York County as "a country . . . gravel and dirt road," same as a lot of the terrain in this part of the state. There were five houses on the section of the road where Wallace was heading.

When he arrived, Wallace saw that several other investigators from the sheriff's office had gotten there before him. As a member of the YCSO's violent crimes unit, Alex Wallace generally worked death investigations, sex crimes, armed robberies, aggravated assaults, and missing person cases.

The rough stuff: the types of crimes that hardly ever come with happy endings and keep good cops up at night, wondering, shaking their heads in disbelief.

After parking and getting out of his vehicle, Wallace walked over to an area where several additional officers had gathered. There was a "little drainage area" coming from a nearby creek that ran underneath the road. Three ribbed metal pipes, side by side with several feet of space between them, directed the water toward the woods, away from the road.

Looking closely as he approached the area, Wallace saw something sticking up out of the brush between two of the pipes.

A body.

"I observed . . . a white female in a culvert, amongst some bushes and trees and stuff," Wallace said.

Her leg and foot were actually stuck up out of the brush, a multicolored sock still on her naked leg.

"Someone riding an ATV saw her," an officer on the scene explained to Wallace.

Where Wallace stood on this day, staring down into the short culvert where the three pipes dumped water, the body came into clear view. Although there was a mailbox maybe twenty-five yards away from the body on the edge of the road, there were no houses or businesses in this particular section of the road. It was woodsy, filled in with trees and brush and weeds. There was a house nearby that could be seen, but it wasn't close enough for law enforcement to think that a witness could have seen what happened here. As far as bodies went, this area seemed to be a hasty dump site—not the perfect place to hide a body, but also not out in a wide open space, either.

Wallace stepped down into the culvert and took a closer look. The woman's body was bent over. She was naked from the waist down (except for those rainbow socks). All she had on was a sweatshirt.

As he took it all in, there was something about the scene that struck the detective immediately.

"You could see her breasts, butt, and vagina area," Wallace said later. "There was bugs crawling all over her. . . ."

This told investigators that she had been down in the small culvert for a while. She had not been dumped there just recently, in other words. Not the night before, or that day, for certain.

Studying her body (she was young, a teenager, many on scene thought right away), the girl had "a deep scratch in her side from a claw or something." Wallace noticed this as he got down on one knee and stared at her. And looking even closer, the detective saw more scratches, maybe three or four "deeper cuts" along her body, "like she scraped across something."

Had she been dragged? the detective wondered.

There appeared to be some "redness" around her neck, too, just above an area where her sweatshirt had been pulled up to expose her breasts.

Ligature marks? Strangulation?

The signs were faint, but it just might be. Although, with the redness being so subtle, it could mean a host of things.

There was an issue here, however, the YCSO now faced: How to identify her? And a bigger issue, of course: How to explain to the public that a teenager had shown up dead in a culvert, nearly naked, with scratches all over her, along with indistinct red marks around her neck?

"Fingerprint her," someone suggested. It was the only way to begin the process of finding out who the young girl was.

After all, there had to be someone out in the world looking for her.

CHAPTER 2

AS THE CRIME SCENE off Robinson Yelton Road, located just south of the North Carolina/South Carolina state line, filled in with investigators of all types, and yellow CSI tape was unspooled and wrapped around trees, an on-scene supervisor called in YCSO K-9 sergeant Randy Clinton. The idea was that the rest of the girl's clothing was maybe somewhere in the woods. But maybe more shocking and immediate: Were there any additional bodies out there waiting to be found?

Sergeant Clinton had nearly three decades on the job, the last seventeen dedicated to the K-9 unit. If there was a need for something to be sniffed out, a trail of a criminal at-large, the possibility of drugs inside a house or a car, or maybe even up someone's ass, Clinton and his dogs were the go-to team of law enforcement for those jobs.

"We work on break-ins, armed robberies, anything that a person left on foot, missing persons . . . ," Clinton said later.

The dogs are trained to pick up a trail and follow it.

"I want you to search along the roads to see if you can find any clothes that might have been tossed out of a vehicle," the captain explained to Clinton. This seemed like a logical approach. The dead girl in the ditch was missing some of her clothes. If she had been raped and murdered, as some suspected, her killer might have hastily tore off her clothing and tossed it wherever the confrontation had started, or taken it with him and gotten rid of it elsewhere. Finding that type of evidence could produce big results—and those three magic letters.

DNA.

When Clinton met with several other investigators to discuss the best way to go about searching the area, one suggested walking along the roadside with the dogs. There were three other officers to assist Clinton, and they could cover a lot of ground quickly.

Respectfully, Clinton didn't like that idea. His thought was to have two cars drive along the roadside and conduct a cursory search first, to see if they spotted anything out in the open. The incident likely occurred at night, under the cloak of darkness. There could be evidence left behind in plain sight, which the killer had not seen.

Those in charge agreed with Clinton.

Sergeant Clinton and a colleague hopped in one vehicle, and two additional officers took another. Each went separate ways along Robinson Road, north, toward the state line between North and South Carolina. The small town of Clover, where the woman's body had actually been found, is directly due south of Gastonia, North Carolina, a mere thirty-minute, twenty-mile ride up the 321. These cops see lots of crimes generated by people from nearby Charlotte and other North Carolina towns. Not that there aren't the same types of crooks, dopers, and all-around criminals in South Carolina, but this region of the state is prone to people coming down from the north and bringing their trash and trouble with them.

Clinton and his colleague took off south down Robinson toward Lloyd White Road, the 148. Both cars drove slowly on the side of the road, officers peering out the window looking into the brush and patches of gravel off to the side of the road to see if anything stood out. Their thought was to conduct a cursory search by eye first and see what they came up with. If they didn't see anything, they could always double back with the dogs and go deeper into the brush and woods alongside the roadway.

Not long after they started, Clinton and his partner came to a stop sign at Crowders Creek, on the North Carolina/South Carolina border.

"Take a right," Clinton suggested. He kept his eyes on the side of the road.

They drove for a mile and a half, when Clinton thought he spotted something.

"Stop."

There was a concrete bridge there. They were now in Gaston County, North Carolina. Something red in color was half on the edge of the roadway and half in the brush, almost directly in front of a striped orange-and-black road sign indicating a bridge.

Clinton got out.

He walked along the roadside a bit and there it was. . . .

Oh, my . . .